PATRICIDE

IN THE

HOUSE DIVIDED

PATRICIDE

IN THE

HOUSE DIVIDED

A Psychological Interpretation

of Lincoln and His Age

GEORGE B. FORGIE

W. W. NORTON & COMPANY · NEW YORK

BOOK DESIGN BY ANTONINA KRASS
TEXT TYPE IS LINOTYPE GRANJON
MANUFACTURED BY VAIL-BALLOU PRESS, INC.

Library of Congress Cataloging in Publication Data
Forgie, George B
Patricide in the house divided: a psychological interpretation
of Lincoln and his age
Includes index.
1. United States—Politics and government—
1845–1861. 2. Lincoln, Abraham, Pres. U.S.,
1809–1865. I. Tiitle.
E415.7.F7   1979   973.7'019   78-26074
ISBN 0-393-05695-3

1 2 3 4 5 6 7 8 9 0

To my mother and father

CONTENTS

ACKNOWLEDGMENTS

In undertaking to become a historian, and in writing this book, I have had a number of advantages which I want to record here. At Stanford University, Don E. Fehrenbacher guided my course as a graduate student, served as adviser for the dissertation that became an early version of this book, and commented critically on the final draft of the manuscript. More important to my work even than his encouragement and willing aid has been the example he set for me through the standards his own work reveals he sets for himself. The other historian at Stanford who influenced me decisively was David M. Potter. Probably anyone who knew the man will understand me when I say that once I had observed him as he thought about historical problems and as he expressed himself, I was no longer able to distinguish the effect on me of his scholarship from that of his manner and his character. I am certain only that the impact of the whole on my work has been profound. That, after studying with these two historians, I now present a book on the origins of the American Civil War that deals hardly at all—and then indirectly—with the sectional conflict, slavery, or political parties is a measure not of my rejection but of my assimilation of their work.

The manuscript benefited greatly at various stages of writing from careful, critical readings given it by historians and other scholars. I want to note my gratitude especially to James M. Banner, Jr., Michael Bell, Sacvan Bercovitch, James Bieri, Carl N. Degler, Barnes F. Lathrop, James M. McPherson, Standish Meacham, Carl E. Schorske, Peter Stansky, Charles B. Strozier, and Bernard Wishy. It cannot come as news to readers of these names that I have been the recipient of superb advice. I have taken it all seriously. Even the advice I have declined to follow has improved the book by compelling me to reassess my purpose and method.

James L. Mairs, who edited this book, has treated both it and me with generosity, patience, and care. The cost of the preparation of the final typescript was borne by the University Research Institute at the University of Texas at Austin.

If it is difficult to measure the importance to my work of people whose role in its progress has been direct, it is all the harder to measure the shaping effect my friends have had upon it. I do know, however, that four of them—Richard W. Crosby, Ann Douglas, James D. Gilmore, and Mark R. Schwehn—have permanently affected my values and marked my life. So certain am I that their spirit has vitalized my book that I do not hesitate at all to implicate them in what I have done.

PATRICIDE

IN THE

HOUSE DIVIDED

INTRODUCTION

Sentiment is the great conservative principle of
society.

HENRY T. TUCKERMAN, 1856

The leaders of American politics and culture in the middle
decades of the nineteenth century belonged to a generation
that was born and socialized in the early Republic, when the
memory of the Revolution was still fresh and the founding
heroes still held political power. This book argues that this
simple fact provides a key to understanding more clearly not
only the mentality of mid-century leadership but also the structure and style of the long struggle to preserve the Union and
hence the origins of the American Civil War. In the course of
explaining what I mean by this assertion I will make particular
use of two terms which, though their meaning will become
fully clear only as the argument builds, should be fixed with
some precision here at the start.

The first of these is *sentiment*. In 1845 Alexander Sims, a
Democratic congressman from South Carolina, spoke in protest against the pervasive influence in public matters of a sensibility that was peculiar to his lifetime. Speaking in the House

of Representatives (whose stenographer recast the tense of his words), he attempted to revivify a distinction he correctly perceived was often ignored in American speech and thought. "There were two sorts of government existing in human society—the government of the family and civil government," he observed.

> Family government rested for its efficiency and its happiness on the feelings of the heart; but civil government . . . was founded on considerations of justice. . . . Men submitted themselves to government mainly for the purpose of obtaining and securing justice. It was no sickly dream of childhood-recollections, but a stern reality of actual life. While in the soft twilight a man with melting bosom might indulge his memory and his feelings in the holy contemplation of the delights of his early years, he clung beneath the glare of day to that which secured to him justice and . . . social protection.[1]

Sims's desire to distinguish sharply between these two forms of government was not widely shared. It was a convention of American public language between the 1790s and the Civil War to speak of the Union and the relationships among Americans in familial and domestic terms. Political language borrowed readily from "sweet household talk, and phrases of the hearth,"[2] and nothing in rhetoric was more common than the formulation that Americans were "the brethren of one great household."[3] Behind this language rested the conservative assumption, sometimes articulated but more often not, that the survival of the Union depended on offsetting the centrifugal and atomistic tendencies of an amorphous and rapidly expanding democracy by the cohesive force of emotion. In this essay I use the word *sentimentalist* to characterize a person who

[1] *Congressional Globe,* 29 Cong., 1 Sess. (December 30, 1845), pp. 115–16.
[2] "America for the Americans," *Putnam's Monthly* 5 (1855): 539.
[3] Boston *Daily Advertiser,* July 7, 1858.

believed that feeling was not only a legitimate but also an important category of public concern, and that it was essential for Americans to extend natural affections, originally directed toward objects close at hand, to the far wider realm of the Republic. In the words of one of them, sentimentalists looked in particular to the "enlargement of home—the extension of family union beyond the little man-and-wife circle" to society generally.[4] Similarly I use the word *sentiment* when speaking of this tendency to superimpose the categories of private, domestic life upon the public realm in order to encourage the transference of emotion from natural and close to abstract and distant objects.[5] My concern here is with people whose chief conscious object was to preserve the Union, and, as we will see, sentimentalism was almost always not only conservative but also regressive in its persistent exploitation of nostalgic impulses. But the rhetoric of gentle feelings was by no means limited to such unambiguously preservationist efforts. Reform

[4] John Humphrey Noyes, *History of American Socialisms* (Philadelphia: J. B. Lippincott Co., 1870), p. 23. Noyes was speaking here of the purposes of the Fourierists and Owenites. The entire statement is emphasized in the original. William Cullen Bryant called the Union an "immortal league of love." "Ode, Written for the Fiftieth Anniversary of the Inauguration of Washington, April 30, 1839," *United States Magazine and Democratic Review* 5 (1839): 498.

[5] It was as common in the nineteenth century as it is now to distinguish at the level of definition between sentiment (genuine or spontaneous emotion) and sentimentality (exaggerated or artificial feeling). See, for examples, [Margaret Fuller], "Goethe," *Dial* 2 (1841): 7; "Athenian Orators," *Southern Quarterly Review* 20 (1851): 374. It was also just as common to ignore the distinction in practice. I use the words interchangeably; one person's sentiment is another's sentimentality, and in any case the point of my use of the term(s) is to stress the *displaced* quality of public emotion. The feelings I am talking about may have become—doubtless did become—real enough. But they did not begin spontaneously, at least not to the extent that the spokesmen for sentiment could rely on their natural emergence. In the sense I use it, sentiment is thought out. It is, never mind the paradox, rationalized emotion.

Sentiment was of course also commonly used as a synonym for "opinion." This sense provides no basis for confusion.

movements of all kinds, including most conspicuously the assault upon slavery, employed the language of domesticity with great effect.[6] However it was used, and for whatever purpose, sentimental language did not simply decorate but also structured the central concerns of the age. I have set for myself the task of explaining how and why this was so.

The second term is *post-heroic*. This book is a study of the ways in which a generally prosperous and peaceful age was shaped by the memory of the revolutionary age that preceded it. I speak throughout of the period from about the mid-1820s to 1861 as the "post-heroic age" and the people whose mature adulthood was passed in this time as the "post-heroic generation." It is paradoxical but true that one of the greatest obstacles in the way of reaching and understanding the mentality of Americans whose actions led to civil war is the ineffably immense fact of the American Civil War itself. From the moment it began, that conflict distorted perceptions of the events that occurred before it. For example, historians naturally use the term *antebellum* when writing of the period before 1861, although it is obvious that (this particular sense of) the word would have been meaningless to people living through the time it describes.[7] Their tortured political struggles presupposed, after all, that disunion and war could be avoided. When

---

[6] John L. Thomas, "Romantic Reform in America, 1815–1865," *American Quarterly* 17 (1965): 656–81. But cf. pp. 667–68. Much of the power of *Uncle Tom's Cabin*, which was published in 1852, came from Harriet Beecher Stowe's awareness that if she could not arouse white sympathy for slaves on the grounds that they were slaves, she could arouse it on the grounds that they were denied the stability and emotional security of family ties they could count on. See Kenneth S. Lynn, Introduction to *Uncle Tom's Cabin; or, Life Among the Lowly* (Cambridge, Mass.: Harvard University Press, Belknap Press, 1962), pp. vii–xxiv. Stowe was the most famous but by no means the first antislavery spokesman to adopt this tactic. See, for example, Timothy Jenkins, *Congressional Globe,* 30 Cong., 2 Sess. (February 17, 1849), appendix, p. 103.

[7] David M. Potter, *The Impending Crisis, 1848–1861,* completed and ed. Don E. Fehrenbacher (New York: Harper & Row, 1976), p. 145.

Americans of the 1850s spoke of their perception of their place in historical time, they almost always spoke in terms of their relationship to the American beginning—the founding age—rather than any age or events to come.

Plato pointed out in *The Laws* that "the beginning is like a god which as long as it dwells among men saves all things,"[8] and probably all beginnings have a power exceeding that of any other moment in a historical process that still continues. To American adults living in the middle of the nineteenth century that power was doubly strong, for—if we may fix its boundaries generously—the national beginning was simultaneous with their own. Abraham Lincoln's remark about Henry Clay, who was born in 1777, applied to many other people, including the man who made it: "The infant nation, and the infant child began the race of life together."[9] The fact of being born too late to experience the Revolution, but in time to be raised by the generation that had fought it, informed the way that many members of this later generation identified and thought about themselves. For instance, in 1837, observing that he was the first president who had been born after the winning of the Revolution, Martin Van Buren declared, "I feel that I belong to a later age."[10]

The sense of having been born with the Republic and of belonging to a later age than the beginning was the basis of a peculiarly deferential mentality that was characteristic of most

[8] Quoted in Hannah Arendt, *Between Past and Future: Six Exercises in Political Thought* (Cleveland: World Publishing Co., Meridian Books, 1961), p. 18.

[9] Roy P. Basler, ed., *The Collected Works of Abraham Lincoln,* 8 vols. (New Brunswick, N.J.: Rutgers University Press, 1953), 2:121; [Joseph G. Baldwin], " 'Representative Men.' Andrew Jackson and Henry Clay," *Southern Literary Messenger* 19 (1853): 522.

[10] James D. Richardson, ed., *A Compilation of the Messages and Papers of the Presidents,* 10 vols. (Washington: Government Printing Office, 1897), 3:313.

American political leaders of Van Buren's time and forever conditioned the way they attempted to deal with the questions that finally got beyond the reach of peaceful settlement. Almost all important political, moral, and personal matters (and many matters that were not so important) were referred to, and most policy choices measured against, the heroic standards of the founding period and the lives of the founders themselves. Citizens of the new Republic talked almost unremittingly about the need to imitate the private virtues of the founders and preserve their public achievements. "It is by a constant recurrence," ran a characteristic example of this pervasive belief, "to the first principles of our government, and the upright character of her earlier statesmen, that our glorious Union is to be nurtured and preserved."[11]

In this deferential context sentimental language knew its greatest use. George Washington was the "father of his country"; the founders were collectively and possessively referred to as "our fathers."[12] Nineteenth-century Americans spoke of themselves as "the sons of those heroes"—the children of Washington and the other founders.[13] The Union, the "beautiful house of our fathers," had been inherited by the next generation, which saw its historical position generally as similar to that of inheritors of paternal property.[14] The sons had not

[11] "Notices of New Books," *United States Magazine and Democratic Review* 26 (1850): 191.

[12] The phrase "our fathers" commonly included all participants in the founding process since the first colonial settlements. Thus: "We look back to the earliest struggles of our fathers; we follow their records down to the establishment of our country, and see them brought out from bondage, and led through the desolations of famine, pestilence and war, to this, the promised land. We look around and find the nation which they planted, multiplied with unprecedented rapidity, and now enjoying an accumulation—we had almost said an intensity, of blessing, which no other nation has known." "Thoughts Upon the Character of the Age," *United States Literary Gazette* 1 (1824): 42.

[13] "Declaration of Independence," *Casket* 7 (1832): 50.

[14] Rufus Choate, in Samuel Gilman Brown, ed., *The Works of Rufus Choate with A Memoir of His Life*, 2 vols. (Boston: Little, Brown and Co., 1862), 2:414.

themselves created or established this fortune of liberty, but were born rich. The fathers "bequeathed to us almost all we have that is worth having."[15] Like men who had successfully made themselves wealthy, the fathers had built an estate to leave to the next generation, an estate of liberty "purchased with PRECIOUS BLOOD."[16] Their sons saw themselves as "inheriting as children the liberty thus won."[17] The inheritance brought burdens as well as gifts. The first obligation was a debt of gratitude that could never be paid off.[18] Second and more important, theirs was an entailed inheritance, one that "the sons never will divide." The successors of the founders had a life estate in these blessings. The inheritance was to be enjoyed, but not squandered. It must be preserved intact so that it could be transmitted to posterity.[19] Made part of their thinking throughout the post-heroic period, this formulation was naturally used by Northerners explaining their intention to defend the Union against secession. "We inherited it from our fathers," a newspaper editor wrote in 1861, "and it is our duty to preserve it for those who come after us."[20]

Like Martin Van Buren, other Americans of his time tended to divide American history sharply into two parts: the time "of

[15] "Reminiscences of a Walker Round Boston," *United States Magazine and Democratic Review* 3 (1838): 80.

[16] "Address of the Bunker Hill Monument Association to the Selectmen of the several Towns in Massachusetts," October 1, 1824, in George Washington Warren, *The History of the Bunker Hill Monument Association during the First Century of the United States of America* (Boston: James R. Osgood and Co., 1877), p. 87.

[17] "Thoughts Upon the Character of the Age," p. 30. See also John Quincy Adams, in Richardson, *Messages of the Presidents*, 2:294; "The Perilous Condition of the Republic," *New-England Magazine* 1 (1831): 289; Daniel Webster, *The Writings and Speeches of Daniel Webster*, 18 vols. (Boston: Little, Brown and Co., 1903), 1:282; [George H. Colton], "Washington and his Generals," *American Whig Review* 5 (1847): 534.

[18] Webster, *Writings and Speeches*, 1:323.

[19] George Ticknor Curtis, quoted in Warren, *Bunker Hill*, p. 325.

[20] Quoted in Howard Cecil Perkins, ed., *Northern Editorials on Secession*, 2 vols. (New York: D. Appleton-Century Co., 1942), 1:298.

the fathers and the present,"[21] a heroic age and a later (and
frequently lesser) one, the division line marked by events in
the lives of the fathers rather than their own. The heroic age
gave way to a post-heroic one not with the founding but with
the deaths of the founders. Thus a focal point of mid-century
nostalgia was the decade of the 1820s, the last one that could
be seen as part of the beginning. It was "still the heroic age
of the Republic," a magazine, looking back thirty years, said
of the twenties.

> The heroes . . . were still walking among the people; linger-
> ing a little as if to give their farewell benediction to the nation
> whose infancy they had baptized with blood. Still the golden
> age of the sentiments of the people continued, still the brazen
> age of the commerce of the people had not opened.[22]

From the same distance, using similar language about the same
period, Edward Everett recalled that "there were still lingering
among us distinguished leaders of the revolutionary struggle.
Our heroic age . . . was prolonged. . . . This tended to lift
events from the level of dry matter of fact into the region of
sentiment."[23]

This division of history corresponded to a prevailing sense
of the movement of time. In the 1820s a heroic generation of
founders ("our fathers") had been, for good or ill, succeeded
in power by a post-heroic generation of sons. People whose
consciousness was structured around their awareness of their
exclusion by the timing of their birth from the heroic founding group ("fathers") and of their shared membership ("our")

---

[21] [Joseph Cook], "Conversational Opinions of the Leaders of Secession:
A Monograph," *Atlantic Monthly* 10 (1862): 622.

[22] "Henry Clay as an Orator," *Putnam's Monthly* 3 (1854): 495.

[23] Edward Everett, *Orations and Speeches on Various Occasions,* 4 vols.
(Boston: Little, Brown and Co., 1850–68), 1:x. "The leading spirits of the
Revolution survived, and imparted their own patriotic aspirations to the rising
generation." [Henry T. Tuckerman], "American Society," *North American
Review* 81 (1855): 31.

in a different group formed what sociologists call a cohort.[24] As we shall see, some members of the cohort celebrated and others suffered under the weight of this particular dispensation of history. Some celebrated *and* suffered. However different their lives were in other respects, and however different their attitudes toward this one, the point is that their lives were structured by shared experience.[25]

The post-heroic cohort encompassed a generation of metaphorical "sons," but the psychological boundaries of the generation are wider than a strict chronological usage of the term would ordinarily permit.[26] Consider, for example, the disparate cases of Henry Clay, a Kentucky Whig who was born in Virginia in 1777, and Stephen A. Douglas, an Illinois Democrat who was born in Vermont in 1813. At first look it might seem to do violence to the language to speak of these two men as belonging to the same generation. After all, on the day Doug-

[24] In facing the methodological problems involved in using "generation" as a unit of historical time, I have benefited from Karl Mannheim, "The Problem of Generations," in *Essays on the Sociology of Knowledge,* ed. Paul Kecskemeti (London: Routledge & Kegan Paul, 1952), pp. 276–320; Norman B. Ryder, "The Cohort as a Concept in the Study of Social Change," *American Sociological Review* 30 (1965): 843–61; Peter Loewenberg, "The Psychohistorical Origins of the Nazi Youth Cohort," *American Historical Review* 76 (1971): 1457–1502; Alan B. Spitzer, "The Historical Problem of Generations," ibid. 78 (1973): 1353–85.

[25] Involved as an obscure youth in the action of the Revolution and as a heroic leader in post-heroic politics fifty years later, Andrew Jackson (1767–1845) stands outside—and thereby obscures—the categories I am defining here. Born later than the celebrated "fathers" and sooner than the celebrating "sons," he identified fully with neither generation. He nevertheless managed to exploit with facility the sentimental language that worked to structure and legitimate these categories. See Michael Paul Rogin, *Fathers and Children: Andrew Jackson and the Subjugation of the American Indian* (New York: Alfred A. Knopf, 1975), esp. pp. 19–74, 140–57.

[26] Of course, the setting of *any* precise boundaries for a cohort of the sort I have described is arbitrary. See Johan Huizinga, *Men and Ideas: History, the Middle Ages, the Renaissance; Essays,* trans. James S. Holmes and Hans van Marle (Cleveland: World Publishing Co., Meridian Books, 1959), pp. 73–74; Spitzer, "Historical Problem of Generations," pp. 1355–56.

las was born Henry Clay was the Speaker of the House of Representatives. The differences between them, not to mention the differences among other people born between the 1770s and the 1810s, were of course enormous and varied, and they will not be neglected here. But Clay and Douglas belonged to the same cohort because psychologically they shared an age, with each other and with other Americans born in the period between their birth years. Politically they were united by neither section nor party, but they were nonetheless united—by having to face the same set of public problems, by coming to these problems from common and often unarticulated assumptions that lay deeper than party or section, and, occasionally, by offering the same solutions to these problems. In the great sectional crisis that followed the Mexican War (when, except for Lincoln, all of the figures whose actions were decisive in the secession crisis were already prominent on the political stage), both men sought in complementary ways to save the Union of their fathers. Clay devised the pieces of legislation that accurately became known as the Compromise of 1850 and Douglas pushed them, one by one, through Congress. The accomplishment of Clay would have been futile had it not been for Douglas; the accomplishment of Douglas would have been impossible had it not been for Clay.

The common psychological background of the post-heroic cohort defined its members' relationship to each other in fraternal terms: "Reminded of our fathers, we should remember that we are brethren," Rufus Choate advised.[27] This outlook encouraged the kind of solidarity that prevented disunion in 1850, but, as we shall see, it also underlay the peculiarly emotional rivalry that made the measures of 1850 necessary in the first place, and that would frustrate later efforts at similarly all-encompassing compromises.

[27] Brown, *Works of Choate,* 1:344.

THE FOUNDING HEROES
AND THE POST-HEROIC GENERATION

Oh! may the youths of this free land,
Columbia's proudest rising sons,
Become with every virtue fraught
A RACE OF GOD-LIKE WASHINGTONS.

THOMAS DUNN ENGLISH, 1837

No sooner did Americans create their Union than they began
to speculate fretfully about how long it would last. That the
new Republic survived and even flourished through one crisis
after another in domestic and international politics between
the 1780s and 1815 did little to put this question to rest. Indeed, throughout the early part of the nineteenth century it
was a common observation that the Union was evanescent. It
was characterized by various writers as "metaphysical and theoretical"; as "a sort of *forced state* . . . of life"; as a mere lin-
guistic creation that had been "spoken into existence"; and
that "exists, so to speak, only in the mind."[1] Vagueness had

[1] [Edward Everett], "Memoir of Richard Henry Lee," *North American Review* 22 (1826): 374; Rufus Choate, in Samuel Gilman Brown, ed., *The*

been less a problem to the founders, for whom the Union was made real enough by the act of creating it. Nor would it be a problem for Americans after 1865: they virtually dropped the word *Union* from their political vocabulary, as if to underscore the most obvious result of the Civil War.[2] But before 1865 the very pervasiveness of the term testified to the tentative quality of the political bonds among Americans. The word *Union* seemed to be synonymous with "not a nation," "not quite a nation," or "not yet a nation."

It was taken for granted from the start that the survival of the Republic for any length of time would depend heavily on the virtue of its citizens. Character was perceived to be the point of contact between individual lives and national fate. The sum of "the characters of individuals," Noah Webster wrote, "forms the general character of a nation."[3] Two additional beliefs, related to this and each other, focused attention on children. The first was that the national character was not yet set. The second, to quote Noah Webster again, was that "the impressions received in early life usually form the characters of individuals."[4] Here then was a magnificent opportunity for all who believed—and according to one scholar everyone did[5]—in Locke's concept of the tabula rasa. National character and national destiny could be formed by a careful molding of the characters of the rising generation. The nurturing of the in-

Works of Rufus Choate with a Memoir of His Life, 2 vols. (Boston: Little, Brown and Co., 1862), 2:315; "American Poetry," *Southern Quarterly Review* 1 (1842): 495; Alexis de Tocqueville, *Democracy in America,* ed. Phillips Bradley, 2 vols. (New York: Alfred A. Knopf, 1945), 1:172.

2 Robert Penn Warren, *The Legacy of the Civil War: Meditations on the Centennial* (New York: Alfred A. Knopf, 1961), p. 6.

3 Noah Webster, "On the Education of Youth in America," in Frederick Rudolph, ed., *Essays on Education in the Early Republic* (Cambridge, Mass.: Harvard University Press, Belknap Press, 1965), p. 43.

4 Ibid.; see also p. 45.

5 [Edward Everett], "Letters from Geneva and France," *North American Review* 11 (1820): 31.

fant nation and the infant generation would proceed in tandem. It was crucial, Noah Webster asserted, to "implant in the minds of the American youth the principles of virtue and of liberty and inspire them with just and liberal ideas of government and with an inviolable attachment to their own country."[6] The little strangers appearing among them presented an opportunity both so obvious and so pressing that probably no other generation of American children was as self-consciously socialized as the post-heroic one. The connection between child rearing and the future of the Republic elevated child rearing to a concern of the highest order—too important, indeed, to be left to the vagaries of the teachings and examples of parents. Outside assistance was required to compensate for the "deficiencies of parental government."[7]

To make the Union real and children virtuous—and thereby secure the Union—was a complex goal that post-heroic Americans sought to reach in a number of ways. One in particular interests us here because of its later importance. Many people who shared these concerns attempted to present the political and historical world to the child in understandable terms that would serve to bind him to it, and at the same time to inculcate the principles of virtue. It was with these purposes in mind that people began to compare the amorphous and invisible Union to a family or a house. To do so was to give the Union an image and a shape at once, thereby making it both more comprehensible[8] and a magnet for that displaced emotion I have called sentiment. To invoke these images was also to imply a certain lack of interest in close theoretical exploration of the meaning of Union. The natural cohesiveness of

[6] Webster, "Education of Youth," p. 45.

[7] Benjamin Rush, "Plan for the Establishment of Public Schools," in Rudolph, *Essays on Education*, p. 16.

[8] See Michael Walzer, "On the Role of Symbolism in Political Thought," *Political Science Quarterly* 82 (1967): 191–204.

families did not require explanation. Daniel Webster did not need to spell out the particular principles he had in mind when he declared that "the bonds of political brotherhood, which hold us together from Maine to Georgia, rest upon the same principles of obligation as those of domestic . . . life."[9] Nor did anyone need to explain why houses, once built with skill by immortal architects, should continue to stand.

Americans did not invent these metaphors. Two propositions—that nations structurally resemble the family and that nations originated in families—are as old as political thought.[10] But to post-heroic Americans unsure of the capacity of their new constitutional machinery to withstand the onslaught of modernity, the analogy had obvious appeal. In a society that valued progress and equality, and in which authority of any kind, no matter how mild, was on the defensive, the family was one archaic, hierarchical institution compatible with modernity and with democracy.[11] It was not subjected to serious challenge partly because, in addition to being historical, the family was also "natural," and because although hierarchical, the authority in the family was so entangled with gentle affection that external control was imperceptibly transformed by love into self-control, making the line between paternalism and self-reliance impossible to draw.

[9] Daniel Webster, *The Writings and Speeches of Daniel Webster,* 18 vols. (Boston: Little, Brown and Co., 1903), 4:249.

[10] Gordon J. Schochet, *Patriarchalism in Political Thought: The Authoritarian Family and Political Speculation and Attitudes Especially in Seventeenth-Century England* (Oxford: Basil Blackwell, 1975), pp. 18–36. Family metaphors played a crucial role in shaping American understanding first of their difficulties with, and then of their break from, Great Britain in the 1760s and 1770s. See Edwin G. Burrows and Michael Wallace, "The American Revolution: The Ideology and Psychology of National Liberation," *Perspectives in American History* 6 (1972): 167–306.

[11] "The Progress of Society," *United States Magazine and Democratic Review* 8 (1840): 69; "California Gold and European Revolution," *Southern Quarterly Review* 17 (1850): 283.

It might seem, however, that the turn into the nineteenth century was among the least propitious of times to call upon the family to bolster any other institution. Historians have analyzed the institution of the family in terms of the progressive loss, beginning in the preindustrial age, of its traditional functions (economic, educational, health care, police, and so forth) and the assumption of these functions by other, specialized social institutions such as factories, schools, hospitals, courts, and asylums. They have gone on to say that the family, thus weakened by the loss of the socializing services that had made it the door to the wider world, retreated, so to speak, into its own "sphere," where it made the best of its historical fate by magnifying its remaining tasks—to nurture children for, and to shield adults from, the escalating demands of modern life. The family, in other words, has been seen by modern observers as narrowed and isolated, and consequently put on the defensive in order not to lose the few functions it retained.[12] It is one thing, however, to describe the family as becoming specialized; it is quite another to equate specialization with either narrowing or isolation, for in no way does the term specialization necessarily connote either. Just to state the above proposition is to reveal some of the exaggerations it contains. Nurture takes place with the child's prospects in the world clearly in mind; it takes into account the needs of society and therefore socializes. The adult who returns to the

[12] See David J. Rothman, *The Discovery of the Asylum: Social Order and Disorder in the New Republic* (Boston: Little, Brown and Co., 1971); William R. Taylor and Christopher Lasch, "Two 'Kindred Spirits': Sorority and Family in New England, 1839–1846," *New England Quarterly* 36 (1963): 23–41; Kirk Jeffrey, Jr., "Family History: The Middle-Class American Family in the Urban Context, 1830–1870" (Ph.D. diss., Stanford University, 1972); Mary Patricia Ryan, "American Society and the Cult of Domesticity, 1830–1860" (Ph.D. diss., University of California, Santa Barbara, 1971); Kathryn Kish Sklar, *Catharine Beecher: A Study in American Domesticity* (New Haven: Yale University Press, 1973).

family hardly leaves the world behind, much as he might like to.

In fact, as an increasingly complex and rapidly transforming society committed itself to the values of economic competition, political democracy, geographic expansion, and individualism, and reveled in a general busy-ness, it self-consciously and with scarcely less zeal committed itself to the counterweight of familial bonds. But perhaps the effect of these opposing commitments was not to make the spheres of family and society more distinct and antithetical, but rather less so. For one thing, as society preempted functions that once were monopolized by the family, it looked for ways to model its performance on that of an idealized family, and described what it was doing in sentimental language. The effect was arguably to make society seem like the family writ large, embracing the whole country.

Training in patriotism is perhaps the most important example of this phenomenon; certainly it was in this realm that society moved most conspicuously to correct the "deficiencies of parental government." For Americans searching for models of virtue more certain than parents, the founding heroes provided natural and obvious choices. Individual imitation of the characters of the founders would tend to the development not only of a common national character, but one of the most desirable kind.[13] It was, further, widely assumed that since the characters of the founders provided the foundation for the Republic, imitation of their characters by the rising generation could preserve it.[14] Publications of the period suggested to parents that

---

[13] At least one writer believed that imitating the fathers was not only natural but unavoidable. "So deeply rooted is the principle of imitation in our nature and so ceaseless is our reverence for those who have gone before us, that the habits and opinions of the people are almost moulded after those of their fathers and especially the first founders of the state." "Machiavel's Political Discourses Upon the First Decade of Livy," *Southern Literary Messenger* 5 (1839): 820.

[14] "Everett's *Orations*," *New-York Review* 1 (1825): 335; "Characteristics of the Statesman," *Southern Quarterly Review* 6 (1844): 95–129.

they accustom their children, from the earliest moments of their lives, to revere the founders and think of them as fathers. Noah Webster wrote that "every child in America . . . as soon as he opens his lips . . . should rehearse the history of his own country; he should lisp the praise of liberty and of those illustrious heroes and statesmen who have wrought a revolution in her favor."[15] "We would exhibit that example to our children in every stage of education," another writer advised, extending the notion. "We would teach the personal narrative of our revolution in our schools; we would make it so completely elementary and systematic, that no one would dare to neglect it."[16]

Rufus Choate once said that patriotic feeling

> comes uncalled for, one knows not how. It comes in with the very air, the eye, the ear, the instincts, the first taste of the mother's milk, the first beatings of the heart. The faces of brothers and sisters, and the loved father and mother,—the laugh of playmates, the old willow-tree, and well, and schoolhouse, the bees at work in the spring, the note of the robin at evening, the lullaby . . . all things which make childhood happy, begin it. . . . [As] love and the sense of home and of security and of property under law, come to life . . . there is a type of patriotism already.

This patriotism extended to the boundaries of personal experience—to local surroundings, even to the state, perhaps, but not necessarily beyond. The problem, as Choate saw it, was how to "direct this spontaneous sentiment of hearts to the Union . . . [how to] transform this surpassing beauty into a national life . . . which shall last while sun and moon endure." He came up with a suggestion at once: history should be cen-

[15] Webster, "Education of Youth," pp. 64–65.
[16] "Diplomatic Correspondence of the Revolution," *American Quarterly Review* 10 (1831): 418.

tral to the emotional life of the child from the start. " 'Americans, . . . begin with the infant in the cradle. Let the first lisps be Washington.' "[17]

With their emphasis on the personal quality of history, these prescriptions envisioned a means of assisting children to comprehend the Revolution, which must have seemed to them a mysterious event indeed. For on the one hand, the War for Independence came down to the post-heroic generation as a cosmic, half-fabulous occurrence, whose events appeared "so strange and heroic that they resemble ingenious fables, or the dreams of romance, rather than the realities of authentic history."[18] Certainly nothing more grand had ever occurred. The Revolution was often said to be the pivotal event in time, toward which all history tended, and from which flowed everything that had happened since. The causes of the Revolution lay "far back in the history of Europe." "Our Independence was the fruit of centuries; the whole previous civilization of the world was the condition, under which the glorious event was possible." "All things conspired, all things wrought, toward it." "All past events [had] been preparing the way for it . . . all past generations [had] been laboring in its cause." Accordingly the Revolution was seen as a climax, "a finishing act," "the great political consummation of the ages," and as "the winding up of a great drama, of which the opening scene begins with the landing of our fathers."[19]

[17] Rufus Choate, "Oration before the Young Men's Democratic Club, in Tremont Temple," Boston *Daily Advertiser*, July 7, 1858.

[18] "Address of the Bunker Hill Monument Association to the Selectmen of the several Towns in Massachusetts," October 1, 1824, in George Washington Warren, *The History of the Bunker Hill Monument Association during the First Century of the United States of America* (Boston: James R. Osgood and Co., 1877), p. 85.

[19] "The National Anniversary," *Southern Quarterly Review* 18 (1850): 170; [George Bancroft], "Force's Documentary History," *North American Review* 46 (1838): 486–87; John S. Holmes, Boston *Daily Advertiser*, July 7, 1858; [Jonathan Chapman], "The Progress of Society," *North American Review* 36

On the other hand, the Revolution was as close and as commonplace as the people one loved. Abraham Lincoln once observed that almost every adult male of the 1770s and 1780s actually participated in at least some of the events of the War for Independence. "The consequence was, that . . . in the form of a husband, a father, a son or a brother, a *living history was* to be found in every family."[20] The fathers of several important figures in the sectional conflict—Daniel Webster, Jefferson Davis, Robert J. Walker, John J. Crittenden, and Robert E. Lee, for examples—had fought in the War for Independence.[21] They were literally the sons of revolutionary fathers. In the 1850s, Samuel Griswold Goodrich, a writer who was born in 1793, recalled his own postrevolutionary childhood in Connecticut, and captured the sense of what it meant to appear not too long after the war ended.

> The existing generation of middle age, had all witnessed it; nearly all had shared in its vicissitudes. . . . Every old man,

(1833): 423; D[avid] H[atch] Barlow, "Mission of America," *Graham's Magazine* 38 (1851): 44; Edward Everett, *Orations and Speeches on Various Occasions*, 4 vols. (Boston: Little, Brown and Co., 1850–68), 4:26; ibid., 1:395.

20 Roy P. Basler, ed., *The Collected Works of Abraham Lincoln*, 8 vols. (New Brunswick, N.J.: Rutgers University Press, 1953), 1:115.

21 Charles M. Wiltse, ed., *The Papers of Daniel Webster, Correspondence* (Hanover, N.H.: University Press of New England, 1974–), 1:5; [Varina Anne Howell Davis], *Jefferson Davis, Ex-President of the Confederate States of America: A Memoir by His Wife*, 2 vols. (New York: Belford Co., 1890), 1:3, 4; Frank Moore, ed., *The Rebellion Record: A Diary of American Events, with Documents, Narratives, Illustrative Incidents, Poetry, etc.*, 11 vols. (New York: G. P. Putnam, 1861–63; D. Van Nostrand, 1864–68), documents, 1:89; Mrs. Chapman Coleman, ed., *The Life of John J. Crittenden, With Selections from His Correspondence and Speeches*, 2 vols. (Philadelphia: J. B. Lippincott Co., 1871), 1:13; Douglas Southall Freeman, *R. E. Lee: A Biography*, 4 vols. (New York: Charles Scribner's Sons, 1934–35), 1:2–3. "The son of a revolutionary soldier, attachment to this Union [*sic*] was among the first lessons of my childhood," Jefferson Davis said in 1850. "I look upon it now with the affection of early love." *Congressional Globe*, 31 Cong., 1 Sess. (February 14, 1850), appendix, p. 156.

> every old woman had stories to tell, radiant with the vivid
> realities of personal observation or experience. Some had seen
> Washington, and some Old Put; one was at the capture of
> Ticonderoga under Ethan Allen; another was at Bennington.
> . . . The time which had elapsed since these events, had
> served only to magnify and glorify these scenes, as well as
> the actors, especially in the imagination of the rising gen-
> eration.[22]

As near and as far as early childhood, the Revolution presented to this new generation a problem of scale.

The extraordinary and the commonplace were fused in the
person and experience of George Washington, who was so
central to the great event as to be synonymous with it and yet
could be known by the close title of father. According to a
stylized pattern of thought and speech that was worked up
by hundreds of people from different backgrounds and that
prevailed with little change from 1799 to the 1850s,[23] Washington was the central and crucial presence in the Revolution
and in the founding period generally. His admirers took it as
a matter of course that the Revolution probably would not
have occurred and certainly would not have been successful
had he not existed and been prepared to fight it. So closely
was he linked to the central event of the eighteenth century,
so perfectly did he represent the "spirit of the age," that his
life story was as good as "an abstract of the history of the
country while he lived."[24] Early biographies of Washington,
indeed, are as much histories of the Revolution as accounts of
the life of the man, going into detail for pages and even chap-

[22] S[amuel] G[riswold] Goodrich, *Recollections of a Lifetime, or Men and
Things I have Seen: in a Series of Familiar Letters to a Friend, Historical,
Biographical, Anecdotical, and Descriptive*, 2 vols. (New York: Miller, Orton
and Mulligan, 1857), 1:22–23.

[23] I deal in Chapter 6 with the changes that did occur.

[24] Alexander Rives, *An Address Delivered February 22nd, 1840, before the
Charlottesville Lyceum* (Charlottesville: James Alexander, 1840), p. 5; Everett,
Orations and Speeches, 4:18.

ters at a stretch on matters with which he had no connection whatever.[25]

For all his importance, it was nevertheless a convention of Washington iconography that he was but acting as the agent of a power greater than himself. His role in history was designed by Providence, which chose him and prepared him to play it.[26] In what seems a reworking for great men of the Puritans' concept of grace, it was said of Washington as well as the other founders that they "well understood the part which Providence had assigned to them," and that they clearly "perceived that they were called to discharge a high and precious office to the cause of civil liberty; that their hands were elected to strike the blow, for which two centuries . . . had been [preparing] on one side or the other of the Atlantic."[27] Beverley Tucker believed that Washington had an "early consciousness of something distinguishing him from other men," and he considered it likely that even in his childhood Washington realized that "he might be a father, and that his children might find an humble pride in looking over the unspotted page of his unpretending life." "It is the most striking instance on record of the *instinct of greatness.*"[28]

[25] The leading example of this habit is John Marshall, *The Life of George Washington, Commander in Chief of the American Forces, During the War which Established the Independence of His Country, and First President of the United States,* 5 vols. (Philadelphia: C. P. Wayne, 1804–7). On Washington biography generally during this period, see William Alfred Bryan, *George Washington in American Literature, 1775–1865* (New York: Columbia University Press, 1952), pp. 86–120.

[26] Henry Lee, in *Eulogies and Orations on the Life and Death of General George Washington, First President of the United States of America* (Boston: Manning & Loring, 1800), p. 13; "Sketches of American Character," *Ladies' Magazine* 1 (1828): 157; Rives, *Address,* p. 5; Everett, *Orations and Speeches,* 4:41.

[27] Ibid., 1:105. See also [Alexander H. Everett], "Origin and Character of the old Parties," *North American Review* 39 (1834): 248; "Benjamin Franklin," *Southern Literary Messenger* 31 (1860): 192.

[28] [Nathaniel Beverley Tucker], "The Writings of George Washington," *Southern Literary Messenger* 1 (1835): 592.

Thus aware of the great deeds he was to perform, Washington prepared himself by developing "a system of moral discipline . . . he trained himself to greatness and virtue."[29] His great guide was natural law, whose precepts he learned by figuring out and then imitating the workings of the cosmos itself. He replicated in human form "that deep repose and silent equilibrium of mental and moral power which governs the universe."[30] Once set in his course he moved inexorably and yet serenely "like some mighty planet along its predestined path" through the eighteenth century changing things forever.[31] This act of mimesis of the Newtonian system—an "impersonation" of "principles" as Alexander Rives expressed it—was the very definition of reason.[32] His success at imitation was what made Washington "the brightest ornament" of the century of light.[33]

As if anticipating and consciously contributing to the development of this myth about himself, Washington in the first years of the Republic had moved actively to make his persona the link between the principles of virtue and the future of the Union. In public he customarily employed a vocabulary that blurred the distinction between the political and the private realms of life. On entering the presidency in 1789 Washington made a highly personal statement, dealing at length

29 Ibid.

30 Everett, *Orations and Speeches,* 4:39.

31 "The Federal Administrations of Washington and the Elder Adams," *Southern Literary Messenger* 13 (1847): 561; Edwin P. Whipple, *Character and Characteristic Men* (Boston: Houghton Mifflin Co., 1866), p. 306. The planetary image appealed to conservative people who longed not only for order but also for quiet. Edward Everett suggested that one difference between most so-called great men and Washington was like that between a thunderstorm—noisy but local and transitory—and a planet, which moves in silence. Everett, *Orations and Speeches,* 4:39–40. See also [Henry T. Tuckerman], "The Character of Washington," *North American Review* 83 (1856): 20.

32 Rives, *Address,* p. 3.

33 Everett, *Orations and Speeches,* 4:24.

with the "conflict of emotions" he experienced as he began this new, last task. The First Inaugural was an aggressively didactic piece, asserting an "indissoluble union between virtue and happiness" and promising that the "foundation of our national policy will be laid in the pure and immutable principles of private morality."[34] On leaving the presidency Washington issued another statement, in which he returned to this sentimental-didactic path. His Farewell Address, which was published in 1796, was characterized throughout by the paternal, personal voice, linking "collective and individual happiness" with virtue, and both to the Union, and urging "brotherly affection" to preserve the last.[35] To nineteenth-century Americans, the Farewell Address stood almost with the Declaration of Independence and the Constitution as an important founding document. In emotional terms it stood ahead of either, for here the father was speaking personally. Although the address contained advice that was exclusively political, it was, Daniel Webster said, "the solemnity with which it urges the observance of moral duties [that] gives to it the highest character of truly disinterested, sincere, parental advice."[36] Andrew Jackson alluded to its prophetic "paternal counsels."[37] Mason Locke Weems wrote that the paper should be studied "with the feelings of children reading the last letter of a once-loved father now in his grave"—that is, with a sense of filial subordination against which only the basest would rebel.[38]

Yet it is important to recognize that it was not so much Washington's advice that was the key to his role in the life of

[34] James D. Richardson, ed., *A Compilation of the Messages and Papers of the Presidents,* 10 vols. (Washington: Government Printing Office, 1897), 1:51–53.

[35] Ibid., pp. 215, 220, 214.

[36] Webster, *Writings and Speeches,* 2:77.

[37] Richardson, *Messages of the Presidents,* 3:295.

[38] Mason L. Weems, *The Life of Washington,* ed. Marcus Cunliffe (Cambridge, Mass.: Harvard University Press, Belknap Press, 1962), p. 141.

the next generation, for the world had never lacked expert moral wisdom serenely presented. Rather it was Washington's life—his life as a model—that set him apart from other moralists, for he had demonstrated that the world was hospitable to virtue.[39] American children were not asked to memorize a list of copybook maxims which might or might not have played a role in the life of the man who claimed to represent them and who demanded that they (if not he) be followed. Such rote lessons were not likely to take in any case; models were far more efficacious. "Do not suppose, young man," Walt Whitman lectured in a story he wrote about Washington, "that it is by sermons and oft-repeated precepts we form a disposition great or good. The model of one pure, upright character, living as a beacon in history, does more benefit than the lumbering tomes of a thousand theorists."[40] Children would internalize the values through identification with the man.

No word in the eulogistic vocabulary was more frequently used than "character." Two of the most famous speeches ever given about the first president are titled "The Character of Washington."[41] People reached for the word as though it explained him—in fact, insisted that it did explain him.[42] His character was "the purest and most effective in all history."[43] Indeed it was the "beauty" of his character rather than anything he did that distinguished him from all other men.[44] A popular magazine of the 1820s acknowledged that there is

[39] Webster, *Writings and Speeches,* 2:70.

[40] Walter [*sic*] Whitman, "The Last of the Sacred Army," *United States Magazine and Democratic Review* 10 (1842): 264.

[41] Webster, *Writings and Speeches,* 2:69–82; Everett, *Orations and Speeches,* 4:3–51.

[42] "American Biography," *American Quarterly Review* 1 (1827): 26–27; James K. Paulding, "Washington and Napoleon," *Graham's Magazine* 25 (1844): 60.

[43] [Tuckerman], "Character of Washington," p. 2.

[44] Everett, *Orations and Speeches,* 4:34; [William H. Prescott], "Bancroft's *History of the United States,*" *North American Review* 52 (1841): 102.

no such thing as a perfect man, but asserted that Washington came close to that ideal, surely closer than any other mortal had ever come.[45] The result of a desire to resemble God by conforming to His works, character was the key to Washington's role in history (and was also the key to the mechanism of history generally). It explained the purity of his ideas, his influence over others, his tenacity—in other words, it explained his own success as well as that of his cause.[46] Character was also the key to his role in the life of posterity. The design of Providence was that Washington go beyond his deeds to become a model on which other Americans could build their own characters.[47]

"It should . . . be the pride of us his children," Beverley Tucker wrote in 1835, "to read the history of his life . . . to study the system of moral discipline by which he trained himself to greatness and virtue . . . and to mould ourselves by his precepts and example."[48] "The ingenious youth of America," Daniel Webster expected, "will hold up to themselves the bright model of Washington's example, and study to be what

---

[45] "Life of Washington," *Casket* 2 (1827): 409. One could criticize Hamilton and Jefferson of course, even Franklin, but "no man whispers a syllable against the name of George Washington." "Character of Jefferson," *New-York Review* 1 (1837): 6.

[46] It was "the moral sublimity of character, which actuated the heroes and sages of the revolution." *United States Literary Gazette* 2 (1825): 295. On this point see also [Andrews Norton], "Dr. Franklin," *North American Review* 7 (1818): 311; [Tucker], "George Washington," p. 592; Brown, *Works of Choate,* 1:351; Henry T. Tuckerman, "Governeur [*sic*] Morris," *Graham's Magazine* 38 (1851): 288. Character was said to be the force that gave "life and movement to society" and that "forms and reforms institutions." Whipple, *Character and Characteristic Men,* p. 2.

[47] Everett, *Orations and Speeches,* 4:41; John J. Crittenden, in William Hincks and F. H. Smith, eds., *Washington's Birthday: Congressional Banquet in Honor of George Washington, and the Principles of Washington* (Washington: Buell & Blanchard, 1852), p. 6.

[48] [Tucker], "George Washington," p. 592. See also "Charles Carroll, of Carrollton," *Casket* 5 (1830): 457–58.

they behold."[49] "The best eulogy" to the fathers, yet another
moralist wrote, "would be for Americans to study his character . . . and then bow their hearts before Heaven, and in a
spirit of pious patriotism fervently ask 'make me like Washington.' "[50] Thomas Dunn English summarized these hopes in
a poem:

> Oh! may the youths of this free land,
>   Columbia's proudest rising sons,
> Become with every virtue fraught
>   A RACE OF GOD-LIKE WASHINGTONS.[51]

Mothers in particular were advised to teach their sons from
infancy to revere and imitate Washington.[52]

We thus confront an important historical coincidence. Society began to concern itself with child nurture as a political
matter and to summon models from history at the same time
that for essentially economic reasons actual fathers ceased to
provide more or less automatic models of roles their sons
would grow up to play. One of the corollaries of the changes
in family life I mentioned earlier is that postrevolutionary
American society ceased to take it almost as a matter of course
that a son would eventually step into the occupation of his
father or that of a village neighbor, and that he would then
spend the rest of his life residing near and attached to his
parents.[53] At a time when expanding economic opportunity

---

[49] Webster, *Writings and Speeches,* 2:71.

[50] "To Whom Does Washington's Glory Belong?" *Southern Literary Messenger* 9 (1843): 589.

[51] Thomas Dunn English, "Young Washington's Reply to Gov. Dinwiddie,"
Casket 12 (1837): 385.

[52] See, e.g., Kate Berry, "How Can an American Woman Serve Her Country?" *Godey's Lady's Book* 43 (1851): 364.

[53] Joseph F. Kett, *Rites of Passage: Adolescence in America, 1790 to the
Present* (New York: Basic Books, 1977), pp. 30–31.

meant that boys were beginning to need a wider range of models than their surroundings were likely to provide, history stepped in to supply them in the form of the founding heroes. That there was not a close fit of model to need—it was not, after all, for their commercial exploits that Americans celebrated the fathers—was a realization that came later when it came at all.

The rest of this study starts from the proposition that the prevalent use of familial metaphors in public discourse reflected the increasingly deep and strong emotional bonds that joined Americans to each other and to their past. The personal nature of the metaphors suggests the nature and the dynamic of the emotions—an extension of natural affections to the public realm. In certain respects, to claim this is not to claim very much. "Causes such as these," wrote a Southerner in the 1830s, referring to the personalization of history I have been discussing,

> all co-operating together to the same end, could scarcely fail of their effect. It is not surprising . . . that the present generation in the United States should have grown up with a love of Union impressed upon their minds, with a strength little short of that of religious veneration. It is the first political lesson inculcated on the infant mind.[54]

The statement comports with the way most people probably assume that the mysterious sense of patriotism becomes part of us.

Nor would most people have much difficulty accepting the proposition that the practically incessant appeals to George Washington in some sense "took"—that, as John J. Crittenden

[54] [Abel P. Upshur], "The Partisan Leader," *Southern Literary Messenger* 3 (1837): 74.

said in 1852, "his name has sunk deep into the . . . inner recesses of the hearts of his countrymen; and, like an oracle, is continually whispering lessons of patriotism and of virtue."[55] One can find many statements that are more or less like that, or like the following one, also made in the 1850s about Washington:

> From our earliest dawning of intelligence, that name had been uppermost in all our fondest recollections and associations. Some how or other, perhaps it was "distance lent enchantment to the view," but we early came to associate some of the purest and best feelings of our nature with the character and conduct of this our great countryman.[56]

Statements like these come provocatively close to modern notions of the way that "the purest and best feelings" become part of "our nature." It is a process more complex—and far more emotional—than simply the imitation of role models. Internalization—the incorporation of values into "our nature"—is achieved only in the process of great struggle between the narcissistic, ambitious self and authority figures around it.[57]

But American children at the turn into the nineteenth century did not, of course, "struggle" with Washington. How then did they internalize the values he represented? Sigmund Freud once observed that for children there is no gap between the word and the thing, between metaphor and referent. On the contrary, they "treat words in every sense as things. . . . They are never ready to accept a similarity between two words as having no meaning; they consistently assume that if two things

---

[55] Coleman, *Life of Crittenden,* 2:28.

[56] E. Kennedy, "Mount Vernon—A Pilgrimage," *Southern Literary Messenger* 18 (1852): 53.

[57] A comprehensive and clear guide to modern psychoanalytic understanding of this process is Roy Schafer, *Aspects of Internalization* (New York: International Universities Press, 1968).

are called by similar-sounding names this must imply the existence of some deep-lying point of agreement between them."[58] In the case at hand there is every reason to suspect that children, urged to identify with the founders as the fathers who held the key to what they should be like and what they might become, would think of them as fathers generally—transferring to them the entire range of attitudes, feelings, memories, and so forth that they had come to associate with the father who was the figure who towered over their childhood, but whose role as model was now compromised by history.[59] Thus, in a sense that goes beyond and deeper than metaphor, the revolutionary fathers collectively became the fathers of the post-heroic cohort, and it is this relationship that gives the cohort its distinct identity in history.

Taken to an extreme degree, transference to historical beings (or abstractions such as "Nature") can take the form of what Freud called "the family romance"—the fantasy that one is actually the child of heroes.[60] Close observers of children have often remarked that one of the most common of their fantasies is to suppose that "one doesn't really belong in this dreary little

[58] Sigmund Freud, *Totem and Taboo, The Standard Edition of the Complete Psychological Works of Sigmund Freud,* ed. and trans. James Strachey, 24 vols. (London: Hogarth Press and the Institute of Psycho-Analysis, 1953–73), 13:56.

[59] Paul Roazen, *Freud: Political and Social Thought* (New York: Alfred A. Knopf, 1968), p. 149; Harold P. Blum, "Transference and Structure," in Mark Kanzer, ed., *The Unconscious Today: Essays in Honor of Max Schur* (New York: International Universities Press, 1971), p. 191; Leonard Shengold, "Freud and Joseph," ibid., p. 473; Fred Weinstein and Gerald M. Platt, *Psychoanalytic Sociology: An Essay on the Interpretation of Historical Data and the Phenomena of Collective Behavior* (Baltimore: Johns Hopkins University Press, 1973), p. 11.

[60] Sigmund Freud, "Family Romances," in Strachey, *Works of Freud,* 9:236–41; Phyllis Greenacre, "The Family Romance of the Artist," *Psychoanalytic Study of the Child* 13 (1958): 9–36; John Frosch, "Transference Derivatives of the Family Romance," *Journal of the American Psychoanalytic Association* 7 (1959): 503–22.

house . . . with these boring ordinary people—that one's real parents are very rich and important and exciting, and live in a great mansion, if not a castle."[61] The fantasy represents two conflicting desires: first, "the child's longing for the vanished happy time, when his father still appeared to be the strongest and greatest man, and the mother seemed the dearest and most beautiful woman"; and, second, a wish for heroic accomplishments of one's own.[62]

A central part of growing up is reducing one's parents to human scale, but some young people, particularly very intelligent and ambitious ones, respond to the discovery of ordinariness with a disappointment so great that they get rid of their parents in fantasy and supplant them with others who better comport with their sense of their own worth and prospects for immortality. Sometimes they suspect, and look for evidence to demonstrate, that they are adopted, or that only one of their parents is a natural parent. Such children are likely to choose a certain kind of figure. As Eva M. Rosenfeld has written, "a genius finds his family from among heroes."[63] After all, heroes have already been idealized by their culture. Their heroic credentials are secure, and they will not disappoint the child the way that ordinary parents are bound to do. Storybooks can play an important role in giving substance and structure to

[61] Alison Lurie, "Happy Endings," *New York Review of Books*, November 28, 1974, p. 39.

[62] Otto Rank, *The Myth of the Birth of the Hero: A Psychological Interpretation of Mythology*, trans. F. Robbins and Smith Ely Jelliffe (New York: Journal of Nervous and Mental Disease Publishing Co., 1914), pp. 63–68. I have removed the emphasis from the quotation, which is at p. 67.

[63] Eva M. Rosenfeld, "Dream and Vision: Some Remarks on Freud's Egyptian Bird Dream," *International Journal of Psycho-Analysis* 37 (1956): 100. On the "family romance" see also Roazen, *Freud*, p. 177; Karl Abraham, *Clinical Papers and Essays on Psycho-Analysis*, ed. and trans. Hilda C. Abraham (London: Hogarth Press and the Institute of Psycho-Analysis, 1955), pp. 271–72; Linda Joan Kaplan, "The Concept of the Family Romance," *Psychoanalytic Review* 61 (1974): 169–202.

such fantasies. The greater the materials at hand in the culture, the greater the number of heroes and the greater the culture's ability to exalt them, the more widespread and deep such fantasies are likely to be. Hence it would seem that a post-heroic historical setting—and one moreover in which the developing mass medium of cheap books could make the contrast between the heroic past and the commonplace present dramatically sharp—would particularly encourage the fantasy of the family romance.

The historical coincidence that encouraged transference has perhaps been obscured by the idea of the self-made man, which seems to imply that once the pattern of traditional authority was broken, no equivalent external authority moved to replace it. Its name notwithstanding, however, the concept of the self-made man did not so much assert that men made themselves without assistance or that there were no longer relevant models, as it did the much less dramatic proposition that people could now look elsewhere for those models. In other words, the self-made man theme is as parricidal as the term implies, but not in the service of autonomy. Emotions and expectations once directed to actual fathers could now be transferred to metaphorical fathers.

Consider, for instance, the case of Abraham Lincoln, who seems twice in his life to have half abandoned fathers who let him down—not to become the self-made man he has been so often called, but to become the obedient and ultimately sacrificial son of yet another father. His famous wartime statement to the 166th Ohio Regiment—"I happen temporarily to occupy this big White House. I am a living witness that any one of your children may look to come here as my father's child has"—was once used by Richard Hofstadter to exemplify what he called "the self-made myth." Lincoln measured his own success in what he called "the race of life" in terms of the distance he put between himself and the obscurity of his father, an obscurity that was ratified in the quoted remarks, for the man was not mentioned by name at all, or even referred to again.[64]

Lincoln's disinclination to model his life on that of his father, or even to pay much attention to him, is notorious. The reasons for this estrangement are evidently lost to us, but the depth of it is clear. After Lincoln set out on his own, at the age of twenty-two in 1831, he never lived more than 100 miles from his father, but they rarely met again in the twenty years that turned out to remain of Thomas Lincoln's life. When Lincoln was repeatedly told in late 1850 and early 1851 that his father was dying, and urged to make a parting visit, he first ignored the letters from his family and then finally wrote to his stepbrother saying he would not come. The press of business was one excuse; the minor illness of his wife was another. He did not try hard to disguise his wish not to go. "If we could meet now," he said, "it is doubtful whether it would not be more painful than pleasant." Thomas Lincoln died a few days later. His son did not go to the funeral.[65]

When Abraham Lincoln was very young he is said to have written down these lines:

> Good boys who to their books apply
> Will all be great men by and by.[66]

There can be little doubt that he took the prospect seriously. Long before he departed from his father geographically, he had used books to put great psychological distance between

[64] Basler, *Works of Lincoln,* 7:512; Richard Hofstadter, *The American Political Tradition and the Men Who Made It* (New York: Alfred A. Knopf, 1948), p. 92.

[65] Lincoln to John D. Johnston, January 12, 1851, in Basler, *Works of Lincoln,* 2:96–97; Stephen B. Oates, *With Malice Toward None: The Life of Abraham Lincoln* (New York: Harper & Row, 1977), p. 95.

[66] William H. Herndon and Jesse W. Weik, *Abraham Lincoln: The True Story of a Great Life,* 2 vols. (New York: D. Appleton and Co., 1892), 1:38.

himself and his origins. Indeed, books served for Lincoln to measure the distance between himself and his father. That his own father was illiterate was to Lincoln one of the most salient aspects of the man. To his son, Thomas Lincoln was a "wholly uneducated man" who could write only his own name, and even that he did "bunglingly." In his memory Lincoln associated his own skill with language with his departure from his parent. Using the third person for a campaign biography in 1860, he wrote: "After he was twentythree, and had separated from his father, he studied English grammar, imperfectly of course, but so as to speak and write as well as he now does." To a man who lived by his skill with the written and spoken word, language was the measure of the difference between father and son.[67] Language was the means of Lincoln's self-creation, but it was also the means of his transference and renewed dependence.

After he had been elected president, Lincoln recalled one of the books that had shaped for him a world beyond his immediate surroundings. He told a group of New Jersey legislators that "away back in my childhood, [in] the earliest days of my being able to read," he had "got hold" of *The Life of Washington* by Mason Locke Weems. By his own account the impression the book made upon him was profound.

> I remember all the accounts there given of the battle fields and struggles for the liberties of the country, and none fixed themselves upon my imagination so deeply as the struggle here at Trenton. . . . The crossing of the river; the contest with the Hessians; the great hardships endured at that time, all fixed themselves on my memory . . . and you all know, for you have all been boys, how these early impressions last longer than any others. I recollect thinking then, boy even though

[67] Lincoln to Solomon Lincoln, March 6, 1848, in Basler, *Works of Lincoln,* 1:456; ibid., 4:61, 62.

I was, that there must have been something more than common that those men struggled for.[68]

A pioneering work in mass culture, Weems's book probably
has had more influence on popular thinking about George
Washington than any other ever published. Almost all subsequent writing on Washington has been affected by the image
of the man that the biography calcifies. Weems worked as if
to secure exactly this result. An itinerant preacher and pro-
moter as well as writer of books, he carried his interpretation
to the boundaries of literacy. He had every reason to know
what people wanted to read, and in his *Life of Washington*
(as well as other books he turned out, including "lives" of
Benjamin Franklin and Francis Marion) he provided it. The
book was evidently highly responsive to public taste. Originally
a pamphlet that was first printed in 1800, the work gradually
developed into a book, incorporating material through several
editions until by 1809 it had reached its final form. By 1825 at
least 29 "editions" had been published.[69] Apparently it proved
just the sort of work to fill the patriotic prescriptions of Noah
Webster and people who thought like him. William Russell
Smith, who read the biography when he was growing up in
Alabama in the 1820s, wrote years later that for his generation
the book had achieved its purpose: "that was, to make the
American youth feel and believe with all his soul that Washington was the greatest man that ever lived . . . , and that the
country he delivered was the greatest country on the globe."[70]

It is not difficult to understand why Lincoln remembered
Weems's description of the battle of Trenton, for the account

[68] Ibid., pp. 235–36.

[69] The history of the reputations of this famous book and its author is
traced by Marcus Cunliffe in his introduction to Weems, *Life of Washington,*
pp. ix–lxii.

[70] Anne Easby-Smith, *William Russell Smith of Alabama: His Life and
Works, Including the Entire Text of The Uses of Solitude* (Philadelphia: Dol-
phin Press, 1931), p. 19.

is nothing if not vivid and suspenseful. By December 1776, according to the author, so dismal were the military fortunes of the rebels that "to most people it appeared that the cause of liberty was a *gone cause.*" But then Washington roused his despondent troops, and on Christmas night led them across the Delaware despite the ice that clogged it. The "GENIUS of LIBERTY" followed the crossing, but she was almost without hope. "*Pale* and in tears, with eyes often lifted to Heaven, she moved along with her children to witness perhaps the last conflict." Meanwhile Washington, seeing his men again falter, took to imitating the lion that calls "his brindled sons to battle against the mighty rhinoceros . . . [by shaking] the forest with his deepening roar, till, kindled by their father's fire, the maddening cubs swell with answering rage, and spring undaunted on the Monster." As an "eager wish for battle flushed over his burning face," Washington waved his sword, exhorted his countrymen to *"remember what you are about to fight for,"* and led their charge as they fell upon the surprised Hessians.[71]

Yet there is reason to doubt that the impact the book made on Lincoln or the countless other children who read it derived from Weems's description of a military encounter, no matter how dramatic his prose. We do not suppose, after all, that the Genius of Liberty or rhinoceri were prominent on the list of childish concerns even then. It is much more likely that Weems's appeal had to do with the way he aided children to understand the Revolution and the meaning of Washington's life.

Weems wrote about Washington in the year after the hero's death—when, he said, "his eulogists . . . have trick'd him up" so that "you see nothing of Washington below *the clouds. . . .* You see nothing of his *private virtues.*"[72] In fact the eulogies did discuss Washington's character in detail, and the main themes by which he was known throughout the post-heroic

[71] Weems, *Life of Washington,* pp. 82–85.
[72] Ibid., p. 3.

period were already well developed. The connections between Washington's virtue and Washington's Union were carefully drawn. The eulogies virtually institutionalized Washington's paternal role. Something like Gouverneur Morris's exclamation—"AMERICANS! he had no child—BUT YOU"—was central to nearly all of them.[73] Even then people having care of children were advised to teach them to think of him as a father and to imitate his character.[74] Weems doubtless realized this, and it may seem ironic that he first exaggerated the seriousness of a problem and then proceeded to exacerbate it; no one tricked Washington up more than he did.

Weems's criticism of the eulogies was not that they were historically inaccurate, but that they left Washington out of reach. People, particularly children, who heard them would not find in them meaning for their own lives. When Weems said that the eulogists showed nothing of Washington below the clouds—nothing of his private virtues—he meant that one could see nothing of his virtues in private, that they were always portrayed in connection with his heroic deeds, and thus were of questionable relevance to children who heard about them. The argument he made is similar to Bruno Bettelheim's observation that children, uncertain about their own prospects in the world but quite certain that they are not perfect, are apt to be more discouraged than otherwise by any suggestion that they imitate a virtuous hero who won immortality by performing glorious deeds.[75]

---

[73] Several of the Washington eulogies were collected in *Eulogies and Orations on the Life and Death of General George Washington, First President of the United States of America* (Boston: Manning & Loring, 1800). The statement by Gouverneur Morris appears on p. 46.

[74] "Shall we not . . . teach our children, and they theirs, to lisp his venerable name, to read his martial exploits, and reverence and copy his godlike virtues?" Jonathan Mitchel Sewall, in ibid., p. 41.

[75] Bruno Bettelheim, *The Uses of Enchantment: The Meaning and Importance of Fairy Tales* (New York: Alfred A. Knopf, 1976), pp. 39–41.

Nineteenth-century iconography of Washington, always more concerned with moral applicability than historical accuracy, tacitly took such concerns into account. Godlike though he turned out to be, Washington made himself what he was through the mastery of ordinary virtues practiced in ordinary situations. "To deal wisely with the events of each day was the great object of his life."[76] "The simple, secret truth of his greatness was that by training, by moral discipline, he gathered together each and every particular virtue, and . . . bundled them in himself to form one great whole of manly strength and beauty, which made him what he was 'beyond compare.' "[77] Washington was not, it was sometimes said, born great or with a character intrinsically superior to that of other men.[78] Indeed, he was known to have been naturally impulsive, passionate, and aggressive, qualities that he managed to control only after a protracted internal struggle. "His excitability was immense and his anger was awful," but he combated and subdued his natural temperament by calling on the tremendous force of his will.[79] In the words of Gouverneur Morris, "his first victory was over himself."[80] In this connection, even the imagery of the solar system could be encouraging rather than forbidding. A planet seems to move on its course serenely and

[76] Robert M. T. Hunter, "Inauguration of the Equestrian Statue of Washington: Oration," *Southern Literary Messenger* 26 (1858): 177.

[77] "Gov. Wise's Oration, at Lexington, Va., 4th July, 1856," ibid. 23 (1856): 7.

[78] [Tuckerman], "Character of Washington," p. 29.

[79] "Gov. Wise's Oration," p. 15; David Ramsay, *The Life of George Washington, Commander in Chief of the Armies of the United States of America, Throughout the War Which Established Their Independence; and First President of the United States* (New York: Hopkins & Seymour, 1807), p. 328.

[80] Morris, in *Eulogies and Orations on Washington*, p. 44. The correct view of Washington, George H. Colton wrote in the 1840s, was of a man "of feelings and passions like those of other men, but subdued by a native loftiness of deportment, a dignity of soul, and the serenity of a great and fearless heart." [Colton], "Washington and his Generals," *American Whig Review* 5 (1847): 521.

without effort, but it is held in its orbit by the balance of opposing forces. In a similar way Washington's character was the
result of a "sublime adjustment of powers and virtues."[81]

Weems organized and thereby greatly advanced the shift of
approach that these comments reflect. More effectively and
thus more memorably than anyone else, he brought Washington to human scale, relating his life to those of more common
people by transforming historical experience into moral possibility. As was common in accounts of the Revolution, Weems
made the struggle comprehensible by identifying it with Washington. But there is a subtle difference between Weems's account and others, because in his the history is clearly incidental
to the life—and the life in turn is incidental to the character
it revealed. Washington's character is the central concern of
the book from the start, and the only subject of the last four
of its sixteen chapters. As was common in didactic pieces on
patriotism, Weems believed that character was firmly set in
childhood.[82] Indeed, he apparently believed that so strong and
clear were the links between childhood and adulthood that one
could deduce the source from the result. Weems, who invented
the story of the hatchet and the cherry tree and others of varying degrees of implausibility, has been much criticized on historical grounds for writing at length about Washington's
childhood, a subject about which almost nothing was known.
The criticism is accurate, but it is beside the point. It misses
the dual nature of Weems's book, which is as much a contribution to the early literature of child nurture as to historiography.

Placed in this broader context, the book seems more complex, though whether the complexities reflect subtlety or confusion is difficult to say. Weems evidently had, for example,
two audiences in mind: children, who could absorb his lessons

[81] Everett, *Orations and Speeches*, 4:39.
[82] Weems, *Life of Washington*, p. 10.

directly; and their parents, who were meant to use the book as a guide. But even this division may press his intent too far. The book seems to address throughout an undifferentiated audience thought to be permanently childlike, unboundedly credulous, and highly anxious to form or reform itself according to the model of Washington. There is complexity—again perhaps unintentional and unrealized—in his view of childhood. Indeed, his remarks about Washington's early years reveal as well as any other part of the book what the reader could expect Weems to offer. On the one hand, Washington's childhood appears as a temporary incapacity to be gotten over as soon as possible. Augustine Washington reminds his son that he is "but a poor little boy yet, without *experience* or *knowledge*," and sets about transforming him directly into a *"little man."*[83] On the other hand, Weems advises his readers to

> listen delighted while I tell of . . . Washington in the days of his youth, when his little feet were swift towards the nests of birds; or when, wearied in the chace of the butterfly, he laid him down on his grassy couch and slept, while ministering spirits, with their roseate wings, fanned his glowing cheeks, and kissed his lips of innocence with that fervent love which makes *the Heaven!*[84]

This kind of writing sports with efforts at serious analysis, but it cannot obscure the idea that childhood, in addition to being a temporary infirmity, was seen also as an idyll to be protected, a separate portion of life to be understood in terms other than a mere preparation for something else.

Parents were meant to pay close attention to Weems's account of the way the child George was raised and then apply

[83] Ibid., p. 11. Weems attributes many statements of this sort to Augustine Washington, although elsewhere in the book he readily acknowledges that "of [Washington's] father, tradition says nothing." Ibid., p. 27.

[84] Ibid., p. 10.

these obviously successful practices to their own children.
("Parents that are *wise* will listen well pleased . . ." he presses
at one point.) Yet in the case at hand the transaction was entirely masculine. Weems describes Washington's birth and
childhood up to the age of eleven without once directly involving his mother at any point. He does not call attention to
her, in fact, until with the death of Augustine (who expires
"luxuriously" in the arms of his son), her presence as lone surviving parent seems to leave him no choice. Even then it is
only to report that she sent him off to live with a half brother.[85]

Augustine Washington "carefully [systematically, indeed
single-mindedly] inculcated" the lessons of virtue in his son.
We see the way that George, because he loved his father before he loved virtue, internalized paternal standards until they
were "interwoven with the fibres of his heart,"[86] and until
having transformed parental control into self-restraint, he was
in a position to "set such bright examples of *human perfecti-
bility.*"[87] The father's didactic method was to lead his son
through a series of lessons which taught not that virtue is its
own reward in a corrupt world, not even that virtue is related
to justice, but that virtue works: it brings notice, love, power,
and other desirable results.[88] The lesson of the barked cherry
tree is not, of course, that thoughtless, careless acts will be
justly punished, but that truth will bring a merciful response.
By exploiting his love and appealing to his interest—speaking
to "both his *heart* and *head*" as Weems puts it—"Mr. Washington conducted George with great ease and pleasure along

[85] Ibid., pp. 10, 18. On one of the few occasions on which he subsequently
mentions her, Weems relates Mary Ball Washington's reaction to the triumph
at Trenton: "Instead of showing the exultation of a Spartan dame," she declared, " 'Ah, dear me! This fighting and killing is a sad thing! I wish George
would come home and look after his plantation!!' " Ibid., p. 27.

[86] Ibid., p. 18.

[87] Ibid., p. 4.

[88] See ibid., p. 186.

the happy paths of virtue."[89] With good cause, however, Augustine is not at all confident that George is internalizing these values so that as an adult he will be kept from vice by his conscience, independent of hope of reward or fear of punishment. The sentimental calculus of virtue suggests that George will always need a father.

Accordingly, Augustine's "heart throbbed with the tenderest anxiety to make him acquainted with that GREAT BEING, whom to know and love, is to possess the surest defence against vice." He decides that the most effective way to do this is to "startle George into a lively sense of his Maker." With the plausible hope of arresting his son's attention, Augustine plants some cabbage seeds in the family garden in such a way that when the sprouts appear they spell out the boy's full name. When the amazed lad tells his father of the sight, Augustine suggests that the plants have grown there by chance. George rejects the hypothesis at once.

> I did never see the little plants grow up so as to make *one single* letter of my name before. Now, how could they grow up so as to make *all* the letters of my name! and then standing one after another, to spell *my name* so *exactly!*—and all so neat and even too, at top and bottom!! O Pa, you must not say *chance* did all this. Indeed *somebody* did it; and I dare say now, Pa, *you* did do it just to scare *me*.

The trickster admits the act, although not the motive. Rather his purpose, he tells the boy, is to "introduce you to your *true* Father." When George wonders about the existence of a God he has not seen, Augustine pushes the lesson through: neither had he seen his father plant the cabbage seeds. And just as George knows that chance could not spell his name perfectly, neither could it achieve the infinitely greater perfection of the

[89] Ibid., p. 12.

world about him.[90] Through the mediation of his father George learns the importance of "imitating God in his glorious works of wisdom and benevolence; and all the rest followed as naturally as light follows the sun."[91]

The virtues Washington develops bring him earthly glory and power and ultimately the reward of being taken to the Father he has presumably served well. Most biographers end their accounts of their subjects' lives with the end of their subjects' lives. Weems does not. He goes on beyond that event to describe Washington's arrival at the gates of heaven, attended by myriads of angels—some of them "warbling" hymns, others playing golden harps—and welcomed by Benjamin Franklin and other patriots, who "embrace him in transports of tenderness unutterable."[92] Earlier, as his narrative approaches Washington's death, Weems slips briefly from the past to the present tense, summoning his readers to "gather yourselves together around the bed of your expiring father—around the last bed of him to whom under God you and your children owe many of the best blessings of this life."[93] He thereby extends the hierarchical chain of fathers, which already links God and the Washingtons, to all Americans, whose own lives would now be connected to the great events of history and, beyond them, to their Providential source.

This small rite brings Weems to the message he has all along been preparing: the Union that Washington developed his

[90] Ibid., pp. 13–15.

[91] Ibid., p. 179.

[92] Ibid., pp. 166–69. Weems restrains himself from describing Washington's actual entrance into heaven and his meeting with God. Evidently concerned that what he does describe might be misconstrued, Weems acknowledges that he is being fanciful here.

[93] Ibid., p. 166. According to Ramsay, the American people's "heart-felt distress" at Washington's death "resembled the agony of a large and affectionate family, when a bereaved wife and orphan children mingle their tears for the loss of a husband and father." Ramsay, *Life of George Washington*, p. 326.

character to create is worth the imitation of his character to preserve. But the message is confused and finally confounded because Weems cannot conceive of preservation in any sense that is historically meaningful or rewarding. He seemed to sense, without fully realizing, what will become clear to us as a major dilemma of the post-heroic period: how to reconcile ambition for distinction or even immortality with the need to be a good son. At places in his book he appears to hold out to the next generation the promise of immortal fame similar to Washington's. An epigraph on the title page reads:

> Lisp! lisp! his name, ye children yet unborn!
> And with like deeds your own great names adorn.

At the end of the book he renews, if less emphatically, the promise: "Young Reader! go thy way, think of Washington, and HOPE. Though humble thy birth, low thy fortune, and few thy friends, still think of Washington, and HOPE. Like him, honour thy God, and delight in glorious toil; then, like him, 'thou shalt stand before kings.' "[94]

Yet Weems, who was well aware that he wrote in the afternoon of a heroic age, was consciously concerned to make a point precisely opposite to this: that there would be no great names performing like deeds, that there would be no opportunities for the display of human greatness. It was unwise to hold up Washington the hero as a model for the young to imitate.

> For who among us can hope that his son shall ever be called, like Washington, to direct the storm of war, or to ravish the ears of deeply listening Senates? To be constantly placing him then, before our children, in this high character, what is it but

[94] Weems, *Life of Washington*, pp. 213–14.

like springing in the clouds a golden Phoenix, which no
mortal calibre can ever hope to reach?[95]

He attempted to resolve the dilemma by creating a sharp
distinction between the public deeds and the private character
of Washington. The public character of a man is often artificial and thus misleading. Conscious of being on display, he
behaves according to the expectations of people around him.
"It is not then in the glare of *public,* but in the shade of *private life,* that we are to look for the man. Private life is always
real life. Behind the curtain, where the eyes of the million are
not upon him . . . there he will always be sure to act *himself.*" Children could not expect to imitate Washington's
achievements or equal his fame, but they could imitate what
Weems called his private virtues. In this realm, "every youth
may become a Washington—a Washington in piety and patriotism,—in industry and honour."[96] Other biographers of
Washington drew the same distinction for the same reason.
David Ramsay, for instance, declared:

> Youths of the United States! Learn from Washington what
> may be done by an industrious improvement of your talents,
> and the cultivation of your moral powers. . . . You cannot all
> be commanders of armies, or chief magistrates; but you may
> all resemble him in the virtues of private and domestic life, in
> which he excelled, and in which he most delighted.[97]

But the distinction between the public and the private realms
was one that the nature of Weems's project would not permit
him to sustain, and indeed it collapsed around him even as he
created it. For one thing, he knew that people wanted to read

[95] Ibid., p. 4.
[96] Ibid., pp. 2, 5.
[97] Ramsay, *Life of George Washington,* p. 338.

about Washington's public exploits, and he was not one to deny the wishes of his audience. Moreover, although some men behaved one way on display and another in private, this was not the case with Washington, whose private character led obviously and directly to the acts that made him immortal. "It was to those *old-fashioned virtues* that our hero owed every thing," Weems acknowledged. "For they in fact were the food of the great actions of him, whom men call Washington. It was they that enabled him, first to triumph over *himself*, then over the *British*."[98]

Weems's method of obliterating his distinction while seeming to maintain it, his license for dwelling on the battles after indicating he would not do so, was to impose private categories on the public realm—in effect to domesticate the world and terminate history retrospectively. Whatever he does or wherever he goes, Washington never really leaves home or the family context. When, for example, he joins Braddock's army, he is said to join his "family." All the major events in his life occur in a highly personal, emotional atmosphere. The man without actual children moves to become the father of all the people he meets. Weems was not the first person to call Washington the father of his country—it was a common title by the time of his death in 1799—but no one before him had elaborated the metaphor so fully. Washington loves his soldiers "as his children." When he is angry with them he shows "Parental displeasure." When they go their own ways at the end of the war, "nature stirred all the father within him, and gave him up to tears." Military victory means that at last the tranquillity and prosperity of his own domestic scene could be extended to the nation. "With a father's joy he could look around on the thick settled-country, with all their *little ones,* and flocks, and herds, now no longer exposed to danger."[99]

[98] Weems, *Life of Washington*, p. 4.
[99] Ibid., pp. 38, 116, 119, 122, 123.

Weems implicitly defines history as the interaction of domesticity with the wilderness that was most of America:

> The whole country west of the Blue Mountains, was one immeasurable forest, from time immemorial the gloomy haunts of ravening beasts and of murderous savages. No voices had ever broke the awful silence of those dreary woods, save the hiss of rattlesnakes, the shrieks of panthers, the yells of Indians, and howling tempests.

To Weems this wilderness is more than geographical: it becomes a metaphor for anarchy wherever it exists—in war, for instance, which he calls "that monster of hell . . . roaring against America"; or in the hearts of men. The wilderness is the antithesis of home, and so frightful that from it "the hearts of youth are apt to shrink with terror, and to crouch more closely to their safer fire-sides."[100] Washington in his life extends the safety of the fireside to the boundaries of the Republic he has made.

Singular as Weems's book is, this episode in the history of popular culture should not be pushed too far. There is no way to measure with precision the influence of one book either on a person like Lincoln or on its age. We can move progressively toward such a measurement by showing that a book was widely diffused, widely read, and much quoted. Still, its actual influence remains elusive. But my point in discussing Weems's *Life of Washington* in detail is that there is little of substance separating his book from Washington iconography generally during the first half of the nineteenth century. His excesses should not obscure the typicality of his treatment. Similar hagiographies preceded his, and many more followed it, until the sentimental myth of Washington and the other founding heroes seemed to take on an existence of its own as an independent structure through which life generally was viewed. If Weems's

100 Ibid., pp. 29, 186.

book was and is more memorable than others, it is probably
less because of his undeniably original and dramatic contributions to the Washington story, than because he helped vividly
to shape the strong but unfocused impressions about Washington and his time that most Americans already shared by the
time the book appeared.

Events during the first quarter of the nineteenth century—
or rather the lack of certain kinds of events—seemed to cooperate with Weems's suggestion that one of the fathers' historical functions, paradoxically, was to end history and replace
it with a kind of domestic timelessness. In many ways the
heroic age of the beginning seemed prepared to extend itself
indefinitely. The first five presidents of the United States, who
served from the beginning of the government in 1789 to 1825,
had all been participants in one way or another in the founding process. They were all fathers and their hold on the paternal role was tenacious. Long after they left office John Adams
and Thomas Jefferson lingered in "patriarchal simplicity,"
seeming to Americans "the embodied spirit of the revolution
itself, in all its purity and force."[101] The memories of the con-
troversies that had surrounded these two men during their
presidencies, and the political parties that for a time had institutionalized hostility, had faded over the years. Nostalgia
had taken hold and rancor was largely forgotten. As long as
the founders survived and led, the golden age of the beginning
continued. During his presidency, James Monroe would on
ceremonial occasions appear in his old Revolutionary War uni-
form, as if to ward off not the British, but time itself.[102] In-

[101] John Sergeant, in *A Selection of Eulogies, Pronounced in the Several
States, in Honor of Those Illustrious Patriots and Statesmen, John Adams
and Thomas Jefferson* (Hartford: D. F. Robinson & Co., and Norton & Russell, 1826), p. 98.
[102] George Dangerfield, *The Awakening of American Nationalism, 1815–
1828* (New York: Harper & Row, 1965), p. 22.

deed, it was as if for Americans there was not yet "a past" but only a continuous present—as if they were somehow exempted from the running of time. Even then some people were conscious enough of this to mention it. "The presence of these few Revolutionary patriots and heroes among us seems to give a peculiar character to this generation," Edward Everett wrote in the 1820s. "It binds us by an affecting association to the momentous days, the searching trials, the sacrifices, and dangers, to which they were called."[103]

The association in many cases was indeed binding and affecting. The continuing presence of the fathers meant continuing dependence on the part of the sons. Political careers in particular were developed tentatively and haltingly, like little plants in the shade of giant oaks. The pilgrimages of people like Daniel Webster and Martin Van Buren to Monticello in 1824 are striking examples of a pervasive tendency to consult with the fathers—in person,[104] by correspondence, and, once that was no longer possible, through careful study of their lives and writings.

But by the middle of the 1820s events were occurring that both promised to end this sense of dependence and inspired a retrospective cast of mind, for they symbolized the passing of the founding era and the transition to a post-heroic age.[105] For

[103] [Everett], "Circular" of the Bunker Hill Monument Association, September 20, 1824, in Warren, *Bunker Hill,* p. 112.

[104] Irving H. Bartlett, *Daniel Webster* (New York: W. W. Norton & Co., 1978), p. 104; John C. Fitzpatrick, ed., *The Autobiography of Martin Van Buren, Annual Report of the American Historical Association for the Year 1918,* 2 vols. (Washington: Government Printing Office, 1920), 2:182–88.

[105] Although the events marking the transition I am describing were most conspicuous in the 1820s, the transition itself occurred gradually, of course, and the sense of generational shift did not go unremarked before this time. "Most of the actors in the great scenes of [revolutionary] times have departed; a new generation supplies their place." [*Niles'*] *Weekly Register,* September 28, 1811, p. 70. "The old Revolutionary generation has passed away." J. W. Barbour to John J. Crittenden, May 31, 1820, in Coleman, *Life of Crittenden,* 1:47. For a similar reaction to the death of James Madison, who survived until

one thing, the decade was crowded with significant anniversaries, which generated self-consciousness about change and its meaning. In 1820 Americans celebrated the bicentennial of the landing of the Pilgrims in Massachusetts.[106] The year 1825 marked the fiftieth anniversary of the beginning of the Revolution. In 1824 and 1825 the Marquis de Lafayette, returning to the United States for the first time since the winning of independence, triumphantly and indefatigably toured the country as the "Nation's Guest." Now his very presence called attention to the passage of time, as people everywhere pridefully pointed out to him how the face of the country had changed in the half century since he had last seen it. As poignant as any other aspect of his visit was the realization by people who welcomed him that surely they would never see him or his like again.[107] Next, when President Monroe retired in 1825, he was succeeded by John Quincy Adams, only nine years younger than himself, but clearly of a different generation. Adams was born two years after the Stamp Act crisis, and he was literally the son of a revolutionary father. In his Inaugural Address he announced that a generation had passed.[108]

An event then occurred that summarized while it overshad-

1836, see John Quincy Adams, *An Eulogy on the Life and Character of James Madison, Fourth President of the United States; Delivered at the Request of the Mayor, Aldermen, and Common Council of the City of Boston, September 27, 1836* (Boston: John H. Eastburn, 1836), pp. 84–86.

[106] Wesley Frank Craven, *The Legend of the Founding Fathers* (New York: New York University Press, 1956), pp. 83–84.

[107] On Lafayette's return see Anne C. Loveland, *Emblem of Liberty: The Image of Lafayette in the American Mind* (Baton Rouge: Louisiana State University Press, 1971); Fred Somkin, *Unquiet Eagle: Memory and Desire in the Idea of American Freedom, 1815–1860* (Ithaca: Cornell University Press, 1967), pp. 131–74. Lafayette died in 1834. The memory of this visit, as the century wore on, became a powerful factor in the growth of sentimental nationalism. "One electric thrill of feeling ran through the whole nation. . . . The whole land spoke in one voice and with one language. The great heart of the nation throbbed with one impulse." G[eorge] S. H[illard], "Everett's Orations and Speeches," *Christian Examiner* 49 (1850): 397.

[108] Richardson, *Messages of the Presidents*, 2:294.

owed all the others. On July 4, 1826, the day that Americans celebrated the fiftieth anniversary of the Declaration of Independence, both John Adams and Thomas Jefferson suddenly and peacefully passed away. Now, as if for the first time, Americans collectively had to face the phenomenon of passing time—of a past. For by this dazzling coincidence the world of the Revolution seemed wrenched away at a stroke. "The revolutionary age of America," Edward Everett declared, was "closed up" by their deaths. To C. C. Cambreleng the period of the Revolution suddenly seemed a remote age. To Samuel L. Knapp the deaths meant that "we are no longer the new men of the new world." Daniel Webster, who delivered a eulogy on the two founders in Boston, acknowledged that an age had ended. "The drama was ready to be closed. It has closed." By the deaths, a "great link, connecting us with former times, was broken." He understood that Americans had "lost something more . . . of the presence of the Revolution itself . . . and were driven on, by another great remove from the days of our country's early distinction, to meet posterity, and to mix with the future."[109]

Of the men who had signed the Declaration of Independence, only Charles Carroll of Carrollton survived after 1826. Adams and Jefferson had extended the golden age into the present. But Carroll was spoken of in a different way. Webster called him a "relic of the past."[110] "Carroll is alone," a popular magazine of the period pointed out. "He is the link which connects us with the past."[111] These applications of the word "past" to the Revolution reflected the developing sense of Americans in the 1820s and 1830s that they lived in a time

[109] Everett, *Orations and Speeches,* 1:131; *Eulogies in Honor of Adams and Jefferson,* pp. 59, 190; Webster, *Writings and Speeches,* 1:290. See also L. H. Butterfield, "The Jubilee of Independence, July 4, 1826," *Virginia Magazine of History and Biography* 61 (1953): 119–40.

[110] Webster, *Writings and Speeches,* 1:323.

[111] "Charles Carroll, of Carrollton," p. 457. Carroll died in 1832.

that was separate from the beginning, and that the few remaining cords to the heroic age were as frail as the old man
who symbolized them.

Yet for the fathers to die literally was in a way hardly to
die at all. If anything, their departure only served to lengthen
their lives. The eulogies that marked their deaths were rituals
of apotheosis that contained a paradoxical double message:
on the one hand, the fathers are gone, and a new generation
has succeeded them to power; on the other, the fathers are immortal and they will always rule. As the physical ties to the
beginning grew weaker, the psychological ties to the same period grew ever stronger, until some people began to fear that
the danger facing the Republic was not that these cords would
snap, but that they would be used by the dead to strangle the
living.

2

LINCOLN AT THE LYCEUM:

THE PROBLEM OF AMBITION IN

THE POST-HEROIC AGE

We can win no laurels in a war for independence.
Earlier and worthier hands have gathered them all.
Nor are there places for us by the side of Solon, and
Alfred, and other founders of states. Our fathers
have filled them. But there remains to us a great
duty of defence and preservation.

DANIEL WEBSTER, 1825

Familial language provided a way for Americans of the post-
heroic generation to comprehend and express the transition
from the founders' age to their own: one generation was passing to another, which now inherited the blessings of liberty—
and the responsibility for preserving them so that they could
be transmitted intact to posterity. Seeing the great men to their
graves, the "whole family of Americans"[1] united in bidding a
sentimental farewell to the fathers and then set out to find
their own role in history. "The great trust now descends to

---

[1] Edward Everett, *Orations and Speeches on Various Occasions,* 4 vols. (Boston: Little, Brown and Co., 1850–68), 1:131.

new hands," Daniel Webster said in 1825. "Let us endeavor to comprehend in all its magnitude, and to feel in all its importance, the part assigned to us in the great drama of human affairs."[2] Almost invariably when people spoke in such terms of the definition of a role for the post-heroic generation, they began by acknowledging their duty to preserve the achievements of the heroic age. To be sure, as Webster said in 1826, "this lovely land, this glorious liberty, these benign institutions, the dear purchase of our fathers, are [now] ours,"[3] but they were "ours" in a particular way. The difference between this inheritance and the inheritance of material possessions originally acquired by a deceased parent is that normally in the latter situation the inheritance is divided. The opposite was the necessary case with the inheritance from the revolutionary fathers. It must be preserved and transmitted intact to posterity. The sons had only a life estate.

Desire was as clear as duty: many of the self-named sons sought for themselves an immortality like that the fathers had attained. One of the characteristics for which the fathers were most highly praised was their lack of personal ambition, a trait that became starkly clear when they were compared with their counterparts in both ancient and contemporary Europe. The ambition that flawed the characters of men like Caesar and Napoleon eventually consumed them, but not before they brought great woe to the people they led. Even men with admirable goals, like Simón Bolívar, for instance, were eventually "stranded on the shoal of personal ambition."[4] Impervious to the desire for power for its own sake, the fathers withstood the temptations to which others succumbed; therefore, the American people escaped the disasters that others suffered. The example cited time and again to support this line of

---

[2] Daniel Webster, *The Writings and Speeches of Daniel Webster,* 18 vols. (Boston: Little, Brown and Co., 1903), 1:252–53.

[3] Ibid., p. 323.

[4] "Portrait of Washington," *Casket* 6 (1831): 49.

praise was Washington's refusal to take a crown at the end of the Revolutionary War or at that point to keep power of any sort. He returned instead to farm and plow.[5] Still, it was often acknowledged that although he did not want office, he did want love and immortal fame.[6] In other words, he was praised for renouncing a political hold over the present in favor of a psychological hold over the present and the future.

Considered a respectable ambition in both the eighteenth and nineteenth centuries,[7] immortal fame was the only self-seeking motive attributed to the fathers generally.[8] It was also the only conceivable selfish motive that placed a filial burden on the sons: the immortality of heroes was obviously a function of the memory of their successors. To win immortal fame was to stake out a piece of territory in the memory of the next generation and others beyond it. Therefore, fame was a conservative bond of continuity, a "golden cord" that "binds us to our fathers and to our posterity."[9] The desire to be im-

[5] Gouverneur Morris, in *Eulogies and Orations on the Life and Death of General George Washington, First President of the United States of America* (Boston: Manning & Loring, 1800), p. 47; "Washington," *Casket* 4 (1829): 505; [E. A. Lynch], "Remarks, On the Essay entitled 'Washington and the Patriot Army,' published in the August No. of the S. L. Messenger," *Southern Literary Messenger* 4 (1838): 658; James K. Paulding, "Washington and Napoleon," *Graham's Magazine* 25 (1844): 60–61; Edward Everett, *The Life of George Washington* (New York: Sheldon and Co., 1860), p. 272.

[6] "He had indeed one frailty—the weakness of great minds. He was fond of fame. . . . He loved glory." Gouverneur Morris, in *Eulogies and Orations on Washington,* p. 47; "Life of Washington," *Casket* 2 (1827): 409; "Washington," ibid. 7 (1832): 229; [Nathaniel Beverley Tucker], "The Writings of George Washington," *Southern Literary Messenger* 1 (1835): 592.

[7] Alexander Hamilton, for instance, wrote that "the love of fame" is "the ruling passion of the noblest minds." *The Federalist,* No. 72. See Douglass Adair, *Fame and the Founding Fathers,* ed. Trevor Colbourn (New York: W. W. Norton & Co., 1974), pp. 3–26.

[8] J[oseph] G. Baldwin, "The Genius and Character of Alexander Hamilton," *Southern Literary Messenger* 22 (1856): 379.

[9] Rufus Choate, in Samuel Gilman Brown, ed., *The Works of Rufus Choate with a Memoir of His Life,* 2 vols. (Boston: Little, Brown and Co., 1862), 1:339.

mortal was the very opposite of narcissism, Edward Everett believed, for it

> tells us, that we who live, and move about the earth, and claim it for our own, are not *the human race;* that those who are to follow us when we are gone, and those that here lie slumbering beneath our feet, are with us but one company, of which we are the smallest part.[10]

As this formula suggests, when the sons made payments on the debt of fame, they began to inquire into their own prospects for immortality. Indeed, celebrations of the fathers contained an unmistakable element of self-interest. The prospect that the sons could attain the same reward the fathers had received was implicit in most exhortations to praise and imitate them. In some remarks the prospect was explicit: "He, whose fancy delights to call up the images of his ancestors . . . is constantly reminded that the same embalming genius, which thus preserves the memory of his ancestors, may also bear down his own name . . . to an indefinite posterity."[11] Imitation of character, therefore, at least pointed in the direction of the personal reward of fame.

Giving the fathers the praise they wanted was just, but it was also expedient and prudent. It was quite obvious that in order for the prospect of immortality to be credible, there could be no default in paying the reward to those whose virtues and actions had earned it. "If we would perpetuate the race of national benefactors," John Knapp wrote in 1818,

> we must be just to the deceased; we must acquaint ourselves with their worthy deeds and sufferings, and take delight in the recital of their praises. This would not fail to create a higher

10 Everett, *Orations and Speeches,* 1:179–80.

11 [Charles W. Upham], "National Gallery," *North American Review* 40 (1835): 410–11.

estimation of posthumous fame among all classes, and an in-
citing thirst for it.[12]

Conversely, it was "obvious that a regard for posthumous fame
. . . must perish . . . in a community where the living generation is ignorant of the past."[13] In these formulations, immortal fame takes on the characteristics of an implied bargain:
the sons remember, imitate, and act in order that they in their
turn may be remembered, and so forth through the ages. Seen
in this way, the desire for immortality pointed directly toward
virtue as the means to obtain it. Giving blessings to posterity
brought fame from posterity, who could be expected to celebrate the virtuous and contemn or ignore the base. Thus it was
variously said that the hope of immortality was "a noble principle of conduct"; that it was, indeed, "one of the strongest in-
centives to good conduct" generally; and that hope for the
world's "applauses after death [is a] sure means of exciting
the mind to virtue."[14]

Alexis de Tocqueville, that acute viewer of shimmering surfaces, remarked of ambition in America that it was a prevalent
desire that was nevertheless low in its objects.

> The first thing that strikes a traveler in the United States is
> the innumerable multitude of those who seek to emerge from
> their original condition; and the second is the rarity of lofty
> ambition to be observed in the midst of the universally am-
> bitious stir of society. No Americans are devoid of a yearning
> desire to rise, but hardly any appear to entertain hopes of
> great magnitude or to pursue very lofty aims. . . . I believe
> that ambitious men in democracies are less engrossed than any

[12] [John Knapp], "National Poetry," *North American Review* 8 (1818):
169.

[13] [Upham], "National Gallery," p. 411.

[14] Ibid.; Everett, *Orations and Speeches,* 2:112; "The Love of Fame,"
Casket 14 (1839): 246.

others with the interests and the judgment of posterity; the present moment alone engages and absorbs them.[15]

This observation is probably correct as far as the ambitions of the masses were concerned, but in some members of the post-heroic generation the wish for immortal fame was evidently quite strong. Edward Everett claimed to be generalizing about human nature when he said in 1828 that the "craving to be remembered by those who succeed us . . . is not the first passion which awakens in the soul, but it is the strongest which animates, and the last which leaves it."[16] Nathaniel Hawthorne in 1832 suggested that everyone dreamed of becoming "the father of a race, the patriarch of a people, the founder of a mighty nation," so that "the men of future generations would call him godlike."[17] According to another writer, the post-heroic generation looked upon the "deeds of 'the fathers' as examples for imitation, as well as subjects for exultation, and strives to perpetuate, by its own exploits, the renown in which it so justly rejoices."[18] To this prospect there sometimes seemed to be no limits. "Providence has left man a free agent," one writer declared in 1840, to become if he could "the Washington of his age."[19]

To some people, then, there seemed to be a happy marriage of duty and desire. Rufus Choate told Americans of his generation that, if they performed their task of preservation successfully, posterity would celebrate

[15] Alexis de Tocqueville, *Democracy in America,* ed. Phillips Bradley, 2 vols. (New York: Alfred A. Knopf, 1945), 2:256, 261.

[16] Everett, *Orations and Speeches,* 1:179.

[17] Nathaniel Hawthorne, "Roger Malvin's Burial," *The Complete Works of Nathaniel Hawthorne,* 13 vols. (Boston: Houghton Mifflin Co., 1883), 2:397–98.

[18] "To Whom Does Washington's Glory Belong?" *Southern Literary Messenger* 9 (1843): 588.

[19] L[ucian] M[inor?], "Bulwer," ibid. 6 (1840): 405.

in one common service of grateful commemoration, their fathers of the *first* and of the *second* age of America,—those who through martyrdom and tempest and battle sought liberty, and made her their own,—and those whom neither ease nor luxury . . . could prevail on to barter her away![20]

Just as his reading of Weems exemplifies the hope of the 1820s that the accomplishments of one generation would be honored by the next, so Abraham Lincoln's experiences and ideas in the 1830s exemplify a developing awareness by some Americans that the attempt to imitate the fathers was a much more complex matter than they had previously suspected. In January 1838 he delivered to the Young Men's Lyceum of Springfield, Illinois, an address that is surely the most interesting and significant of all his pre-1854 speeches. It is also the most profound contemporary study (that I know anything about) of the problem of ambition in the post-heroic age. The formal subject of the speech was "the perpetuation of our political institutions." The major policy question that informs it is: given our duty to preserve, what can we, the sons, do in history? Behind this question lay another: why are we not like the fathers, and why is it impossible for us to become like them? The speech carefully explicates the different roles history had assigned to the fathers and to the sons; it agrees with but then goes far beyond Weems's handling of this theme to indicate that a major crisis in the life of republican institutions was at hand.[21]

As he would do often to the end of his life, Lincoln spoke ritualistically on this occasion of "gratitude to our fathers." He

[20] Brown, *Works of Choate*, 1:370.

[21] Roy P. Basler, ed., *The Collected Works of Abraham Lincoln*, 8 vols. (New Brunswick, N.J.: Rutgers University Press, 1953), 1:108–15. For a commentary on the Lyceum speech see Harry V. Jaffa, *Crisis of the House Divided: An Interpretation of the Issues in the Lincoln-Douglas Debates* (Garden City, N.Y.: Doubleday & Co., 1959), pp. 182–232.

praised them according to rhetorical convention, but there was a dutiful quality to his obeisance. The fathers' historical role, he indicated, had been to take possession of the land and to build upon it a "political edifice of liberty and equal rights." They performed this task well, even nobly, but the nobility of their actions was qualified by the self-interest of their motives. Moreover, that their work had lasted until the 1830s was "not much to be wondered at." Lincoln believed that the act of creation was motivated by the desire of the fathers for immortality. "If they succeeded, they were to be immortalized; their names were to be transferred to counties and cities, and rivers and mountains; and to be revered and sung, and toasted through all time. . . . They succeeded." By implication Lincoln rejected the charge—one that was frequently made—that the characters of the fathers were superior to those of the present generation. Historical circumstances merely created the illusion of difference. The fathers were no more naturally immune to corrupt passions than people of any other age. But the need to win the Revolutionary War and to establish and maintain institutions that would protect liberty suppressed some of "the basest principles of our nature" (among which Lincoln listed "jealousy, envy, and avarice") and channeled others toward the British. Passion therefore actually cooperated with the patriot cause.[22]

Historical opportunity worked with natural passion to permit great deeds. In the case of the sons there was no such fortunate conjunction. The central fact of their lives was that they were born second. They had "toiled not" in building the nation, but were merely "inheritors" "of the fairest portion of the earth" and the best "system of political institutions" in history. The accident of the timing of their birth dictated the post-heroic role. It was the duty of this generation, required

[22] Basler, *Works of Lincoln,* 1:108, 113, 114.

by gratitude, among other reasons, to preserve those institutions and transmit them undecayed to the next generation.[23] Now Lincoln never explicitly and probably never consciously questioned the correctness of this role. Nor did he challenge the prevailing convention that virtue was essential to preservation (unless utter silence on the matter may be interpreted in dismissive terms). But Lincoln and others did challenge the assumption that virtuous characters of the "make me like Washington" category could still bring immortality.

Although virtue might be a necessary starting point on the road to immortality, immortality ultimately depended, of course, not on virtue alone but on the occasion to demonstrate it. Nothing should have been more obvious to careful students of the fathers than the idea that although immortality of the *Union* might depend on personal character, immortality of the *self* depended on a "field for action," which the task of preservation did not promise to provide.[24] In addition to being necessary for immortality, action provided the only way to know for certain whether one had developed a virtuous character. It took "great exigencies" to "bring out the nerve and excellencies of character. . . . We know not what can be done, until an opportunity and a stimulant to effort is presented."[25] In other words, as it certainly did in the case of the fathers, history must complement and bring out latent character. "There never was a great character," said Rufus Choate, "never a truly strong, masculine, commanding character,—which was not made so by successive struggles with great difficulties. . . . All history, all biography verify and illustrate it, and none more remarkably than our own."[26] James Russell Lowell said

[23] Ibid., p. 108.

[24] Edwin P. Whipple, *Character and Characteristic Men* (Boston: Houghton Mifflin Co., 1866), p. 130; "Was Napoleon a Dictator?" *Putnam's Monthly* 5 (1855): 18.

[25] "Richard Henry Lee," *Casket* 5 (1830): 223.

[26] Brown, *Works of Choate*, 1:361.

virtually the same thing: "It is only first-rate events that call for and mould first-rate characters."[27] And Nathaniel Hawthorne too: "A hero cannot be a hero, unless in a heroic world."[28] It is doubtful that people would have been led to make this observation in this manner unless they had reason to know that they did not live in a heroic world.

But the fathers had. Not only were they virtuous, but they were lucky besides, for they lived in that most magic of ages—the right time. Were it not for the Revolution, they would have had no opportunities either fully to develop or to display the characters that won them immortality. That conflict, as David Ramsay noted, "called forth many virtues and gave occasion for the display of abilities which, but for that event, would have been lost to the world."[29] Of no one was this more true than George Washington. In addition to developing virtues, he was "blessed by Providence with a vast and comprehensive sphere for their exercise."[30] Heroes "are made by the times and the necessities of the occasion," a writer asserted in 1860, adding that, had there been no American Revolution, "Washington would have lived upon his farm a worthy squire, and gone down to posterity with the local reputation of a good, although not a great man."[31] Jefferson was another man who "undoubtedly owed much to fortune. He was placed in a country . . . prepared for the reception of new truths and the abandonment of ancient errors," William Dorsheimer wrote.

> To be called upon to give symmetry and completeness to a political system which seemed to be Providentially designed

27 [James Russell Lowell], "Self-Possession *vs*. Prepossession," *Atlantic Monthly* 8 (1861): 763.

28 Claude M. Simpson, ed., *The American Notebooks, The Centenary Edition of the Works of Nathaniel Hawthorne* ([Columbus]: Ohio State University Press, 1972), 8:501.

29 Quoted in Adair, *Fame and the Founding Fathers*, p. 5.

30 Paulding, "Washington and Napoleon," p. 62.

31 "Great Men, a Misfortune," *Southern Literary Messenger* 30 (1860): 313.

. . . was certainly a rare and happy fortune, and must be considered, when we claim superiority for him over those who were placed in the midst of apathy and decay.[32]

In similar language, Abel Upshur observed that Jefferson was "fortunate in this respect. . . . He came into active life precisely at the moment when the situation of his country most strongly demanded the exertion of his peculiar talents and qualifications."[33]

Disagreeing with optimists who spoke of a second age of godlike Washingtons, Lincoln concluded that in present circumstances immortality of the Republic not only made immortality of the self unlikely—it actually precluded it. For how could such a treasure be attained? By participating in the act of founding? The act was done. "This field of glory is harvested, and the crop is already appropriated."[34] The historical paradox that Weems had sensed at the turn of the century had become clear to many people three decades later as the post-heroic generation, now in charge, sought its role. Many people became aware that the sons, unlike their fathers, were sharply constrained in what they could do. The flamboyance of the genuinely heroic Andrew Jackson obscured to later observers but not completely to contemporaries the reality that an age almost officially hospitable to the common man was inhospitable to heroes. In the year before the Lyceum speech an anonymous writer developed the theme:

Take, for example, a youth who feels both the desire and ability to achieve the loftiest distinction. He embarks in the career of his hopes, believing that all the glorious lessons he has learned are now to be reduced to practice—that the great

[32] [William Dorsheimer], "Thomas Jefferson," *Atlantic Monthly* 2 (1858): 802.

[33] [Abel P. Upshur], "Mr. Jefferson," *Southern Literary Messenger* 6 (1840): 643.

[34] Basler, *Works of Lincoln*, 1:113.

models whom he has before his eyes, and in whose footsteps it has always been his fondest wish to walk, he may now perchance triumphantly imitate—that he, too, may one day read his blessings in a nation's eyes. Almost at the first step he finds he must truckle to what he knows to be caprice, or delusion, or vice, which he will not flatter; . . . with hopes and spirits bruised, he retires from the contest, abandoning it to the mercenaries whose struggles alone are applauded by the people. . . . This is no fancy picture. What has happened, and is happening around us, affords a melancholy illustration of its truth.[35]

The problem such statements recognize is not that there were no careers. There were many careers, but the paths that were opened were the ones that Tocqueville mentioned when he mistook opportunity for desire—paths that could lead at most only to wealth, or power in workaday politics. There was plenty of action, as long as one were content to define action as busy-ness. Moreover, there was much to be said, and it was, in defense of the historical mission of the post-heroic age: democratization, economic transformation, and expansion— that is, carrying out the implications of the fathers' work, and getting rich, if possible, along the way. The problem was not the absence of things to do and the rewards for doing them, but the nature of the things to do and the nature of the rewards for doing them. It was common for young people to dream of seeking out great men to adopt as models, Ralph Waldo Emerson said in *Representative Men*. But the seductive promises of the times soon intervened: "We are put off with fortune instead."[36] He wrote elsewhere of a pervasive "feeling

[35] "The United States by Chevalier," *American Quarterly Review* 21 (1837): 351.

[36] Ralph Waldo Emerson, *Representative Men: Seven Lectures, The Complete Works of Ralph Waldo Emerson*, 12 vols. (Boston: Houghton Mifflin Co., 1903–4), 4:1.

of the most ingenious and excellent youth in America[:] . . . that we have no prizes offered to the ambition of virtuous young men,"—none, that is, except "plenty of bribes for those who like them."[37]

The irony of the fathers' achievement, then, was that it raised the possibility that their example was irrelevant.

> Are such characters possible in public life, when that life is no longer a contest of great minds for great ends, but a pot-house squabble—when the despotism of party machinery excludes from public service every man who is not sufficiently base to stoop to its arts, and to roll in its ordure?[38]

Even some of the people who believed in the importance of celebrating the founders saw the possibility that after all their virtuous preparation, they might not be "called to follow the example of our fathers."[39] Daniel Webster, who in 1825 had called on his age to appreciate the magnitude of its task, acknowledged in 1843 that "Heaven has not allotted to this generation an opportunity of rendering high services, and manifesting strong personal devotion, such as [the fathers] rendered and manifested. . . . But we may praise what we cannot equal, and celebrate actions which we were not born to perform."[40]

Even the conventions of language that summoned the post-heroic generation to duty sharply differentiated its role from that of the fathers. To define that role in terms of preservation was in effect to rule out creation—in other words to rule out true imitation. "It is for us to *preserve*," Charles Francis Adams emphasized, "and not to create."[41] "We can win no laurels

---

37 Emerson, "Aristocracy," *Complete Works,* 10:59.

38 "American Despotisms," *Putnam's Monthly* 4 (1854): 528.

39 Everett, *Orations and Speeches,* 1:78.

40 Webster, *Writings and Speeches,* 1:262.

41 [Charles Francis Adams], "Hutchinson's Third Volume," *North American Review* 38 (1834): 157.

in a war for independence," Daniel Webster said even in one of his most hopeful speeches. "Earlier and worthier hands have gathered them all. . . . But there remains to us a great duty of defence and preservation."[42] Into such comments crept a note of self-disparagement on moral grounds that chronological difference alone does not imply. That is, Webster suggested that the fathers were earlier *because* they were worthier.

To be sure, it was possible for nineteenth-century people to reassure themselves that if need be they could be as great as the fathers. A popular magazine asserted in 1830 that

> if occasion demanded, the sons of the sages and heroes of the revolution would shew that the spirit of their fathers still lingered, and only required the kindling spark of kindred circumstance, to send forth as bright and strong a flame as ever cheered the darkest night of the revolutionary struggle.[43]

Certainly such an occasion could not be ruled out. Daniel Webster warned, for instance, that "days of disaster . . . come upon all nations" and therefore "must be expected to come upon us also."[44] But the irony of pursuing immortality through the role of preservation was that if it was done well it would not even be noticed, let alone remembered or celebrated. As a Whig journal pointed out, a "heroic age . . . never comes to a nation but once."[45] If its achievements are preserved there is no need of another. Because the fathers had been heroes, their sons did not need to be and, indeed, could not be heroes.

[42] Webster, *Writings and Speeches*, 1:253–54.

[43] "Richard Henry Lee," p. 223. The theme is developed at length by an anonymous Whig writer in "Our Political Errors," *American Quarterly Review* 22 (1837): 53–76, esp. 74. See also "Ode for the Fourth of July, 1847," *American Whig Review* 6 (1847): 57.

[44] Webster, *Writings and Speeches*, 1:238.

[45] "Memoirs of the Administrations of Washington and John Adams," *American Whig Review* 4 (1846): 614.

Thus we can detect among many ambitious men in the post-heroic period a gradual shift from a concern over how posterity would judge them to a concern that posterity might not take the trouble to judge them at all. Americans could be exhorted to imitate Washington, and they could be promised fame—by some people at least—if they did so. But the Jacksonian 1830s clearly revealed that a stable democracy dedicated to impersonal social progress, a society that counted among its most pressing concerns the question of the provenience of bank charters or the funding of internal improvements, did not demand a "RACE OF GOD-LIKE WASHINGTONS" or even another generation of heroes. Among men of genius and ambition, the endless eulogies on the revolutionary fathers succeeded not so much in demonstrating the need for heroic virtues as in calling attention to a society so arranged and so destined that it did not require those virtues, did not inspire them, and, indeed, could find no place for them at all. In this situation Samuel Tilden later found the germ of the Civil War. "A race had grown up formed amid the discussion of the small administrative questions, and amid the competitions of professional politicians, for the petty honors and emoluments of office," he wrote. "Generations, like individuals, do not completely understand inherited wisdom until they have reproduced it in their own experience."[46]

Although the post-heroic generation had a role to play in history, that role was not historic and therefore would not be memorable. This is the implication that can be seen prospectively in Weems's domestication of history; and it is the implication that can be seen retrospectively in a much later assessment by James Russell Lowell. "Our position as a people," he wrote in 1861, "has been such as to turn our energy, ca-

[46] Frank Freidel, ed., *Union Pamphlets of the Civil War, 1861–1865,* 2 vols. (Cambridge, Mass.: Harvard University Press, Belknap Press, 1967), 1:544.

pacity, and accomplishment into prosaic channels." The meaning of the success of the fathers, as these two men and countless others knew, was that when their heroic tasks were completed, so was the story. "Why," Lowell remarked, "does the novelist always make his bow to the hero and heroine at the church-door, unless because he knows, that, if they are well off, nothing more is to be made of them?"[47]

Unlike Weems and Lowell, Lincoln did not believe the story was over just because history no longer provided obvious dangers to challenge heroes. It was precisely because preservation would comport with prosperity but not with glory that preservation would not be easy. In the Lyceum speech Lincoln predicted that an ambitious man would eventually emerge to present a major challenge to the deceptive stability of a post-heroic age. Ambition is natural, he observed. That the nature of the times did not require it did not mean that it would not appear.

> New reapers will arise, and *they,* too, will seek a field. It is to deny, what the history of the world tells us is true, to suppose that men of ambition and talents will not continue to spring up amongst us. And, when they do, they will as naturally seek the gratification of their ruling passion, as others have *so* done before them.

The existence of this passion in the mind of a genius was the reason preservation would be difficult. Although most men could be satisfied with the self-effacing task of preservation—knowing that the Union would survive even if their own names were forgotten—the ambitious genius could not. "Can that gratification be found in supporting and maintaining an edifice that has been erected by others? Most certainly it cannot." Nor would such roles as the expansionistic age of Jackson provided—among them the very role that Lincoln was playing during the period of his life when he made this speech—be sufficient. "Towering genius . . . sees *no distinction* in adding story to story, upon the monuments of fame, erected to the memory of others. . . . It *scorns* to tread in the footsteps of *any* predecessor, however illustrious." Not even the presidency itself would satisfy the passion. It is not that this genius is naturally evil. He is naturally ambitious and he is made evil by his place in historical time. If there were opportunities to win fame in founding and building, he would probably pursue them. But there are none. "Nothing left to be done in the way of building up, he would set boldly to the task of pulling down." Just as it blocked certain paths to immortality, a post-heroic age created a situation in which other, more destructive paths were opened. Indeed a post-heroic age not only permitted strong but frustrated ambition to take a patricidal course; it actually encouraged it to do so.[48]

No times were more dangerous than prosperous ones, for it was then that would-be tyrants were likely to be most restless and everyone else would be least on guard. Lincoln once formulated the proposition quite starkly: "Feeling prosperity we forget right."[49] The fathers' awareness of this prospect constituted a major purpose of the Declaration of Independence. Lincoln argued that they "knew the proneness of prosperity to breed tyrants, and they meant when such should re-appear in this fair land and commence their vocation they should find

[48] Basler, *Works of Lincoln*, 1:113–14. Lincoln may have expressed better than anyone else the precise nature of the gravest challenge that could face a stable middle-class society, but he was by no means the only one to state it. Another Whig wrote some years later, for example, that the "noblest work in which a man of great spirit can be engaged" was the work of founding. But the opportunity of "composing constitutions and building up institutions of freedom is rare." Americans living in "those ages which offer none of these fortunate occasions" should watch out for ambitious men whose "only chance for distinction lies in being the first to pull down what their fathers established." "The New Machiavel," *American Whig Review* 7 (1848): 207.

[49] Basler, *Works of Lincoln*, 2:274.

left for them at least one hard nut to crack."[50] Lincoln's use of
the word "prosperity" here was typical of that of his time in
that the meaning of the term extended beyond the happier
phases of the economic cycle to the general well-being of the
nation. Prosperity stood for all that the sons inherited; and it
explained why the sons could not act. The very word seemed
to be one more announcement that heroism was not needed.

Perhaps because the "age of Jackson" was dominated by a
self-dramatizing hero who managed to contrive the kinds of
exploits that since his youth seemed to make his life anything but dull, we tend to think of the 1830s as an exciting
time. Actually, many people who lived through the Jacksonian
period believed that by comparison to the heroic past they lived
in confined and boring times. As early as the 1820s Ralph
Waldo Emerson was complaining that the United States since
the Revolution had moved progressively to "strength, to honour, and at last to ennui."[51] In the 1830s, to be sure, there were
events that passed and still do pass for "great" on a historical
scale, but even these seemed pale in comparison to the action
available in the past. The phrase "Bank War" attempts to dramatize the great conflict of the 1830s, but only calls attention
to the reality that the metaphor of "war" cannot give life to
the intractably technical questions implicit in "bank." Moreover, in contrast to Jackson's life, those of great numbers of
ordinary people were characterized by a relative eventlessness
as they adjusted to the structured conditions of the developing
bourgeois-domestic style of living that soon would be called
"middle class."[52] In the magazines that reflected the rise of

[50] Ibid., 2:406.

[51] Emerson to John Boynton Hill, July 3, 1822, in Ralph L. Rusk, ed., *The
Letters of Ralph Waldo Emerson,* 6 vols. (New York: Columbia University
Press, 1939), 1:120.

[52] "Under every form of government having the benefits of civilization there
is a middle class, neither rich nor poor, in which is concentrated the chief enterprise of the country. The virtues of industry and economy, ambition, and

this style and catered to its interests and needs, articles began to appear that characterized the period as a "prosaic epoch" and worried that ennui, "the desire of activity without the fit means of gratifying the desire," could if not relieved lead to "insanity."[53]

The reason that "nothing more is to be made of them,"—to use Lowell's chilling, dismissive phrase about the people of his generation—is that they were prosperous; and he went on to add, "prosperity is the forcing-house of mediocrity."[54] The great paradox of prosperity was that it was simultaneously the goal of, and the greatest danger to, bourgeois life. That Americans in the post-heroic period were jubilant and self-congratulatory about their economic good fortune has never been in doubt, but that they were at the same time uneasy with this prosperity is also clear.[55] Prosperity was not only the

capacity to increase in knowledge and wealth, a watchful guardianship of their own rights, and a vigilant attention to the public welfare, are their leading characteristics." Timothy Jenkins, *Congressional Globe,* 30 Cong., 2 Sess. (February 17, 1849), appendix, p. 103.

[53] Henry T. Tuckerman, "The Philosophy of Travel," *United States Magazine and Democratic Review* 14 (1844): 527; "Ennui," *American Quarterly Review* 9 (1831): 36, 46. A character in James Fenimore Cooper's novel *Homeward Bound* contemplates democracy in these terms, worrying about the possible effects of the "eternal *ennui* of always walking on a level surface." James Fenimore Cooper, *Homeward Bound; or, The Chase, The Works of James Fenimore Cooper,* 33 vols. (New York: G. P. Putnam's Sons, [1895–1900]), 13:448. On the connection between ambition and insanity as it was perceived during the Jacksonian period, see David J. Rothman, *The Discovery of the Asylum: Social Order and Disorder in the New Republic* (Boston: Little, Brown and Co., 1971), pp. 109–29.

[54] [Lowell], "Self-Possession *vs.* Prepossession," p. 763.

[55] See Fred Somkin, *Unquiet Eagle: Memory and Desire in the Idea of American Freedom, 1815–1860* (Ithaca: Cornell University Press, 1967), pp. 11–54. The uneasiness was chronic, its expression formulaic. For two similar examples from different times, see William H. Winder, "Oration Delivered on the 4th of July, 1812, at the celebration of American Independence, in Howard's Park, (Baltimore)," [*Niles'*] *Weekly Register,* July 11, 1812, p. 307; J. M. Sturtevant, "The Lessons of our National Conflict," *New Englander* 19 (1861): 899.

forcing house of mediocrity—it could generate also greed, self-ishness, corruption, self-indulgence, love of luxury, enervation, effeminacy, and boredom. It was, in the words of one observer, the nation's "only curse."[56] As that, prosperity served as the point of departure for countless exercises in self-abasement. "We speculate how to get rich," ran a typical version,

> but the heroic virtues, the chivalric sentiments . . . we lay aside. . . . The fair dreams of our youth we despise. The dream that this young land . . . should be the home of free-dom and a race of men so manly that they would lift the earth by the whole breadth of its orbit nearer heaven . . . has passed away from the most of us, as nothing but a dream. We yield ourselves, instead, to calculation, money-making and moral indifference.[57]

We might suppose that members of the post-heroic genera-tion, since they could claim little else, would claim the achieve-ment of prosperity, even if they felt they must go on to apolo-gize for its effects. Often the claim was made, but some people believed that prosperity was no more the work of the nine-teenth century than was the Constitution. Indeed, prosperity was seen to be both a gift from the fathers—for which the sons must feel grateful—and a measure of how far the sons had fallen from the fathers—for which they must feel unworthy. "Our liberty *and national prosperity* are a very great inheri-tance," said one writer.[58] "The foundation for that prosperity had been laid by our fathers," said another.[59] "Our existing prosperity and happiness, and the whole of our present mag-nificent possessions," said a third, "are based upon the heroic

---

[56] "British Opinions of America," *American Quarterly Review* 20 (1836): 420.

[57] "The Kansas Question," *Putnam's Monthly* 6 (1855): 431–32.

[58] [George H. Colton], "Washington and his Generals," *American Whig Review* 5 (1847): 534. Emphasis mine.

[59] Freidel, *Union Pamphlets,* 1:405.

darings and endurances . . . of those who have preceded us."[60]
It was characteristic of such remarks that praise of the dead
was often followed by disparagement of the living. Thus, the
"present happy prosperity" was "but the fruit of that harvest
long ago sown in tears and blood—this is but the benign result
of a labor earlier and stronger than ours."[61]

That all the heroic deeds of the fathers were selfless was a
convention of speech that only a few people joined Lincoln in
questioning, and then they did so obliquely. The Revolution
itself was carried out not primarily for the sake of the generation that lived through it, but for posterity. "It was for their
children that the heroes and sages of the revolution labored and
bled," Edward Everett believed.[62] "That principle of *responsibility to posterity,* one of the divinest of Heaven's inspirations,
[was] ever more present to them than personal interests."[63]
They cast aside a quest for prosperity in their own time so that
their children could enjoy it. Their sacrifice made it permanently possible. Yet the sacrifice was not a great one, since in
any case the "thirst for private gain, that is now so engrossing,
was then a feeble passion, compared with the ardor to promote
the public good."[64] At the very least, "the passion for wealth
was *not* the generating cause of our independence."[65] But these
and countless other critics of nineteenth-century mores pointed
out that it was certainly the dominant characteristic of the
present. Thus the gift of the selfless fathers had been narrowed
and perverted into a single-minded pursuit which placed the
second generation morally far below the first.

Of course, we could distinguish sharply here between "happy

60 D[avid] H[atch] B[arlow], "American Literature," *Graham's Magazine*
38 (1851): 328.
61 John S. Holmes, Boston *Daily Advertiser,* July 7, 1858.
62 Everett, *Orations and Speeches,* 1:104.
63 "Claims of the Beautiful Arts," *United States Magazine and Democratic
Review* 3 (1838): 255.
64 "Sketches of American Character," *Ladies' Magazine* 1 (1828): 157.
65 "Claims of the Beautiful Arts," p. 255.

prosperity" and "passion for wealth." This would be one way to resolve, indeed demolish, the paradox of the baneful gift. But as far as people who took this problem seriously were concerned, there was no way to do this: prosperity itself seemed to generate the narrowing materialistic drive and produced "men of small ambitions and cold hearts."[66] People who became prosperous by inheritance—as did all Americans in these formulations—were prone to recklessness in their estate, be it wealth or liberty. Not having earned it through their own efforts, they did not know how to value it accurately. A Civil War pamphleteer surmised that because the fathers had established the political estate, "they, apparently, valued liberty and good government more than we do, just as the builder of a fortune appears usually to appreciate and value it higher, than he to whom it falls without exertion—by inheritance."[67] But he was explaining why efforts to preserve the Union without violence had failed. A quarter century earlier Lincoln and a few other political writers had already made the point that it was inherently difficult for inheritors to be good preservers.

Among the adverse effects sometimes attributed to prosperity was a dangerous restlessness among the people generally. The base passions that were natural to a people, but that had been suppressed or transformed into constructive energies by the demands of the revolutionary era, were now liberated without direction in times that were peaceful and prosperous. Indeed, such times seemed to exacerbate passion, and Abraham Lincoln believed that the mob violence that seemed on its way to becoming a characteristic feature of urban life in the 1830s was the most apparent and worrisome evidence that this was the case. The danger of mob violence lay not so much in the

[66] "The Kansas Question," p. 431. Henry T. Tuckerman, *The Rebellion: Its Latent Causes and True Significance* (New York: James G. Gregory, 1861), pp. 20–21.

[67] Freidel, *Union Pamphlets*, 1:405.

immediate and direct consequences as it did in eventual but no less foreseeable results. Individuals ordinarily might be deterred from committing illegal acts by the likelihood of punishment, but people in mobs were protected by the anonymity of their numbers. That they were unlikely to be punished encouraged the spread of lawlessness. Innocent people were then increasingly likely to become victims of the mob, without possibility of redress, "and thus it goes on, step by step, till all the walls erected" to defend people and property would be destroyed. Most Americans loved law and order, Lincoln was certain, and would make great sacrifices to preserve both. But he knew that if pushed to realize a preference (in a way that the unitary term "law and order" does not demand), they placed a higher value on order, which was absolutely necessary, than on the rule of law, which was only desirable. Their "feelings" could be "alienated" from a government of laws if that government could not protect order. Having little left to lose, the people would become vulnerable to the appeal of the ambitious genius, abetting his patricidal plans to destroy inherited institutions.[68]

The difficulties that beset the effort to preserve the fathers' work only made it that much more important that Americans dedicate themselves to the task. Among the defenses that a post-heroic age could summon against the reappearance of passion were memory and reason. Later in his life Lincoln would

[68] Basler, *Works of Lincoln,* 1:109–12. In his discussion of the obstacles in the way of preserving liberty, Lincoln began by dismissing the possibility of any danger from abroad. His train of thought here was similar to that of Andrew Jackson in his Farewell Address of the previous year. "You have no longer any cause to fear danger from abroad," Jackson said. "It is from within, among yourselves—from cupidity, from corruption, from disappointed ambition and inordinate thirst for power—that factions will be formed and liberty endangered." James D. Richardson, ed., *A Compilation of the Messages and Papers of the Presidents,* 10 vols. (Washington: Government Printing Office, 1897), 3:307–8.

invoke, albeit as an afterthought, "the mystic chords of memory" in an effort to hold at bay the greatest outburst of passion and violence the nation ever faced, but in the 1830s his faith in sentiment was limited. Memory worked by associations. The men who fought in the Revolution kept the heroic age and republican institutions alive by the very fact of their affecting presence. They were a *"living history"* identified with, indeed the pillars of, what Lincoln called the "temple of liberty." Sentiment for them protected the building; they therefore held it up. But now in the 1830s, most of them were dead, and, "like every thing else," their actions "must fade upon the memory of the world." Ambition made possible the creation of the Union and sentiment helped to preserve it; neither worked in that direction any longer. Now that the fathers have "crumbled away, that temple must fall, unless we, their descendants, supply their places with other pillars, hewn from the solid quarry of sober reason."[69] In practical—and for Lincoln impassioned—terms, this meant absolute obedience to law. Having shown where lawlessness could lead, he exhorted not only his Springfield audience but the whole nation: "Let every American . . . swear by the blood of the Revolution, never to violate in the least particular, the laws of the country. . . . Let every man remember that to violate the law, is to trample on the blood of his father."[70] Reverence for laws would frustrate the patricide, and when the last trumpet awoke Washington he would find with satisfaction that his sons "permitted no hostile foot to pass over or desecrate [his] resting place."[71] Holding out to Americans of his generation the offer of a kind of symbolic immortality, through identification with a republic whose immortality they had helped assure, Lincoln at the same time exhorted them to renounce ambition and hence any personal chance of historical immortality.

[69] Basler, *Works of Lincoln,* 1:115.

[70] Ibid., p. 112.

[71] Ibid., p. 115.

The Lyceum speech struggles toward and seems finally to achieve a formula for stability and preservation. Examined more carefully, however, it presents a very different prospect. Lincoln's analysis of ambition and his generation's historical role certainly coincided with and probably proceeded from an intense self-consciousness about the progress of his own career. Lincoln's intense ambition was not channeled toward the pursuit of wealth that in more than one way compensated other ambitious men of his time for the unavailability of heroic opportunity. If he did not flee from money, neither was he ever much interested in it.[72] His ambition was of a different and higher kind. Like the founders, he sought immortality through politics. He had not pursued it far, however, before he found himself thwarted and stifled: his ambition could find no satisfying outlet as long as he was determined to be a good son of the revolutionary fathers.

In her study of what she calls the "Nobel Prize complex," the psychologist Helen H. Tartakoff has described a crisis that often occurs in the lives of extraordinarily intelligent men as they turn from youth into early middle age. Encouraged by a culture that holds out promises of great reward and by their strong awareness of their superior abilities, they can develop fantasies of having become "chosen by virtue of exceptional gifts" to perform great deeds of various sorts. Early successes reassure them of their powers and reinforce their fantasies of ambition. If their upward course is interrupted, however, and they abruptly find themselves caught in a kind of cul-de-sac of history, they are subject to great depression and feelings of hopelessness, as the difference between what society seemed to

[72] "He never had what some people call 'money sense,' " Herndon wrote. "In dealing with the financial and commercial interests of a community or government he was equally as inadequate as he was ineffectual in managing the economy of his own household. In this respect alone I always regarded Mr. Lincoln as a weak man." William H. Herndon and Jesse W. Weik, *Abraham Lincoln: The True Story of a Great Life,* 2 vols. (New York: D. Appleton and Co., 1892), 1:165–66.

offer and what it does in fact offer becomes clear. The greater the fantasies and the deeper into their careers they get before they realize this, the greater the depression is likely to be.[73]

Tartakoff's model should be highly suggestive to students of Lincoln's career in the 1830s and 1840s. Praising the fathers and desiring a fame of his own, he moved into politics with an aggressiveness that suggests he had taken to heart the messages that, since Weems, had promised rewards to young people who would imitate Washington and the other founders. Lincoln began his political career at the age of twenty-three, running for a seat in the Illinois house of representatives just one year after taking up residence in the state. He lost this first contest, but won the next one in 1834, and at the age of twenty-five entered the legislature, where he quickly became a leader of the faction that gradually developed into the Whig party. He was centrally involved in the process of legislating "internal improvements" for the state and was instrumental in moving the capital of Illinois from Vandalia to Springfield. Lincoln moved with the capital, and began to practice law in Springfield. He said during this period that he wanted to become known as the De Witt Clinton of Illinois, which meant that he wanted to be known as a state builder.[74] He found many people willing to assist him. "No man ever had an easier time of it in his early days," one of his associates recalled. Lincoln "always had influential and financial friends to help him; they almost fought each other for the privilege."[75]

This apparent public success was matched and largely viti-

[73] Helen H. Tartakoff, "The Normal Personality in Our Culture and the Nobel Prize Complex," in Rudolph Loewenstein et al., eds., *Psychoanalysis—A General Psychology: Essays in Honor of Heinz Hartmann* (New York: International Universities Press, 1966), pp. 222–52, esp. 236–40.

[74] Herndon and Weik, *Abraham Lincoln,* 1:166.

[75] William H. Herndon to Jesse W. Weik, January 15, 1886, in Emanuel Hertz, ed., *The Hidden Lincoln: From the Letters and Papers of William H. Herndon* (New York: Viking Press, 1938), p. 134.

ated by private depression that sometimes deepened to despair. In the second half of the 1830s and in the early 1840s, from the time that he was about twenty-five until he was nearly thirty-five years old, Lincoln apparently passed through recurring periods of great psychological disturbance. During the early years in Springfield he acted in ways that led some people who knew him to think that he had become "deranged." William H. Herndon, Lincoln's law partner and biographer, believed that the death of Ann Rutledge in August 1835 was the source of the deep and chronic melancholy from which Lincoln never finally managed to free himself.[76] But it may have been that his depression inspired the Ann Rutledge story (and later variants of it involving his internal struggle over whether to marry Mary Todd) rather than that Ann Rutledge's death led to his depression. Herndon himself presented evidence that suggests that Lincoln's emotional condition involved not only sexuality and his relationships with women, but also the encompassing problem of his transcendent ambition.

In the summer of 1841, in flight from a malaise so acute he seemed suicidal, Lincoln traveled to Kentucky with Joshua Speed, his closest friend during this period of his life—or ever. "In the deepest of his depression," Speed recalled to Herndon many years later, Lincoln said

> he had done nothing to make any human being remember that he had lived; and that to connect his name with the events transpiring in his day and generation, and so impress himself upon them as to link his name with something that would redound to the interest of his fellow-men, was what he desired to live for.[77]

At the age of thirty-two he considered himself a failure. To be sure, he was at the center of events in Illinois politics in the

[76] Herndon and Weik, *Abraham Lincoln*, 1:130.
[77] Ibid., p. 203.

1830s, but the ease with which he arrived there might only have called attention to the relative insignificance of the game he was playing. Moreover, he might have considered his "success" deceptive, for it showed no prospect of leading anywhere. He had, after all, cast his lot with Springfield, a city that was to be eclipsed by Chicago, and with a party that on the state level as well as nationally was to be outnumbered and usually outfought by the Democrats. The internal improvements program he championed became an embarrassment as overspending brought Illinois close to bankruptcy by the end of the 1830s.[78] Lincoln had defined his ambitions in terms of the immortality of the founding heroes, only to find himself mired in middle-level politics far from the center of important action. He had trained himself according to the highest principles, only to find that these principles had little apparent relevance to the kinds of questions he was called on to decide. The Lyceum speech, which was a product of this period of his life, reflected—although it hardly resolved—his personal problem with ambition.

Thoughtful American conservatives searching for a role during the transition from the heroic to the post-heroic age were almost always far better at perceiving the transition than they were at defining a positive and noble role for themselves as a consequence of the transition. Daniel Webster's exhortation in 1825, "let our age be the age of improvement," is rather anticlimactic and necessarily unspecific.[79] It is also typical of such remarks. Lincoln was not an exception to this pattern. His great study of ambition in the Lyceum speech is marked by an unmistakable imbalance. The acute analysis of the malaise of his age makes the banality of his prescription for curing its

[78] Paul Simon, *Lincoln's Preparation for Greatness: The Illinois Legislative Years* (Urbana: University of Illinois Press, 1971), pp. 173–88.

[79] Webster, *Writings and Speeches*, 1:254.

effects—reason and reverence for law—all the more sharply apparent. Lincoln's assertion that reason could ensure stable times is almost mocking after his subtle and complex argument that stable times released passion and bred their own demise. Moreover his prophecy of the emergence of the ambitious genius who would be a tyrant is not conditional. He did not say that this man will appear unless reason prevails; he said that the man *will* appear.

It is indeed the prophecy of the tyrant rather than the plea for reason that represents Lincoln's solution to the problem of the post-heroic age. He seemed to look less to the prevention of the emergence of this figure than to combating and vanquishing him once he appeared. The psychological reassurance that this fantasy might have provided is apparent, for only if the prophecy were fulfilled could Lincoln satisfy his ambition for immortality while remaining true to the fathers. To confront and defeat such a villain—to *save* the temple of liberty the fathers had built—would not that deed be rewarded with immortality?

That Lincoln at least sensed this way to resolve the problem of heroic ambition in a post-heroic age there can be no doubt. He evidently enjoyed imagining himself in situations that were both heroic and defensive—in the role, in short, of a savior, and a doomed savior at that. On more than one occasion he made dramatic public statements in which he portrayed himself in the role of the defender in the last redoubt of liberty, prepared to martyr himself regardless of whether the sacrifice would serve any defensive purpose. One of these statements is especially conspicuous because in the context in which he made it, it was both gratuitous and incongruous. Nearly two years after the appearance at the Lyceum, at the end of a long and rather technical presentation on a complex subject (the subtreasury proposal) to a small audience in Springfield, Lincoln abruptly turned to a warning that the Republic was in grave danger. The administration of Martin Van Buren—who was himself an "evil spirit"—was a "great volcano . . . belching forth the lava of political corruption" which threatened to sweep away everything in its path. If the country should lose its liberty, Lincoln said, his proudest boast would be "not that I was the *last* to desert, but that I *never* deserted her." Never did he feel more noble than "when I contemplate the cause of my country, deserted by all the world beside, and I standing up boldly and alone and hurling defiance at her victorious oppressors." Nothing—not the prospect of failure, chains, or torture, not even the prospect of death—would deter him.[80]

In his campaign against Stephen A. Douglas for the Senate in 1858, Lincoln begged his hearers to renew their faith in the ideas that the Declaration of Independence contains. And then, as if from nowhere: "You may do anything with me you choose, if you will but heed these sacred principles. You may not only defeat me for the Senate, but you may take me and put me to death." So much, one would think, for the principles of the Declaration. On his way to his inauguration in 1861 Lincoln asserted on a visit to Independence Hall in Philadelphia that he hoped the Union would be saved on the basis of the founding principles, but even if it could not, he would choose to be "assassinated on this spot" rather than surrender those principles.[81]

In certain striking respects Lincoln's description of the man to guard against resembles my description of Lincoln in the 1830s. We observe an ambitious genius, who saw no distinction in imitating his predecessors, warning against an ambitious genius who "sees *no distinction* in adding story to story, upon the monuments of fame, erected to the memory of others." In a famous essay, Edmund Wilson wrote that Lincoln in the Lyceum speech was warning the public against

[80] Basler, *Works of Lincoln,* 1:178–79.
[81] Ibid., 2:547; 4:240.

himself.[82] Wilson was partially correct, for Lincoln's image of danger is on the one hand so precise and on the other so far removed from any plausible threat that it must have appeared first on some inner mirror. But it is important to clarify or amend (it is not clear which) Wilson's proposition to add that Lincoln was doing so *unconsciously*. So close is the description to certain traits of the describer that only a man completely unconscious of what he was doing would have presented it.

On the other hand, as close as the image is to Lincoln, it is also quite far from him. At a conscious level, as I have shown, Lincoln was among the most devoted of all sons of the revolutionary fathers. There is no evidence that at this level he ever questioned that it was his duty to preserve. That this duty required a renunciation of ambition was the point of the speech, and it was a sacrifice that consciously he was obviously prepared to make. Ambitious as he was, he would not have admitted that, like his imagined antagonist, "distinction" was his own "paramount object." He always insisted on a different order of priorities. "While pretending no indifference to earthly honors," he claimed in the contest with Douglas twenty years later, "I *do claim* to be actuated in this contest by something higher than an anxiety for office. . . . Drop every . . . thought for any man's success. . . . *But do not destroy that immortal emblem of Humanity—the Declaration of American Independence.*"[83] This strong and lifelong filiopiety meant that if he could not be happy adding to, neither could he tear down, the fathers' work. It appears, again at the level of consciousness, that he was trapped—set to be confined in the life of quiet, comfortable, and respectable middle-class domesticity in Springfield, Illinois.

But what the Lyceum speech announces is that Lincoln had

[82] Edmund Wilson, *Patriotic Gore: Studies in the Literature of the American Civil War* (New York: Oxford University Press, 1962), pp. 106–8.
[83] Basler, *Works of Lincoln,* 2:547.

found (but almost certainly unconsciously) a way out of the trap. The distinct implication of his political analysis is that the only way that both ambition and filiopiety could be satisfied in a post-heroic age was if a good (rational, renunciatory, obedient) son were to rescue the fathers' institutions from some *other* ambitious person. Lincoln created this person out of undesirable wishes he could not recognize in himself. Although Lincoln loved the fathers, it is hardly bold to suppose that he was also unconsciously hostile to them. They had, after all, preempted him. Unlike Thomas Lincoln, they could not be left behind; nor would they "die." This was bad enough, but on top of it he was obliged to praise them. Here he sometimes held back. Even in the Lyceum speech, as we have seen, he said their achievements were not much to be wondered at. Still he evidently took great pains to shield himself from the smallest sign of hostility toward the founders, going even to the point of imagining himself dying in defense of them. To avoid having to recognize his antagonistic feelings, he expelled and then reified them into the image of the bad son.[84] This projection served a purpose greater than psychic peace. Contained in the prophecy of attempted patricide is a formula for immortality after all. For presumably if the evil figure did appear, and if Lincoln fought and defeated him, and saved the fathers' work, then Lincoln would be rewarded with immortality. Is there not some likelihood that such a prophecy would tend to be self-fulfilling? If one's chances for immortality depend on the appearance of one's own basest passions embodied in a tyrant, is not the man who desires to become immortal

[84] Psychoanalysts call this operation "projection." Sigmund Freud, "The Unconscious," *The Standard Edition of the Complete Psychological Works of Sigmund Freud,* ed. and trans. James Strachey, 24 vols. (London: Hogarth Press and the Institute of Psycho-Analysis, 1953–73), 14:184; idem, *The Psychopathology of Everyday Life,* ibid., 6:258–59; Anna Freud, *The Ego and the Mechanisms of Defence* (New York: International Universities Press, 1946), pp. 55–57, 128.

going to be prepared to recognize such a tyrant when he appears, and even go in search of him if he does not appear? If the tyrant did not spring up from the dynamics of history as Lincoln explained them, would he then not only have to be imagined, but also invented?

3

THE FAILED REBELLION OF YOUNG
AMERICA AGAINST THE FATHERS
(I): THE ILLUSION OF BOUNDLESSNESS

"Our fathers did so," says some one. "What of that?"
say we.

THEODORE PARKER, 1848

The immortality of the revolutionary fathers conflicted not
only with the ambitions of those nineteenth-century men who
wished to take their place but also as a matter of course with
the democratic order itself, which after all bears an inherent
antagonism to heroes, dead or alive. "We should despair of
democracy . . . if Washingtons were always necessary to it,"
an anonymous political writer of the 1840s declared,[1] thus calling attention to a striking paradox of the post-heroic age:
Americans of the time willingly revered and attempted to imitate men whose true replicas they would have been required
by the fathers' own achievements to reject.

According to sentimentalist convention the relationship be-

[1] "Guizot's Essay on Washington," *United States Magazine and Democratic
Review* 8 (1840): 11.

tween the generations was an example of mortmain—the hand of the dead would control the living. It was with the intent to praise them that nineteenth-century Americans pointed out that in many respects the fathers were not dead at all. "They live in their example; and they live . . . in the influence which their lives and efforts, their principles and opinions, now exercise, and will continue to exercise, on the affairs of men."[2] Immortality of this almost activist sort was therefore conducive to a general hatred directed toward the founders. A character in a late, unfinished work on the Revolution by Nathaniel Hawthorne observes that the immortality of the father did not simply mean that the father would always be remembered. Because "the sire would live forever . . . the heir [would] never come to his inheritance, and so he would at once hate his own father, from the perception that he would never be out of his way." In political terms, "the same class of powerful minds would always rule the state, and there would never be a change of policy."[3] In more personal terms, it meant that psychologically the sons could not grow up.

One might think that this situation would have led to a rejection of the authority of the fathers, and that the most likely time in the post-heroic age for a rebellion against them to have occurred would have been between the late 1830s and the 1850s. Americans in those years seemed preoccupied far less by the memory of the Revolution than by the economic, demographic, geographic, and technological changes that had transformed the landscape since then. At the same time, the surfaces of the lives of countless Americans were being similarly transformed, validating their easy assumptions about fated progress, and fix-

[2] Daniel Webster, *The Writings and Speeches of Daniel Webster,* 18 vols. (Boston: Little, Brown and Co., 1903), 1:291. "Our fathers, from behind, admonish us, with their anxious paternal voices." Ibid., p. 323.

[3] Nathaniel Hawthorne, *Septimius Felton, The Complete Works of Nathaniel Hawthorne,* 13 vols. (Boston: Houghton Mifflin Co., 1883), 11:363–64.

ing their vision on the prospect of an even more dazzling future. Even if the logic of democracy did not call into question the example of the fathers in a self-consciously democratic age, we would expect the social changes of the time to have done so, if only to dismiss precedent in the dust of change. The news Robert Saunders carried to a group of Southern college students in 1846 was just no news at all: "All things are in motion. . . . The movement is all forward. . . . The rushing stream of democracy is sweeping along, bearing on its bosom constitutions, morals, social relations and religious sects. . . . No man or men can arrest the impetuous tide."[4]

The record does not fully accommodate the expectations that logic and such statements create. To be sure, in the late 1830s and especially in the 1840s, a distinctly antisentimentalist rhetoric emerged, which insisted that filiopiety must have limits. "The great revolutionary names—at the head of which stands . . . that of WASHINGTON—are safe . . . and the world admires them," it was said. "But the dead cannot save the living. They acted well their part, and received their reward. We and our successors have also a part to act."[5] It did not go unnoticed by the post-heroic generation that the example set by the fathers called into question its own tendency to defer to the example set by the fathers. Thus: "While we love and reverence our fathers, we are not disposed to think that they attained to all truth. Their path was onward, and we best manifest our duty to them by pressing forward ourselves."[6] One writer, arguing that the experience of the living was a safer and more self-respecting guide to action than precedents set by

[4] Robert Saunders, "Baccalaureate Address. Delivered to the graduates of William and Mary College, in the College Chapel, 4th July, 1846," *Southern Literary Messenger* 12 (1846): 543–44.

[5] J[oshua] N. Danforth, "Thoughts on the Fourth of July, 1847," ibid. 13 (1847): 502.

[6] "The Peace Movement," *United States Magazine and Democratic Review* 10 (1842): 116.

the fathers, observed that "we have all the light they had to guide our feet, and the advantage of half a century's improvement."[7] Attacking "a certain class of thinkers . . . [who] seem wed to the idols of the past," another writer proposed reforms in the training of the young that would elevate the experience of the self over received precepts and encourage children to think "that they may be great themselves" instead of always subservient to dead men.[8]

Nor did it go unnoticed that there were antidemocratic implications in accounts of the Revolution that—as most did— placed Washington in an indispensable role. "The issue depended on no one man," Lewis Cass insisted. "Though the peculiar characteristics of Washington were admirably suited to his station and duties, still the great work would have gone on to its consummation if he had never existed."[9] Where there were not signs of asperity with the overvaluation of the fathers' achievement, there were signs of indifference to it. Americans seemed able, for example, to complete monuments commemorating the founders or battles of the Revolution only after great tribulation, embarrassment, and protracted delay. The *Democratic Review* pointed out correctly that "pages might be filled with the list of the abortive attempts that have been set on foot, in various places, with a view to the erection of statues of Washington." On a different occasion, ridiculing yet another proposal for a monument to Washington, the maga-

[7] "Daniel Webster; His Political Philosophy in 1820," ibid. 22 (1848): 130. "We should always be suspicious of the truthfulness of our father's instructions, until we have proved them for ourselves, and to our own satisfaction." Ibid.

[8] "The East and the West," ibid., p. 408. See also "The Love of Fame," *Casket* 14 (1839): 246.

[9] [Lewis Cass], "France—Its King, Court, and Government," *United States Magazine and Democratic Review* 7 (1840): 368. See also William Maxwell Wood, "The Spirit of Democracy," *Southern Literary Messenger* 9 (1843): 671.

zine insisted that Americans were "too utilitarian" to spend money on a merely sentimental gesture.[10]

Statements critical of the founders, however, are most notable for their scarcity and a tone almost invariably either mild or defensive. Opponents of monuments rarely argued that the fathers did not deserve monuments, but rather that the power of their memory did not require them. The cumulative effect of assertions of the kind quoted here is to call attention to the resilience of the cult of the fathers, which first withstood and then outlasted the forces that threatened to undermine it. So successfully were sentimental conventions settled upon American speech, and beyond speech to internalized belief, that antagonistic feelings toward the fathers seldom reached consciousness, let alone expression.

"No one cares for what occurred before his time," Tocqueville wrote about the Americans he encountered in the 1830s,[11] and historians have nodded concessively at his observation ever since. It is beyond dispute that he accurately read a prevalent national attitude. Americans were fond of boasting that "we have outgrown tradition, and authority no longer seems to us a valid argument."[12] Everywhere exultant claims were heard to the effect that after a "long and very bitter" struggle between past and present, the past was dead. "Probably no other civilized nation has at any period of its history so completely

10 "Thomas's Reminiscences," *United States Magazine and Democratic Review* 8 (1840): 227; "Gossip of the Month," ibid. 21 (1847): 474. See also George Watterston, "To the American People," *American Whig Review* 15 (1852): 464; George Washington Warren, *The History of the Bunker Hill Monument Association during the First Century of the United States of America* (Boston: James R. Osgood and Co., 1877), pp. 285–314 and *passim*.

11 Alexis de Tocqueville, *Democracy in America,* ed. Phillips Bradley, 2 vols. (New York: Alfred A. Knopf, 1945), 1:219. See also 1:55.

12 O[restes] A. B[rownson], "Cousin's *Philosophy,*" *Christian Examiner* 21 (1836): 34.

thrown off its allegiance to the past," the *Democratic Review* stated in 1842. "The whole essay of our national life and legislation, has been a prolonged protest against the dominion of antiquity in every form whatsoever."[13] Earlier the magazine had explained that "such grand though shadowy anticipations are for ever vaguely present before our minds, that the things of the past have but little interest or value for us."[14] "In our country . . . there are no recollections, no institutions consecrated by time," said an orator in 1846.[15] "The spirit of the age throws off the fetters forged by the folly of the past," said a congressman in 1850.[16] As such statements suggest, "the past" was one of the more conspicuous objects of public remark in the United States between the 1830s and the 1850s. Indeed, probably at no other period in American history did people speak of the past as "the past" so often, with so much intensity, and with so little precision.

The suspicion thus arises that people who made claims of this sort wanted to fool themselves and block the awareness that the past was not dead at all. Other interpreters of the age seemed to sense this, for they directly challenged the perceptions of Tocqueville and those who seconded him. In the famous opening passage of his first book, *Nature,* published in 1836, Ralph Waldo Emerson, for example, regretted the hold of the past over the present:

> Our age is retrospective. It builds the sepulchres of the fathers. It writes biographies, histories, and criticism. The foregoing generations beheld God and nature face to face; we, through their eyes. Why should not we also enjoy an original relation to the universe? Why should not we have a poetry and phi-

[13] "Lucian and his Age," *United States Magazine and Democratic Review* 11 (1842), pp. 225–26.

[14] "Thomas's Reminiscences," p. 227.

[15] Saunders, "Baccalaureate Address," p. 543.

[16] David T. Disney, *Congressional Globe,* 31 Cong., 1 Sess. (March 13, 1850), appendix, p. 229.

losophy of insight and not of tradition? . . . Why should we grope among the dry bones of the past, or put the living generation into masquerade out of its faded wardrobe? The sun shines to-day also.[17]

Henry David Thoreau wrote in the 1840s that the dead ruled the world yet, "and the living are but their executors. . . . Like some Indian tribes, we bear about with us the mouldering relics of our ancestors on our shoulders." Far from being swept away by the forces of modernization, "history accumulates like rubbish before the portals of nature."[18] The transcendentalists, in setting out what passed for a creed in their new magazine, the *Dial,* claimed to represent not only themselves but the rising "spirit of the time" generally when they took on (and thereby complimented) the established American culture, "which looks only backward, which asks only such a future as the past, which suspects improvement, and holds nothing so much in horror as new views and the dreams of youth."[19] Not everyone who shared the perception put the same judgment upon it. "The past she ruleth," wrote Lydia Sigourney in 1846 with evident cheer, as though there were no doubt and no dispute.[20]

[17] Ralph Waldo Emerson, *Nature, The Collected Works of Ralph Waldo Emerson,* ed. Robert E. Spiller and Alfred R. Ferguson (Cambridge, Mass.: Harvard University Press, Belknap Press, 1971), 1:7. See also "Self-Reliance": "Whence then this worship of the past? The centuries are conspirators against the sanity and authority of the soul. . . . Man is timid and apologetic . . . he dares not say 'I think,' 'I am,' but quotes some saint or sage. . . . These roses under my window make no reference to former roses or to better ones. . . . But man postpones or remembers; he does not live in the present, but with reverted eye laments the past, or, heedless of the riches that surround him, stands on tiptoe to foresee the future." *The Complete Works of Ralph Waldo Emerson,* 12 vols. (Boston: Houghton Mifflin Co., 1903–4), 2:66–67.

[18] Henry D[avid] Thoreau, *A Week on the Concord and Merrimack Rivers* (Boston: Houghton Mifflin Co., 1867), pp. 140, 404.

[19] "The Editors to the Reader," *Dial* 1 (1840): 1–2.

[20] L[ydia] H. S[igourney], "Memory," *Southern Literary Messenger* 12 (1846): 586.

The prevailing modern understanding of the authority of tradition in the post-heroic period is probably most clearly signaled by the phrase "Age of Boundlessness," which John Higham has convincingly applied to the years from about 1815 to 1848.[21] Without ignoring the strength of contrary tendencies,[22] he and others have emphasized the culture's increasing celebration in those years of centrifugal values and qualities: expansiveness, progress, egalitarianism, individualism, and the power of the imagination;[23] and its rejection of contrary claims, particularly the authority of history, whose limits "dissolved in an ecstatic dedication to the future."[24] The prevalence of the *spirit* of boundlessness is undeniable, but it is important to stress perhaps more than Higham does its essentially illusory quality.[25] The almost desperate insistence with which some

[21] John Higham, *From Boundlessness to Consolidation: The Transformation of American Culture, 1848–1860* (Ann Arbor: William L. Clements Library, 1969), p. 17. The phrase has reached at least one textbook. "New Ways of Thinking: The Age of Boundlessness" is the title of a chapter in Robert Kelley, *The Shaping of the American Past*, 2nd ed., 2 vols. (Englewood Cliffs, N.J.: Prentice-Hall, 1978), 1:177–97.

[22] "It would be absurd to suppose that these expansive sentiments and ideas ever overwhelmed more cautious and traditionalist views." Higham, *Boundlessness to Consolidation*, p. 8.

[23] The association of the imagination with the absence of limits was a subject of frequent (and often concerned) remark. "The imagination is the most illimitable monarch that reigns." "The Imagination; Its Seat, Its Disposition, Its Pleasures, Its Pain, Its Powers," *Southern Literary Messenger* 21 (1855): 228. "It would be difficult accurately to discriminate the limits of this element of mental action, or to exaggerate its influence and importance." "The Culture of Imagination," *United States Magazine and Democratic Review* 22 (1848): 33.

[24] Higham, *Boundlessness to Consolidation*, p. 8.

[25] The focus of Higham's analysis in any event is on what he calls the cultural transformation to "consolidation" after about 1848. Because my understanding of "boundlessness" differs somewhat from what I take Higham's to be, my formulation of the transformation toward consolidation turns out to be somewhat different as well. But I am in general (and admiring) agreement with his perception that an important cultural change did occur in the United States at or just before the middle of the nineteenth century.

Americans argued alternatively that nothing did or that nothing should limit them is a clue pointing both to the objective reality of continuing limits and to an at least half-acknowledged sense that these limits were still quite strong. Perhaps the most challenging historical problem here is not to account for the repudiation in the 1830s and 1840s of the ancient limits on man's thoughts and actions, but rather to account for the persistent and even triumphant strength of those limits during a period when they appeared so weak that the prospect of their disappearance seemed quite real.

Although their entrenched filiopiety prevented Americans from directly confronting the problem of the proper place of the authority of the founders in a democracy, many of them did face it indirectly. Attitudes toward tradition were at least to some extent displaced attitudes toward fathers, whom the founders represented in the public realm. That this was so is by no means obvious, but as the cited examples suggest, the language of the assault on the past was conspicuously personal and of the body. Even more directly to the point, sentimentalists made the above connection at once. As one of their adversaries somewhat defensively pointed out, "a man cannot declare himself a friend of progress, without being at once proclaimed a foe to the Constitution, and a reviler of its honored framers. If he pronounces those who oppose progress 'old fogies,' it is instantly caught up as an attack on Washington, Jefferson, Madison, and our earlier statesmen."[26] But surely the sentimentalists were not completely misreading the celebrants of progress. When we observe a newspaper correspondent demanding, as one did in 1853, that the government act "for the present, and the vast future, and not for the

[26] Quoted in Siert F. Riepma, " 'Young America': A Study in American Nationalism before the Civil War" (Ph.D. diss., Western Reserve University, 1939), pp. 309–10.

mouldering tombs of the eighteenth century," we do not need to wonder whose bones are in those tombs.[27]

There were, after all, several metaphors that Americans of the post-heroic period used to express their Republic in figurative terms. In the 1820s the dominant analogy was to the family; in the 1850s this again was the case—along with the house. The prevailing metaphor in the 1840s, however, was neither institutional nor architectural, but organic: the nation was a growing youth. There was, of course, nothing new in the general habit of which this was a part. Like family metaphors, the analogy of the body politic to the human body has always been a standard item of political thought. In the United States in the nineteenth century, the comparison settled either on the child or the youth and became a commonplace. As the *Southern Literary Messenger* observed in 1849, "there is . . . no similitude more trite and familiar,—certainly there is none more striking and true, than that which likens the origin and progress of nations to the growth and development of children."[28]

Familiar indeed in the American case: it became common in nineteenth-century rhetoric to evoke the myth that the new Republic was the fortunate child of the best of space and time. In addition to being the greatest of "our fathers," George Washington was also, of course, the "father of his country," and in that role he hardly symbolized the repudiation but rather the natural—indeed unavoidable—continuation of the authority of history. Just as the Revolution was the great culmination of all time, so its greatest leader represented the generative power of the past, which according to Richard Henry Dana was "our great ancestor."[29] Herman Melville also understood that "we are the heirs of all time." "Our ancestry is lost in the universal paternity; and Caesar and Alfred, St. Paul and

[27] Quoted in ibid., p. 263.

[28] "National Ballads," *Southern Literary Messenger* 15 (1849): 10.

[29] Richard Henry Dana, "The Past, and the Present," *American Quarterly Observer* 1 (1833): 39.

Luther, and Homer and Shakespeare are as much ours as Washington."[30]

It was through the agency of the last of these that Providence arranged for the greatest act of generation. Before the nation could be born, the carrier of history had to meet maternal (and emotional) space. Barren and wild before the appearance of the fathers, she was transformed by them into a fruitful garden and became the great mother. Here, in one fanciful account, was Nature's reaction to the birth of Washington:

> The snows on Alleghenies' height
> Flushed with red joy that dawn, the pines
>   Bowed low and listened with delight,
> And heard the story from the winds.
>
>   .   .   .
>
> The rivers told it as they passed,
>   Surging on slumberous shores; each hill
> Rocked jubilant with echoings,
>   Repeated o'er and o'er, until
> The eagle heard them on sunward wings.

Nature is jubilant because she knows the appearance of Washington portends her own fulfillment.

> The conscious prairies laughed with glee,
>   Prophetic of the future corn;
> The rivers dreamed of flashing keels,
>   Of snow-winged navies, forest-born,
> And thunders of innumerous wheels.
>
> The rest is History's.[31]

---

[30] Herman Melville, *Redburn: His First Voyage, The Works of Herman Melville,* 16 vols. (London: Constable and Co., 1922–24), 5:217. I have reversed the order of the quoted sentences.

[31] John R. Tait, "The Twenty-Second of February," *Graham's Magazine* 53 (1858): 546.

The revolutionary heroes, Rufus Choate said, "sent forth, scattering broadcast, the seed of life in the ready, virgin soil."[32] Nature responded. "The earth was made to bring forth in one day!" John Quincy Adams exclaimed. "A Nation was born at once!"[33] Explaining the meaning of Jean-Antoine Houdon's statue of Washington to an audience in 1856, Henry Wise pointed out that the figure "stands on the mother earth, the plough-share placed on the left by his foot. These signify the idea of 'Country,'" the offspring of Washington's relationship with Nature.[34] The most famous of all nineteenth-century American speeches owes some of its force to its clean use of the parturient convention. "Our fathers," said Abraham Lincoln, "brought forth on this continent, a new nation, conceived in Liberty."[35]

That the fathers were revolutionaries tended to obscure their strong ties to the past, much as the biggest obstacle to understanding the essential conservatism of the Revolution has always been the Revolution itself. "Our national birth was the beginning of a new history . . . which separates us from the past and connects us with the future only."[36] This assertion, which appeared in the *Democratic Review* in 1839, uses imagery similar to the previously quoted ones, but differs from them in an important respect: its new nation was an orphan. Precisely because no one denied that the nation *was* new, many

[32] Samuel Gilman Brown, ed., *The Works of Rufus Choate with a Memoir of His Life*, 2 vols. (Boston: Little, Brown and Co., 1862), 1:460.

[33] John Quincy Adams, *An Oration Delivered Before the Inhabitants of the Town of Newburyport, at Their Request, on the Sixty-First Anniversary of the Declaration of Independence, July 4th, 1837* (Newburyport, Mass.: Charles Whipple, 1837), p. 12.

[34] "Gov. Wise's Oration, at Lexington, Va., 4th July, 1856," *Southern Literary Messenger* 23 (1856): 3.

[35] Roy P. Basler, ed., *The Collected Works of Abraham Lincoln,* 8 vols. (New Brunswick, N.J.: Rutgers University Press, 1953), 7:23.

[36] "The Great Nation of Futurity," *United States Magazine and Democratic Review* 6 (1839): 426.

Americans were able to avoid seeing that it was no more cut off from the past than the child to whom it was compared. At least one contemporary writer did, however, understand that Americans were made "worshippers of the past" by their up-bringing, and proceeded to argue that therefore the authority of tradition amounted to an "almost insurmountable obstacle . . . against real advancement."[37] Even the most revolutionary of parents are the carriers of tradition, which becomes part of the child before he has a chance to reflect on the matter. If he would get rid of the past, the child must plan not only to throw it off but throw it out.

Metaphors that ascribed human traits to the Republic through the medium of historical actors created a link between broad political and social developments and the psychology of the self. They described a common field on which the emotional conflicts individuals experience privately, at different times, and unconsciously, could be made public, made common by simultaneous repetition, and acted out, without necessarily becoming conscious in the process. Specifically, the analogy that used the growth of the self to illuminate the nature of the Republic worked in the reverse direction as well: to varying degrees the youth of the nation not only recalled but psychologically reinstated the youth of the self.[38]

A substantiating notice of this tendency appeared in an article published in 1851 by David Hatch Barlow, a Unitarian clergyman and essayist. Barlow wrote that he had happened to read almost simultaneously two essays on John Milton, one by an American and the other by an Englishman. Though the

---

37 "Daniel Webster," p. 130.

38 For an excellent discussion of possible effects of group symbols on the self-conception of individuals within the group, see Edwin G. Burrows and Michael Wallace, "The American Revolution: The Ideology and Psychology of National Liberation," *Perspectives in American History* 6 (1972): 268–84.

American writer (whose identity, like that of the other essayist, is not disclosed) was "past fifty" when he wrote his piece, and the Englishman was a "young man when he wrote" his, Barlow was struck by the *"youthfulness"* of the American's essay and the maturity of the other. By this he did not mean simply "a certain young glow and fervency manifest from first to last," though this was certainly present. He meant, rather, the *"species* and *form* of its thoughts and images. These appear to me more like those of a brilliant and able youth, than those of a completely matured man of large and various culture."[39]

On the other hand, the essay by the Englishman gave the "appearance of belonging to a more advanced, older mind. In its cast of thought, and its sources and modes of illustration, it exhibits traces, not perceptible in the other, of that multiform experience, that extended and profound acquaintance with life and the world, which are the customary fruit of a ripe age." The question that Barlow drew from his observations seemed to him to extend far beyond these two cases, and he formulated it in very general terms: "Why is it . . . that, for the most part, Americans write *youthfully,* whatever their age may be, while other nations write *maturely,* however young the individual writer?" He concluded that "a young nation . . . must be reckoned the *commencement of a new train of thoughts,* and consequently somewhat superficial and crude in utterance." The youth of a nation profoundly affected the consciousness of the people within it. "A people, like an individual, must needs pass through a season of youth in its progressive development, and . . . during this season the individual partakes of the youthfulness of the community to which he belongs."[40]

The tendency Barlow observed comported with one of the purposes of sentimentalist rhetoric: to provide an image that would link the self to the Republic, thereby bringing the latter

[39] D[avid] H[atch] Barlow, "American Literature," *Graham's Magazine* 38 (1851): 410.
[40] Ibid.

to human scale, while encouraging the arrested development of both. Americans were urged from many quarters to think of themselves and the nation as children of the fathers—to identify themselves with the child nation and think of it in the same terms of structure, permanence, and deference they supposedly used when contemplating their own family and their place in it. When sentimentalists compared the Republic to a child they implied that it required, perhaps forever, the restraint and discipline of the parental voice they were quite prepared to interpret. Their strategy seemed to work to their satisfaction as long as the Republic was plausibly a "child." But for reasons not difficult to discover, the analogical custom could not be restricted to childhood. The analogy of self and nation shifted as the Republic inexorably grew "from infancy to the vigor and strength of young manhood."[41]

Territorial expansion was the most obvious development that inspired the comparison of the Republic to a rapidly growing youth. A personified young Republic was said by Theophilus Fisk to demand the "immediate annexation of Texas at any and every hazard. It will plant its right foot upon the northern verge of Oregon, and its left upon the Atlantic crag."[42] The image was further inspired by the technological advances that attended expansion. Oliver Wendell Holmes once wrote, for example, that the development of the telegraph gave the nation a "network of iron nerves which flash sensation and volition backward and forward to and from towns and provinces as if they were organs and limbs of a single living body." Similarly, railroads provided a "vast system of iron muscles which, as it were, move the limbs of the mighty organism."[43]

[41] John A. McClernand, *Congressional Globe,* 29 Cong., 1 Sess. (January 8, 1846), p. 168.

[42] Quoted in Frederick Merk, *Manifest Destiny and Mission in American History: A Reinterpretation* (New York: Alfred A. Knopf, 1963), p. 54.

[43] [Oliver Wendell Holmes], "Bread and the Newspaper," *Atlantic Monthly* 8 (1861): 348.

These developments cumulatively produced a new metaphor that, with the possible exception of "manifest destiny," became the most prevalent political slogan of the 1840s: "Young America." Americans of the day who yearned and searched expectantly for a "new order of society" turned as if by reflex to the phrase when they attempted to characterize the ascendent impulses and attitudes that were everywhere called the spirit of the age.[44] Thus: "There is a new spirit abroad in the land, young, restless, vigorous and omnipotent. . . . It is Young America." And: "The spirit of Young America . . . will not be satisfied with what has been attained, but plumes its young wings for a higher and more glorious flight."[45]

Like the child metaphors which are its obvious antecedents, the "Young America" slogan speaks metaphorically of the nation as a single being. In its function, however, the metaphor was very different from those we have been considering up to here. The sentimental family metaphors were meant to oppose or at least obscure the implications of the developments that the Young America metaphor celebrated. Everyone knew that to use the new phrase was to connote a group of related values and wishes as well as a particularly aggressive, boastful, and exploitative style of conduct. People who were identified as spokesmen for a distinctly "Young America" cast of mind called variously for the broadening of majoritarian democracy; for geographical expansion; for the liberation of oppressed peoples, or the self; or for a vital national literature. But what-

[44] M[oncure] D. Conway, "Concerning Hawthorne and Brook Farm," *Every Saturday,* January 2, 1869, p. 14; M. E. Curti, " 'Young America,' " *American Historical Review* 32 (1926): 34–55; Riepma, " 'Young America' "; Perry Miller, *The Raven and the Whale: The War of Words and Wits in the Era of Poe and Melville* (New York: Harcourt, Brace and Co., 1956), pp. 71–117; David B. Danbom, "The Young America Movement," *Journal of the Illinois State Historical Society* 67 (1974): 294–306.

[45] These statements, which appeared in print in 1845 and 1844 respectively, are both quoted in Merk, *Manifest Destiny,* pp. 54, 53.

ever their particular interests were, they shared a commitment to "progress" (whether moral or material) and the autonomy of the present generation—a commitment that implied a hostility to the authority of tradition.[46] Attributing the characteristics of a vigorous and growing youth to the abstraction of the Republic, their leading metaphor recognized the bounds not of history but of nature only, and looked implicitly to the coming manhood of the imagined being. "Our fathers deemed the Revolution a great work," said Theodore Parker, who happened to agree with them. But, he went on, "young America looks to other revolutions."[47] In short, the term suggested an approach to culture and politics that was anything but sentimental.

To the extent that the objective condition of the nation could be translated through metaphors into the self-image of the nation's citizens, it was perfectly foreseeable that when the nation grew and no longer was comparable to a child but now to a youth or even young man, the self-sense of the citizens would tend to reflect the change. This is precisely what took place. "We are young," Lewis Cass said in 1846, by which year he had passed well beyond the age of sixty.[48] "We are a nation of young men," Theodore Parker said in 1848, by which he meant that there was an essential callowness in the bragging, boastful plans and the aggressive actions of American political leaders.[49]

Because we know that although sons love their fathers they also hate them, it is just here that we look for signs of confrontation between the founders in whatever form their pater-

[46] "A 'Progressive' Age," *Emerson's Magazine and Putnam's Monthly* 5 (1857): 481–85.

[47] Theodore Parker, "The Destination of America" [1848], *The Works of Theodore Parker,* 15 vols. (Boston: American Unitarian Association, 1907–13), 11:143–44.

[48] *Congressional Globe,* 29 Cong., 1 Sess. (January 26, 1846), p. 241.

[49] Parker, "Destination of America," p. 145.

nal immortality was felt, and countless men of all ages whose outlooks were shaped and energized by their association with Young America and who thus were as good as young themselves. The imagery associated with the myth of a youth whose father was the past or tradition and whose mother was the earth or Nature could serve as a magnet drawing out the never-resolved feelings of individuals toward their parents, transferring these emotions to the public realm, organizing them there, and then directing them powerfully toward a common object with perhaps revolutionary results.

The possibilities, at least theoretically, were rich, for in combination with the creative intellectual challenges that might have been directed at the sere rationalism of the Enlightenment culture with which the fathers were associated, there was now potentially the concentrated emotion of filial hate to fuel generational conflict. To call up one formulation that everyone knows, if romanticism was a reaction against the Enlightenment, we would perhaps expect romanticism to have flourished most strongly in a culture where the Enlightenment was institutionalized and firmly set, providing such an obvious target. To call up another, if the essence of romanticism lay in its appeal to the authority of nature against that of tradition and the artificialities of civilization, we would perhaps expect romanticism to have flourished in a society where the inspirational potential of nature was almost everywhere visible. But American romanticism is conspicuous by its thin, confined quality and its marginal place in the culture of the time—and this seems to be true almost no matter how one defines it.[50] The fathers' association with Enlightenment culture helped to protect and strengthen that culture, not undermine it. This was because the fathers and perforce the values of the world they created and lived in had been internalized by the sons.

[50] Ann Douglas, *The Feminization of American Culture* (New York: Alfred A. Knopf, 1977), pp. 253–56.

Defenders of progress tended to argue that they were actually imitating the fathers, who were "the 'young America' of that period. They were not satisfied with the existing state of things."[51] The similarity between the generations was perhaps most strongly insisted upon by the militant supporters of expansion. Like the language of sons who obscure conflict with their fathers by displacing it onto their fathers' enemies,[52] the rhetoric of manifest destiny fed on an explicitly derivative Anglophobia at almost every chance. The actual or possible presence of the British in Maine, Texas, California, and particularly Oregon provided the point of departure for countless declarations that the sons would, if need be, confront and defeat that chronic foe as gloriously as the fathers had.[53] More striking to modern ears is the tendency of politicians of the 1840s and 1850s to parody the language of courtship and to speak of potential new states as women being married to the Union. Sam Houston wrote of Texas presenting itself "to the United States as a bride adorned for her espousals."[54] Andrew Johnson described at length an imaginary wedding ceremony between the United States and Texas, "the interesting young virgin of the South," who after having been "compelled to act the coquette a little, finally brought Uncle Sam to his senses, and the Union was consummated."[55] An opponent of immediate statehood for the Mexican cession charged in 1850 that President Zachary Taylor was trying to "drag California into

[51] Quotation from Riepma, " 'Young America,' " p. 310.

[52] Martin Wangh, "Some Unconscious Factors in the Psychogenesis of Recent Student Uprisings," *Psychoanalytic Quarterly* 41 (1972): 209.

[53] Parker, "Destination of America," p. 129; Andrew Kennedy, *Congressional Globe,* 29 Cong., 1 Sess. (January 10, 1846), p. 181; Jacob Brinkerhoff, ibid. (January 14, 1846), p. 205; John Fairfield, ibid. (January 27, 1846), p. 252; Charles W. Cathcart, ibid. (February 6, 1846), p. 324.

[54] Sam Houston to Andrew Jackson, February 16, 1844, United States Congress, *House Executive Documents,* 28 Cong., 1 Sess., no. 271, p. 110.

[55] *Congressional Globe,* 29 Cong., 1 Sess. (January 31, 1846), p. 289.

the Union before her *wedding garment* has yet been cast about her person, and ere she has been regularly bidden to the nuptial."[56]

The difference between the metaphors of Young America spokesmen and those of the transcendentalists provides an unintended opening into the psyches of people in both groups, illuminating the reasons behind their conflicting measurements of the weight of the past. When Emerson was a young man he walked away from a Fourth of July celebration, saying he preferred to "expend" his "patriotism in banqueting upon Mother Nature."[57] In his imagination he seemed to be repudiating not just a particular model of manhood, but adulthood itself, or at least its unavoidable effects. In *Nature* he yearned for a general retention of the "spirit of infancy even into the era of manhood." He wrote that in nature "a man casts off his years . . . and at what period soever of life, is always a child. In the woods, is perpetual youth."[58] As a friendly reviewer of the book noted, Emerson showed himself to be a "devoted child of the great Mother."[59] His disciple Thoreau moved even more radically back beyond childhood to preexistence and then in ambiguous communion with Mother Nature ("Sometimes a mortal feels in himself Nature . . . his Mother stirs within him, and he becomes immortal with her immortality."[60]) created himself anew. He became, as it were, his own father, a transcendental version of the self-made man.

Unlike the transcendentalists' desire to possess and commune permanently with a maternal Nature, however, the courting

56 Henry S. Foote, ibid., 31 Cong., 1 Sess. (February 14, 1850), p. 367.

57 Emerson to John Boynton Hill, July 3, 1822, in Ralph L. Rusk, ed., *The Letters of Ralph Waldo Emerson*, 6 vols. (New York: Columbia University Press, 1939), 1:121.

58 Emerson, *Nature*, pp. 9–10.

59 "Nature—A Prose Poem," *United States Magazine and Democratic Review* 1 (1838): 321.

60 Thoreau, *Concord and Merrimack Rivers*, p. 399.

by expansionists of territorial "women"—Texas and California particularly—meets exogamous standards. The rhetoric of Young America—and hence presumably the outlook of people who employed the phrase—was that of a son who had identified with and now sought to emulate his father, not that of a rebellious son wishing only to be rid of him. This is not the same thing as saying that the United States had passed successfully through its Oedipal phase. Nations do not have Oedipus complexes. It is simply to suggest that the recalled psychic phase of the self from which expansionists drew memories to create Young America imagery was post-Oedipal.

For all the emotional turmoil it involves, the normal outcome of the Oedipus complex is conservative, and this is not just because it occurs at a point in life where the defeat of the son is unavoidable. The murderous impulses of the son are in effect bought off by the prospect that eventually he will be in a position to approximate his true desires. Not only does he settle for this and direct his erotic and aggressive drives outside of the family; he is likely to celebrate his defeat as a victory by claiming his former enemy as an ally and anticipating his coming independence. That is, the son identifies with the father; he internalizes the values of and strives to become like the person he once wanted to kill. The hatred that energized the patricidal wish does not thereby disappear—ever. The illusion that it has or that it never existed at all is permitted by the fact that (and as long as) it can be directed elsewhere. In the case at hand, the repetition of this conflict through the dynamic I have described seems exactly to have imitated its ontogenetic model in that it remained unconscious in the minds of the people who unknowingly contributed to it, and moved on its course to the same result.

Thus the spirit of boundlessness, which we expect to have threatened the fathers, actually protected them in two distinct ways: first, by providing opportunities for those who wanted them to march in their steps; and, second, by creating the illusion that the past was gone and thus obviating any desire to rebel against it. It was exactly the ability of Americans to avoid facing the synonymy of past and father that permitted them to indulge the illusion that they were good sons who revered and imitated the fathers but who had repudiated the authority of tradition and broken free from all ties whatever to the past.

There are two episodes in the fiction of Nathaniel Hawthorne that, if understood with the fullness they deserve, both substantiate and surpass Abraham Lincoln's analysis of the urban social unrest that disturbed many Americans in the 1830s and 1840s. They substantiate his intuition, revealed throughout the Lyceum speech and particularly in his striking metaphor that "to violate the law, is to trample on the blood of [one's] father," that social unrest bore a complex and emotional relationship to the revolutionary tradition and was what we would now call Oedipal. They surpass it by suggesting something that Emerson only partially and Lincoln evidently never realized: that precisely because such acts were Oedipal they were not subversive.

The first piece is "My Kinsman, Major Molineux." In 1832, the year after Lincoln left his father to begin his rise in the world according to the example of the fathers, Hawthorne published a classic short story about a young man leaving his father to begin his rise in the world according to the example of the fathers.[61] A raw adolescent named Robin Molineux

[61] Nathaniel Hawthorne, "My Kinsman, Major Molineux," *Complete Works,* 3:616–41. The story appeared first in 1832 in—rather incongruously—*The Token,* an annual giftbook of sweet prose and poetry published by Samuel Griswold Goodrich in Boston. See Randall Stewart, *Nathaniel Hawthorne: A Biography* (New Haven: Yale University Press, 1948), pp. 30–33. Generally ignored by literary critics before 1950, "Molineux" is now considered to be one of Hawthorne's most important works. For important instances of this

travels from the country to the city to seek the "major" of the title, his wealthy and well-positioned kinsman, who has offered to give him the kind of start in life that the youth's own father is unable to provide. The major represents the promise of upward mobility according to traditional hierarchical principles. Robin is seeking, in other words, both another father and his own manhood. Most of the story is taken up with the double search.

Robin has never been to the city before; he does not know exactly where his kinsman lives, yet not until he has walked some distance into town does he realize that "he knew not whither to direct his steps." He wanders desultorily and confusedly through the city asking directions, but is everywhere baffled. No one is helpful. Some people chase him away; others ridicule him with laughter; one young woman attempts to seduce him. "But Robin, being of the household of a New England clergyman, was a good youth, as well as a shrewd one; so he resisted temptation, and fled away." Increasingly frustrated, he finally halts a man and refuses to let him pass until he is told the location of his kinsman's dwelling. The man tells Robin to wait where he is for "an hour," and his kinsman will "pass by."[62]

recognition see Seymour L. Gross, "Hawthorne's 'My Kinsman, Major Molineux': History as Moral Adventure," *Nineteenth-Century Fiction* 12 (1957): 97–109; Daniel Hoffman, *Form and Fable in American Fiction* (New York: Oxford University Press, 1961), pp. 113–25; Simon O. Lesser, "The Image of the Father," *Partisan Review* 22 (1955): 372–90; Roy Harvey Pearce, "Hawthorne and the Sense of the Past or, the Immortality of Major Molineux," *ELH* 21 (1954): 327–49; Peter Shaw, "Fathers, Sons, and the Ambiguities of Revolution in 'My Kinsman, Major Molineux,'" *New England Quarterly* 49 (1976): 559–76; and Julian Smith, "Historical Ambiguity in 'My Kinsman, Major Molineux,'" *English Language Notes* 8 (1970): 115–20. The most challenging psychological study of Hawthorne's fiction generally is Frederick Crews, *The Sins of the Fathers: Hawthorne's Psychological Themes* (New York: Oxford University Press, 1966).

[62] Hawthorne, "My Kinsman, Major Molineux," pp. 618, 628, 629.

Robin does as he is told, and eventually hears the noise of a crowd growing closer. Suddenly a mob, reveling in bacchanalian frenzy, surges around the corner. A "mighty stream of people" heads Robin's way, some of the men playing wind instruments, some carrying torches, some dressed as Indians, all of them noisy. The mob is led by the man who directed Robin to wait there, and at its center in a cart sits Major Molineux, tarred and feathered. In the crowd are all of the people who had "made sport" of Robin during the evening. As they pass him with the major in tow, some people begin to laugh, and the laughter spreads. Surely Robin will spring to the rescue of his kinsman. Surely he does not! "The contagion was spreading among the multitude, when all at once, it seized upon Robin, and he sent forth a shout of laughter that echoed through the street,—every man shook his sides, every man emptied his lungs, but Robin's shout was the loudest there." Then, when the laughter had died, "on swept the tumult, and left a silent street behind."[63]

It cannot be taken for granted that this story involves postheroic attitudes toward the fathers; it contains not a word on the subject. Rather it seems to concern the American Revolution directly or some excited precursor of it, and to depict the colonials in the very act of throwing out the British. Indeed, Hawthorne at first leads the reader to think that the major himself is a justly deposed royal governor of Massachusetts, for he prefaces his account of the officer's fate by recalling the various miseries and humiliations suffered by most of the colony's royal governors. But the period in which the story occurs is not precisely fixed, and a reading that emphasizes the overthrow of imperial rule makes sense only by making central what occurs for the most part offstage and by ignoring Robin, who, though central to the story, is essentially a bystander to history. He confirms the ouster of the major, but does not

[63] Ibid., pp. 637–40.

bring it about or even actually participate in it. This focus would distort the meaning of the story, which fixes and then keeps its attention on Robin's state of mind.

Close attention to what actually happens in the tale suggests that Hawthorne is dealing with the historical situation of his own generation. Not only does Robin not participate in the act of symbolic patricide except to ratify it; his behavior raises the possibility that unlike the Revolution the rebellious deed does not actually take place—that it is a fantasy within a fantasy. Robin's mind keeps "vibrating between fancy and reality"; he spends much of the story standing or sitting around, sometimes on the edge of sleep or in it, possibly dreaming, certainly hallucinating. His period of forced waiting becomes an occasion for fantasies about his actual father, his mother, and the home he has left behind. So closely do these fantasies precede the appearance of the mob that when we are told by Hawthorne that the procession has a "visionary air, as if a dream had broken forth from some feverish brain, and were sweeping visibly through the midnight streets,"[64] we are prepared to conclude that the feverish brain is Robin's own. That is to say, the ritual of the "slaying" of the father may be nothing more than a primordial and very common wish taking shape as elaborate fantasy.

The emotional origins of Robin's patricidal gesture could have little to do with its victim personally, for Robin scarcely knows him. More likely they derive from his relationship with the father he has always known and just left, and are transferred to the major, who represents a continuation in the public, adult realm of the private world of dependence and childhood from which Robin has only physically departed. Hostile impulses toward his father, successfully repressed until then, burst in disguised form but with "bewildering excitement"

[64] Ibid., pp. 633, 632, 638.

into Robin's consciousness at the appearance of the surrogate[65]
—who is not, however, just any patron.

To Hawthorne's readers, as Roy Harvey Pearce has dis-
cerned, the name Molineux would probably have called to
mind an actual figure of that name in revolutionary politics,
although one who was not a royal governor at all, but rather
a patriot hero—one of the fathers.[66] By appearing (but *only*
appearing) to recount what the fathers did to the British, Hawthorne actually reveals what the sons would like to do to the
fathers. At once replicating and anticipating one of the central
stories in American history in the nineteenth century, Robin
comes to the city seemingly on course to becoming the archetypal self-made man. The city represents the promise of adulthood and independence. But in Robin's case, of course, the
prospect of autonomy is matched and finally vitiated by the
prospect of restraint and permanent dependence which the
authority of his new father represents. Robin's brief excursion
into individualistic adventure—his engagement with the world
—will presumably come to an end or be sharply circumscribed
when he enters the major's house. That he half-realizes this
helps us understand his neglect to plan how to get where he
intends to go, and his evident lack of haste to get there.

The fantasy of the humiliation of the fathers does not end
the dependent relationship but only complicates it. At the end
of "Molineux," when Robin, nearly overcome by feelings of
guilt for his act or his desire (from the standpoint of guilt it
does not matter which), decides to return to his childhood
home ("I begin to grow weary of a town life, sir. Will you
show me the way to the ferry?"), he is told by a nameless bystander to stay. "As you are a shrewd youth, you may rise in
the world without the help of your kinsman, Major Molineux."[67] The last words of the story thus seem to hold out

[65] Ibid., p. 639.
[66] Pearce, "Hawthorne," pp. 327–29.
[67] Hawthorne, "My Kinsman, Major Molineux," p. 641.

to him the promise of becoming a self-made man. But of course what they really signal is that the self-made man is in truth not only a patricidal son but still a dependent one as well.

During the story—before and after the appearance of the major and then right up to the very last words—others take over in fact the paternalistic role which the major never has a chance except in Robin's mind to play. The youth's patricidal guilt not only leads him to seek authority (the wish to go home) but prevents him from realizing that he has already found it in democratic civilization, which is the authority of the fathers dispersed among the thousand nameless burghers who will help him find and keep his place in the community. That these burghers have just orchestrated a mobocratic act detracts not at all from this reality, for the point is precisely that the mob *is* orchestrated. The outrages of the mob, which provided the occasion for Lincoln's speech, give focus also to Hawthorne's story. Unlike Lincoln, however, Hawthorne saw in mob action the promise not of social chaos but of stability. The action of the mob in "Molineux" is ritualistic, preceded by obvious planning, carried out on schedule ("Watch here an hour") in as orderly a manner as the nature of such exercises permits, presided over by the civil establishment, and succeeded by calm. The social order has not been overturned.[68] If anything it has been strengthened as potentially anarchistic passions are organized and focused on the humiliation and ouster of a scapegoat. The implication is that the ritualistic acting out of patricidal fantasies is conservative. A corollary would be that repressing them as Lincoln wished buys trouble.

The second of Hawthorne's episodes takes place at a critical turn in *The House of the Seven Gables,* which he wrote between August 1850 and January 1851, the period during and just after the climactic phase of the political crisis that ended

[68] Cf. David Grimsted, "Rioting in Its Jacksonian Setting," *American Historical Review* 77 (1972): 361–97.

in the historic compromise measures.[69] One need not be on a willful search for symbols to notice a resemblance between the Union and the house of the title, which "presented the aspect of a whole sisterhood of edifices, breathing through the spiracles of one great chimney." As the Union was always said to be, the house was a "dear bought . . . inheritance." It was built, Hawthorne says more than once, with posterity in mind, and was intended to stand for centuries.[70]

Like the Union by 1850, moreover, the house is divided in such a way that whether it will stand much longer has been called into question. Part of the house is bolted off from the rest. But in this separate section lives no alienated Southerner. The division in *The House of the Seven Gables* is not along sectional lines. Although Hawthorne's house is beset by many serious dangers, including the possibility of destruction, potential violence among its inhabitants is not one of them. At the time that he wrote the book, Hawthorne claimed not to share the prevailing belief that slavery was the "great subject of the day."[71] The conflict in his house is psychological. It does not symbolize the struggle between the antagonistic halves of a single nation but between the antagonistic halves of a single mind. Hawthorne, indeed, compares the facade of his house to a human face, its chimney to a throat, and the building itself to a "great human heart, with a life of its own, and full of rich and sombre reminiscences."[72] He takes the conflicted feel-

[69] Stewart, *Nathaniel Hawthorne*, pp. 112–13. The crisis of 1850 is also reflected in the other great American novel to appear in 1851: *Moby-Dick*. See Alan Heimert, *"Moby-Dick* and American Political Symbolism," *American Quarterly* 15 (1963): 498–534.

[70] Nathaniel Hawthorne, *The House of the Seven Gables, The Centenary Edition of the Works of Nathaniel Hawthorne* ([Columbus]: Ohio State University Press, 1965), 2:11, 207.

[71] Quoted in Allen Flint, "Hawthorne and the Slavery Crisis," *New England Quarterly* 41 (1968): 399.

[72] Hawthorne, *House of the Seven Gables*, pp. 5, 277, 27.

ings toward the authority of tradition that many Americans individually experienced, externalizes them into opposing mentalities, and reifies them into characters arranged in a domestic setting, thereby revealing the nature of the emotional forces at work underneath the prosaic surface of politics.

Holgrave, the young protagonist, has come to live in the isolated portion of the house after having traveled widely in search of action and experience in the United States and Europe; worked variously as a peddler, dentist, and lecturer; taken up mesmerism and Fourierism, only to drop them as the fads they were; and written stories, some of which have appeared in *Graham's* and *Godey's,* two of the most fashionable magazines of the day. Nothing if not up-to-date, he now earns his living as a daguerreotypist. Later in the nineteenth century Henry James recognized Holgrave as a "national type."[73] The point, indeed, cannot be missed, for Hawthorne announces that the young man is meant to represent his generation:

> Altogether, in his culture and want of culture; in his crude, wild, and misty philosophy, and the practical experience that counteracted some of its tendencies; in his magnanimous zeal for man's welfare, and his recklessness of whatever the ages had established in man's behalf; in his faith, and in his infidelity; in what he had, and in what he lacked—the artist might fitly enough stand forth as the representative of many compeers in his native land.[74]

Certainly his experiences comport with the spirit of boundlessness. But do they by themselves make him a representative character in an age that celebrated its own rootlessness? When we first hear him talk at any length, Holgrave sounds more

[73] Henry James, Jr., *Hawthorne* (New York: Harper & Brothers, 1879), p. 125.
[74] Hawthorne, *House of the Seven Gables,* p. 181.

like Emerson and Thoreau—hardly typical figures—than an unchastened Young America enthusiast.

Far from exulting in or even acknowledging the spirit of boundlessness which sanctions his way of life, Holgrave announces that he feels oppressed, trapped in a psychic cage for which the house is both an obvious and an unsatisfactory symbol. He locates the source of his wasting malaise in the weight of the paternal past. "This Past," he complains, elevating it to the status of a proper noun,

> lies upon the Present like a giant's dead body! In fact, the case is just as if a young giant were compelled to waste all his strength in carrying about the corpse of the old giant, his grandfather. . . . Just think, a moment; and it will startle you to see what slaves we are to by-gone times. . . . Whatever we seek to do, of our own free motion, a Dead Man's icy hand obstructs us!"[75]

He would like to see the "rotten Past . . . torn down, and lifeless institutions . . . thrust out of the way, and their dead corpses buried, and everything . . . begin anew."[76]

What "lifeless institutions" exactly, how would Holgrave get rid of them, and what, if anything, would he establish in their place? He would unclench the grip of the past first of all by destroying houses, not just the ancient one he lives in, but all houses after a term, for old houses are "expressive of that odious and abominable Past." Public buildings, too, should be constructed of impermanent materials in order that they would "crumble to ruin, once in twenty years, or thereabouts, as a hint to the people to examine into and reform the institutions which they symbolize." That matter arranged, he moves on to assault the permanence of families. "To plant a family! This

[75] Ibid., pp. 182–83.
[76] Ibid., p. 179.

idea is at the bottom of most of the wrong and mischief which men do." At fifty-year intervals "a family should be merged into the great, obscure mass of humanity, and forget all about its ancestors."[77]

Making connections among buildings, families, and the authority of the past was a convention of post-heroic speech. But no defender of the authority of the past would have wished to place the chances of his case with the fate of old houses, whose treatment by Americans, as Theodore Parker observed in 1848, was one of the telling traits of the age: "Such is our dread of authority, that we like not old things. . . . Our house must be new."[78] Nor would such a defender have been likely to rely on the conscious memory of ancestors in a republic where, so Tocqueville said, "no family . . . authority can be perceived," and "every fresh generation is a new people."[79] Holgrave's speech brings to a culmination the antisentimentalist custom of attacking the past which Emerson may be said to have begun in the United States. It is also a parody of that custom that lays bare its ideological vacuity. In hopelessly mixing the metaphors with which such objections were characteristically expressed, and in addressing himself to the uncomprehending Phoebe Pyncheon, Hawthorne's protagonist reveals his ideas to be devoid of political content—though not of political implications.

Phoebe Pyncheon seems on the surface to be a kind of female

[77] Ibid., pp. 184–85.

[78] Parker, "Destination of America," p. 131. To the perplexity of some Americans, however, the new houses being built everywhere were not always new enough. "Since they cannot live in real old houses, our lovers of antiquity do the next best, and imitate old barbarisms in their new structures. . . . The affectation of building new houses to resemble old ones, is quite as ridiculous as it would be for a young man to affect the gait of his grandfather." "Our New Homes," *United States Magazine and Democratic Review* 21 (1847): 392–93.

[79] Tocqueville, *Democracy in America*, 1:55, 97.

Robin Molineux; she, too, is the country cousin who comes to live with relatives in town. Unlike Robin, however, she knows exactly where she wants to go and goes directly there. From virtually the moment of her first appearance in the book it is clear that her function is to take over. Though younger than any of the other central characters, she takes on the role of mother to the elderly but childlike permanent inhabitants of the house, and then transforms the old place itself according to the joyousness of her own pure heart. It is Phoebe to whom Holgrave declares his antagonism to the past—and with whom he then promptly falls in love.

Enchanted by her, Holgrave is easily drawn into her sphere. "After all, what a good world we live in!" he exclaims as he is distracted from radicalism by romance. "How good, and beautiful! How young it is, too, with nothing really rotten or age-worn in it!" His love for Phoebe expands to and informs his view of the entire world. Sitting with her in the Pyncheon garden on a moonlit evening he declares, in the most important political statement in the book: "Moonlight, and the sentiment in man's heart, responsive to it, is the greatest of renovators and reformers."[80] Hawthorne has wrapped the strong band of love around the boundlessness of the 1840s.

When he marries Phoebe, Holgrave abandons his radical dreams altogether. Soon after using the language of domesticity to take his combative stand against the past, Holgrave becomes thoroughly domesticated. The death of Judge Pyncheon, who is Holgrave's paternal antagonist and also Phoebe's cousin, makes Phoebe an heiress. In other words, the rebellious son does not destroy his father's house; he inherits it. "That sworn foe of wealth and all manner of conservatism—the wild reformer" who has advocated the destruction of such dwellings now moves to the dead father's comfortable country-seat and

[80] Hawthorne, *House of the Seven Gables,* p. 214.

begins a family of his own.[81] When domesticity proves such a solvent to radicalism, as is the case here, radicalism is revealed at once as purely personal and emotional in nature. It is not that Holgrave ceases to be a prophet of social revolution. He demonstrates that he never was one.

Holgrave's emotional and hence, in his case, political turn from combative radicalism to sentimental domesticity paralleled a change in American culture generally that began to become evident by the midpoint of the nineteenth century. Just as his early ideas read, for example, like a summary restatement of some of Emerson's early ones, so his later behavior anticipates Emerson's own turn from attacking the past to identifying with the fathers. Perhaps no other act was so strikingly indicative of the psychological direction that Emerson and his generation were taking than a small event that occurred in his home in the summer of 1852: he hung a portrait of George Washington in his dining room. "I cannot keep my eyes off it," he wrote in his journal. In Washington's face he found a "certain Appalachian strength, as if it were truly the first-fruits of America, and expressed the Country. . . . Noble, aristocratic head, with all kinds of elevation in it, that come out by turns." There is only the barest sense of resignation here, and none at all of contradiction. Emerson's praise of Washington is that of a man who has met his match but who does not realize it because he has forgotten there ever was a contest. Though he implied that the fathers through their accomplishments had debilitated their sons, the primary focus of his animus remained where it always was—on the debilitated. The godlike strength and calm of Washington's face suggested to him that "this MAN had absorbed all the serenity of America, and left none for his restless, rickety, hysterical

[81] Ibid., p. 313.

countrymen."[82] The difference is that where once Emerson would have attacked these countrymen for attempting to imitate the fathers rather than relying on themselves, now he attacked them for not resembling the fathers.

Many Americans of Emerson's generation followed him indoors psychologically. Claiming simultaneously to be good sons of the fathers and to be adults unburdened by the past, conspicuous representatives of the post-heroic cohort (among them Holgrave—that "national type"—and many of the Young America expansionists) took their booty (Phoebe Pyncheon with her wealth, the territories with theirs) and moved into their fathers' house—which, as we will see, now became quite crowded. No son lives easily there, filiopietistic sons probably least of all. They were all parties to an unconscious understanding that hatred of the fathers (which was made certain, as Hawthorne wrote, by the heroes' everlasting presence) would remain unrecognized in accordance with the dictates of their proclaimed filiopiety. The strange calculus of patricidal desires did not require that they remain repressed—only that they be understood and dealt with as anything but what they really were.

[82] Edward Waldo Emerson and Waldo Emerson Forbes, eds., *Journals of Ralph Waldo Emerson, with Annotations,* 10 vols. (Boston: Houghton Mifflin Co., 1909–14), 8:300.

4

THE FAILED REBELLION OF YOUNG
AMERICA AGAINST THE FATHERS
(II): STEPHEN A. DOUGLAS AND THE
PROBLEM OF SLAVERY IN
THE TERRITORIES

The sons never will divide the great inheritance.

GEORGE TICKNOR CURTIS, 1843

Brotherhood is always a quarrel over the paternal inheritance.

NORMAN O. BROWN, 1966

The sages of the Revolution decided that the Colonies . . . had the inalienable right to govern themselves in respect to their local and domestic concerns. This is precisely what I now assert on behalf of the Territories.

STEPHEN A. DOUGLAS, 1859

From the founding of the Republic to 1854 a tradition prevailed by which most Americans dealt with the fact that slavery existed among them. Stephen A. Douglas by himself was the first political leader to rebel successfully against this tradition. In passing the Kansas-Nebraska bill he and his followers acted to throw off the past in order literally to prepare the ground for the future. His assault on the authority of tradition reflected the exuberance and boldness but also the recklessness of the Young America mentality he spoke for. When no one else would or could do it, Douglas moved (although it was not his intention) to kill the fathers. He did not get away with it. He made his move at a time when the prevailing attitude toward the authority of tradition had shifted from the indifference or rebelliousness that characterized the 1840s to a new sympathy and deference. The penalty he paid was the deflection of his career and the frustration of his greatest dreams.

One of the most conspicuous, significant, and potentially misleading aspects of the crisis of the Union is that by the late 1840s the debates on the problem of slavery in the territories moved on their course with all the predictability of an ancient ritual. Nearly all responsible politicians played roles that custom had long since made familiar. Custom alone could not, of course, dictate the way people felt about slavery, but it could and did control the way most of them dealt with their feelings in public. It was perfectly possible, for instance, to be hostile to slavery and still be an effective politician, but custom required that a politician wishing to be taken seriously should assault slavery not in the states where it existed, but in the territories where it did not. Everyone knew that in the Constitution the fathers had acknowledged the legitimacy of slavery in the states that chose to have it. Indeed, much of the liturgy of the ritual of sectional confrontation consisted of appeals to "the intent of the fathers," yet these appeals were paradoxical, for the very existence of the ritual presupposed that there was no such clear intent. If the fathers had left an unambiguous will on the matter of slavery in the territories, it would have been automatically applied. In other words, if the fathers in a dozen clear words in the Constitution had stated whether slavery could or could not go into the territories, the history of the first six decades of the nineteenth century would have been exceedingly different from what occurred.[1] It might seem that the nonexistence of such a clause would have served to release the post-heroic age from obedience to the fathers in this realm. The reverse turned out to be the case. Clear instructions would have bound the sons very tightly to the instructions. Their absence bound them ever more tightly to the fathers' lives.

This ritual held to a fixed course throughout the age. Proponents of slavery expansion would assert that a careful reading of the historical record demonstrated that the fathers intended to protect slavery in the territories from interference by Congress, which certainly had no constitutional power to exclude it. The sons must follow this intent or the South would have no choice but to secede from the Union. Opponents of slavery would assert that the same record demonstrated that the fathers intended that Congress could (should, must) prohibit slavery from entering the territories. Any attempt by the South to secede from the Union would be resisted. A middle group would then emerge to declare that neither of these positions was historically accurate, that some of the fathers had taken the first position and some the second, but, whatever their intent, they and everyone since had ended up compromising in order first to create and then to preserve the Union. The fathers knew that there could be no disunion without civil war. From this middle group eventually would emerge a mechanism for compromise that would win enough support (or silent acquiescence) from the others to become law. Harmony would be restored, and fraternal affection would again appear to prevail—until the next time.

The ritual was destroyed by Douglas, who rendered the compromise portion of it meaningless. After 1854, to be sure, Southerners continued to assert what they always had, and Northerners continued to respond as they always had. There

---

[1] This statement of course assumes that a document containing such language could have been ratified, which is, I grant, a large assumption.

was still a middle group (made up of men from both free and slave states) that warned both sides of the dangers of agitation, but the compromise ending to the liturgy had disappeared, leaving in effect the last word to the ritualistic warnings of disaster, which then loomed as ever more vivid prophecies. (As we will see, Abraham Lincoln attempted to supply a new ending to the ritual that would achieve the same psychological result as the old one, but the attempt failed.)

To understand the meaning of what Douglas did, it is important to recognize what he did not do. Although he was often charged with it, Douglas did not upset any accepted understanding of the fathers' *substantive* policy. He no more departed from the intent of the fathers in this respect than did John C. Calhoun or Salmon P. Chase. This is not a comment on his filiopiety, but on the nature of the fathers' record, and the difficulty everyone encountered in deducing intent from it. The problem here is not that they left no clues. The founders in fact left behind many clues that revealed their attitudes on slavery—in what they said about it; how, when, and where they said it; and what they did about it politically and in their personal lives. But this record is so complex and ambiguous that only someone with the desire to make a political case, combined with a high talent for explaining away the starkest contradictions, could torture the record into a single— let alone a coherent—position for or against slavery. On the one hand, some of the fathers on some occasions used language that was unquestionably hostile to slavery. The central precept of the Declaration of Independence is that all men are created equal and are entitled, among other things, to liberty, and that only with their own consent could they even be governed. On the other hand, many of the men who staked their lives on these bracing words were slaveholders at the time, and continued to be slaveholders throughout their lives.

On the specific question of extending slavery into the territories, Congress under the Articles of Confederation passed an ordinance in 1787 that barred slavery from the Northwest Territory. The first Congress under the Constitution reenacted the Northwest Ordinance, and President Washington signed it into law.[2] But Congress did not prohibit slavery in the territory south of the Ohio River when the area was ceded to the federal government by the states that once had claimed it.[3] Indeed, one of the most striking but nevertheless often overlooked facts about the Northwest Ordinance is its uniqueness. Except in that territory by that law, which originated before the completion and ratification of the Constitution, the fathers did not restrict the spread of slavery at all. In other words, at no time between the creation of the federal government and the Compromise of 1820 did Congress prohibit slavery from a single square inch of territory not already closed to it.

The ambiguity of the fathers' actions on this subject was matched by that of the relevant constitutional language. To be sure, Article IV of the Constitution provides that "the Congress shall have Power to dispose of and make all needful Rules and Regulations respecting the Territory or other Property belonging to the United States."[4] The words "all [not some or most but *all*] needful Rules" when considered with the Northwest Ordinance might suggest ample constitutional sanction for slavery restriction by Congress. But looked at in a slightly different way, as opponents of such restriction did not fail eventually to do, the words "dispose of . . . Territory or other Property" cast on the word "Territory" the connotation not of a political community but merely of land.[5] Supporting this interpretation is the fact that another section of

---

[2] Clarence Edwin Carter and John Porter Bloom, comps., *The Territorial Papers of the United States,* 28 vols. (Washington: Government Printing Office, 1934–), 2:49, 203–4.

[3] Ibid., 4:7, 12, 16, 18–19.

[4] U.S., *Constitution,* Art. IV, sec. 3.

[5] Arthur Bestor, "State Sovereignty and Slavery: A Reinterpretation of Proslavery Constitutional Doctrine, 1846–1860," *Journal of the Illinois State Historical Society* 54 (1961): 159.

the Constitution gives Congress power to "exercise exclusive Legislation in all Cases whatsoever" over the federal capital city—much stronger language for a much smaller place.[6] Even James Madison, who certainly was in a position to know, believed (at least by the time of the Missouri crisis) that Article IV did not give to Congress the power in question.[7]

Some political leaders found more certain sanction for their proposals in the Fifth Amendment. The only other constitutional provision to figure heavily in these debates, it was invoked to support slavery extension on the grounds that slaves were property which could not be taken without due process of law, and to oppose slavery extension on the grounds that slaves were persons whose liberty could not be taken away without due process of law. No one has ever been able to cite a single piece of evidence to support the idea that the fathers meant the "due process" provision of the Fifth Amendment either to protect slave property in the territories (as Chief Justice Roger B. Taney asserted in the *Dred Scott* decision) or secure black liberty in the territories (as Chase maintained).[8] What the Fifth Amendment, and much of the rest of the legacy of the fathers, revealed was that they valued liberty and property generally, and sought to protect both.

The conclusion is inescapable that the fathers adhered to no single position on the future place of slavery in American life. Even men who made statements that were clearly hostile to

[6] U.S., *Constitution,* Art. I, sec. 8.

[7] Madison to James Monroe, February 23, 1820, in Gaillard Hunt, ed., *The Writings of James Madison,* 9 vols. (New York: G. P. Putnam's Sons, 1900–10), 9:23–26; idem to Robert Walsh, November 27, 1819, in ibid., pp. 1–13. See also [James Madison], "Jonathan Bull and Mary Bull," *Southern Literary Messenger* 1 (1835): 342–45.

[8] *Dred Scott* v. *Sandford,* 19 Howard 450 (1857); Eric Foner, *Free Soil, Free Labor, Free Men: The Ideology of the Republican Party before the Civil War* (New York: Oxford University Press, 1970), pp. 73–102, esp. 83–87; Robert R. Russel, "Constitutional Doctrines with Regard to Slavery in Territories," *Journal of Southern History* 32 (1966), 468–69.

slavery sometimes turned out to have had mixed, not to say confused, attitudes on the subject. Thomas Jefferson, who was quoted on this matter more than any of the other fathers, may have trembled for his country when he remembered that God is just, but he continued to hold slaves, and he attempted to track down any who fled. He believed that all men are created equal, but he also believed that black people are mentally inferior to white people. He expressed abolitionist principles, but it was almost always in private that he did so. He inspired the Northwest Ordinance of 1787, which restricted the territorial spread of slavery, but he opposed the Missouri Compromise of 1820, which imitated it, not because it did not go as far as the Northwest Ordinance, but because it restricted the territorial spread of slavery.[9]

In the middle of the nineteenth century the record of the fathers was used by different groups who shared little else but their ability to exploit the treasure it contained. At the center of the fray stood the least impassioned group, whose commitment to other priorities allowed them to see with clarity that the statutory results of the mixed attitudes of the fathers were equally mixed, but also balanced.[10] Slavery was barred by Congress north of the Ohio river and 36°30′ north latitude, but not south of them.

Radical groups at either end of the spectrum of attitudes on slavery shared a view of the fathers' record, in both cases with regret. Abolitionists criticized the fathers for holding slaves, for protecting slavery in the states, for their failure to keep it from spreading into the territories south of the Ohio river, and for

[9] William Cohen, "Thomas Jefferson and the Problem of Slavery," *Journal of American History* 56 (1969): 503–26; William W. Freehling, "The Founding Fathers and Slavery," *American Historical Review* 77 (1972): 81–93. Jefferson owned more than 180 slaves in 1776, and more than 260 when he died in 1826. Cohen, "Thomas Jefferson," pp. 503, 519.

[10] Their position was lucidly set forth in [Sidney George Fisher], *The Law of the Territories* (Philadelphia: C. Sherman & Son, 1859).

temporizing with the institution generally. (But the conflicted way in which they sometimes expressed their disappointment was poignant. Wendell Phillips said of the fathers in 1848: "I love these men; I hate their work. I respect their memory; I reject their deeds. I trust their hearts; I distrust their heads."[11] Theodore Parker also sought a way to reject the fathers' politics without completely rejecting the fathers themselves. He came to the conclusion, without revealing how he reached it, that they were not sinful but merely benighted. The aroused modern age knew better than they. "What in them to establish was only an error, in us to extend or to foster is a sin!"[12]) Their counterpart on the opposite, proslavery end of the spectrum criticized the fathers for (and attempted to explain away) their antislavery pronouncements, principles, and expectations. George Fitzhugh thought the writers of the Declaration were "silly, thoughtless, half-informed, speculative charlatans" and that the "bombastic absurdities" of the document were about as appropriate to the independence of the colonies as an oration would be on the occasion of "the teething of a child."[13]

Moderates on both sides of the extension question selectively used the fathers' record in support of their own desires. On one side stood free-soilers and (after 1854) Republicans, whose historical interpretations varied in detail and emphasis but were based on the shared belief that the fathers were hostile to slavery and wished to see it die. Antislavery politicians argued that the Declaration, where the founders were free to express their hopes, was a more accurate guide to their attitudes than the

[11] Quoted in Dwight L. Dumond, "The Controversy over Slavery," in Arthur M. Schlesinger, Jr., and Morton White, eds., *Paths of American Thought* (Boston: Houghton Mifflin Co., 1963), p. 90.

[12] Theodore Parker, *The Works of Theodore Parker,* 15 vols. (Boston: American Unitarian Association, 1907–13), 11:246.

[13] George Fitzhugh, "The Revolutions of 1776 and 1861 Contrasted," *Southern Literary Messenger* 37 (1863): 719.

hard practicalities of the Constitution. The statements regarding equality and liberty never purported to be a statement of reality but rather of an ideal toward which the new nation should ever tend. The fathers were quite aware that they had been born into a world in which some people not only were unequal but also were not free, and in which all who were free were not equal. They could not change this situation at once. Moreover, they found themselves in the paradoxical position of having to protect the enslavement of some people in order to protect liberty for the rest of the people—in the Union, under the Constitution. But they went no further in this direction than necessity dictated. With liturgical regularity, free-soilers and Republicans pointed to the absence of the word "slavery" in the Constitution, arguing that by this avoidance the document permanently stigmatized what it ostensibly protected. The fathers could not themselves destroy slavery, but they could set the stage for its "ultimate extinction" by prohibiting its spread into areas still free from it. This was the purpose of the Northwest Ordinance, the reenactment of which during the Washington administration revealed at the very least that the people who wrote the Constitution did not doubt that Congress could constitutionally prohibit the spread of slavery into new territories.[14]

Pointing to the utter antagonism between the Declaration and historical reality, defenders of slavery argued that the effect of reading the document the way the Republicans interpreted it meant either that the fathers who continued to hold slaves were hypocrites; or that the fathers simply did not have

[14] For instances and elaborations of this train of thought, see the speeches of Salmon P. Chase, *Congressional Globe,* 33 Cong., 1 Sess. (February 3, 1854), appendix, pp. 137–40; William H. Seward, ibid. (February 17, 1854), appendix, p. 150; Charles Sumner, ibid. (February 21, 1854), appendix, pp. 266–70. On Chase's argument see also Foner, *Free Soil,* pp. 73–102. Abraham Lincoln interpreted the fathers' attitudes toward slavery in many of his speeches after 1854. See Chapter 7.

black people in mind when they wrote it. In any case the Constitution was a later and more sobered document. This point was repeated by Southerners more than any other: the fathers protected slavery, and anyone claiming to be a good son will do the same cheerfully and in good faith. The fathers permitted slavery to spread into all areas then generally considered naturally suited to it. If they had been committed to barring its spread into new areas, they could easily enough have taken steps in that direction in the Louisiana Purchase. Although there was slavery in Louisiana at the time it was acquired in 1803, it was certainly no farther beyond control than were the scattered numbers of slaves in the Northwest Territory in 1787. Yet before 1820 nothing was done to keep slavery from going where it would in the Purchase. Moreover, the fathers left to the territories themselves the question of what local laws, if any, were necessary to protect and regulate the institution.[15]

To demonstrate, however, that the fathers held to no single view on slavery in the territories or anywhere else, and that their intentions, if any, are difficult to interpret and impossible to generalize about—to demonstrate this is not to demonstrate that there was no historical tradition regarding slavery in the territories and that therefore no one can be justly accused of violating it. On the contrary, there was a coherent "past" in this realm, and one man did attack it. If we shift our ground slightly here, we can see that it is paradoxical but true that people who used the fathers' record either to restrict slavery or to extend it were both operating within the boundaries of tradition, and not just in the sense that there were enough fathers with enough ideas to support opposing positions.

[15] For representative statements of this position, see Thomas H. Bayly, *Congressional Globe*, 29 Cong., 2 Sess. (February 11, 1847), appendix, p. 390; Jeremiah Morton, ibid., 31 Cong., 1 Sess. (February 6, 1850), appendix, pp. 114–15; John M. Berrien, ibid. (February 12, 1850), appendix, p. 206; Thomas J. Rusk, ibid. (February 28, 1850), appendix, p. 238.

Whether or not they liked to acknowledge it, or were even aware of it, moderates on both sides imitated the fathers in the sense that after pushing hard to arrange the entire world to their liking, they settled for half of it. Considered in terms of results, then, the legacy of the fathers on the problem of slavery was compromise. This is why the institution of slavery is not directly mentioned in *either* the Declaration of Independence or the Constitution, although it was demonstrably contemplated by the framers of both. Some of the fathers tried to protect and extend slavery, others tried to stunt and limit it, and the conflict of opposing desires produced results that no one had originally sought.

Thus Thomas Jefferson proposed in 1784 that slavery be barred from all federal territory after 1800;[16] it was barred in part of that territory.[17] An unsuccessful effort was made in 1812 to prohibit slavery in the Louisiana Purchase above 33° north latitude;[18] in the epochal Compromise of 1820 slavery was prohibited above 36°30′ north latitude, except for Missouri.[19] The territories were more or less evenly divided between land open to slavery and land closed to it. East of the Mississippi River the Ohio River formed a natural boundary between these two regions. The drawing of 36°30′ in 1820 served, in effect, as an artificial extension of that boundary west to the Rocky Mountains. Thomas Hart Benton once compared this situation to that of brothers dividing an estate. It is natural for sons to divide an inherited estate rather than preserve it intact. This division could not occur in the Union, which must be preserved as it was received, but it could take

[16] Julian P. Boyd, ed., *The Papers of Thomas Jefferson* (Princeton, N.J.: Princeton University Press, 1950–), 6:604, 608.

[17] Carter and Bloom, *Territorial Papers*, 2:49.

[18] Glover Moore, *The Missouri Controversy, 1819–1821* (Lexington: University of Kentucky Press, 1953), p. 32.

[19] U.S., *Statutes at Large*, 3:548. The best account of the Missouri Compromise is Moore, *Missouri Controversy*.

place "outside" of it, in the territories. Indeed it was precisely because the inheritance was divided that peace was kept.[20]

The difference between the way the slavery problem was resolved for the Louisiana Purchase and the way it was resolved for territories acquired subsequently is not as great as it might at first seem. After the Missouri Compromise of 1820 the next occasion to confront the problem arose in the 1840s with the prospect of the annexation of Texas and the ending of the joint occupation with the British of the Oregon country in such a way that at least a large portion of it would become United States territory. With Texas and Oregon, the issue was not whether slavery should be permitted or prohibited in territory previously acquired, but whether territory should be acquired in view of the fact that the place of slavery in it was already settled. Although there was great dispute over whether to annex Texas or take over Oregon, it was accepted as settled by most people that the southern area would be slave and the northern area would be free. Indeed, the fact that the two great tracts were acquired roughly simultaneously lends plausibility to the idea that they balanced each other in much the same way that the Southwest Ordinance of 1790 balanced the Northwest Ordinance of 1787. In other words, Texas, which was annexed in 1845, was made possible by the prospect of Oregon; and Oregon, which was partitioned in 1846, was made possible and even necessary by the pressure to balance Texas.[21]

Before 1854 the most serious challenge to this established pattern of balance developed with the Mexican War in 1846—in particular with the prospect, followed by the reality in 1848,

[20] *Congressional Globe,* 33 Cong., 1 Sess. (April 25, 1854), appendix, p. 558. See George Ticknor Curtis, *The Just Supremacy of Congress over the Territories* (Boston: A. Williams and Co., 1859), pp. 33–34.

[21] See Columbus Delano, *Congressional Globe,* 29 Cong., 1 Sess. (February 5, 1846), p. 318; David M. Potter, *The Impending Crisis, 1848–1861,* completed and ed. Don E. Fehrenbacher (New York: Harper & Row, 1976), pp. 25–26.

that Mexico would be forced to cede a large portion of its northern territory to the United States. Unlike the cases of Texas and Oregon, the future of slavery in what became the Mexican cession was not obviously set. For several historical and natural reasons slavery had not flourished there, but very few people who cared deeply one way or the other about the matter were willing to assume that this would always be the case. Many Southerners believed that if natural conditions invited slavery into the new territories it should go there, and no man-made obstacle should be put in its path. Many Northerners sought to extend the principle of the Northwest Ordinance to whatever territory Mexico might give up. Their desire took form in the Wilmot Proviso of 1846, which would have established, "as an express and fundamental condition to the acquisition of any territory from the Republic of Mexico," that "neither slavery nor involuntary servitude shall ever exist" in it.[22] Later versions would have prohibited slavery in "any territory on the continent of America" that the United States "shall hereafter" acquire.[23] The Wilmot Proviso was a direct descendant not only of the Northwest Ordinance but also of Jefferson's 1784 proposal to bar slavery by 1800 from all the territories held by the United States. When backers of the Proviso claimed that their idea came straight from the fathers, they were correct.[24]

An obvious way to balance these conflicting demands would

[22] *Congressional Globe,* 29 Cong., 1 Sess. (August 8, 1846), p. 1217.

[23] Ibid., 29 Cong., 2 Sess. (February 15, 1847), p. 424.

[24] This assertion puts me in disagreement with one argument of an article I very much admire. Arthur Bestor sees the Wilmot Proviso as a break with the established custom of dividing the territories "in an equitable fashion, so as to permit slaveholding in the southerly portions and prohibit it in the northerly." "State Sovereignty and Slavery," p. 154. But to say this is to confuse proposal with result. The Wilmot Proviso, which never became law, was very much within the tradition of other sweeping proposals that never became law but that set the stage for the territorial compromises Bestor describes.

have been to extend the Missouri Compromise line of 36°30′ across the Mexican cession to the Pacific. If this had been done, the dividing line between free and slave territory would have hit the ocean near Monterey, California. Somewhat less than half of the Mexican cession would have been opened at least legally to slavery. The idea suggested itself very early in this new phase of the sectional conflict as a way of settling slavery matters in both Oregon and any acquisition from Mexico, and it gained important support even before the end of the Mexican War. James Buchanan, hoping to win the Democratic nomination for president in 1848, made the idea central to his campaign as early as August of the preceding year. President James K. Polk came out in support of the proposal in June 1848.[25] Stephen A. Douglas was a leader in obtaining Senate acceptance of the line, but the idea failed in the House.[26] Although the debates on the question occurred in the context of the organization of Oregon—that is, slavery would be barred there because it lay north of 36°30′—everyone knew that to deal with slavery on that basis would have had the effect of transforming the line into a principle, and that what they were really debating was the future of slavery in the Southwest. But the moral agitation of the abolitionists had had its polarizing effect, and it is at this point that we can most clearly see their impact on political events by the end of the 1840s.

Because slavery had come, in popular thinking, to be a moral question, it was more difficult than ever for Northerners to accept any plan that would extend the domain of evil. Moreover, many Northerners believed that the line was no longer a fair bargain. At the middle of the century it seemed more likely than not that expansion was simply pausing rather than (as it

[25] On the maneuvers to extend 36°30′ to the Pacific, see Potter, *Impending Crisis,* pp. 22, 55–57, 69–76.

[26] Robert W. Johannsen, *Stephen A. Douglas* (New York: Oxford University Press, 1973), pp. 224–25.

turned out, essentially) ending, and that future growth would be to the south. To have extended and reaffirmed 36°30′ would have made it that much more difficult to find a basis on which to exclude slavery from these areas. At the very least it would have amounted to an invitation to quarrel over Cuba or some similar place. But to rule out a particular formula for compromise was not to rule out compromise itself. It was to meet the need to provide for the Mexican cession a new formula for compromise—one that would respond to the demands of tradition and yet take account of changed perceptions of morality and power—that politicians turned, or rather returned, to the concept of "popular sovereignty."

Any attempt to define popular sovereignty precisely should begin with the observation that much of the appeal of the doctrine lay in its ability to evade precise definition. But let us attempt to mark out the boundaries within which ambiguity reigned. In very broad terms, of course, popular sovereignty meant simply government by the consent of the governed. In the present context it stated that whether slavery should exist in a particular jurisdiction was not a matter for Congress but for the area's white residents to decide. This was the unquestioned constitutional prerogative of states. Now it was proposed to extend the prerogative to the earlier, territorial stage. Popular sovereignty combined three advantages which no competing plan could duplicate. First, it promised to remove the whole vexed question from Congress and isolate it far from the cockpit of the capital city. Second, unlike 36°30′, it permitted its supporters to argue that they were making a decision based on an important principle (majority rule) rather than the expedient of resolving a question of right and wrong by drawing a line. Third, unlike any other plan, it permitted both extensionists and restrictionists to support it with the hope that it would facilitate their own opposing goals. Nothing in the principle of popular sovereignty conflicted with the proslavery interpretation that a territory would be open to slavery throughout the territorial stage, which was tantamount to the creation of a slave state, for no territory open to slavery had ever failed to become a slave state. On the other hand, nothing in popular sovereignty ruled out a free-soil result. It permitted Northerners to tell themselves that a more numerous and seemingly more mobile free-state migration could dominate territorial politics and bar slavery at once. This would be tantamount to the creation of a free state, for no territory closed to slavery in the territorial stage had ever failed to become a free state.[27]

Some moderate Northern politicians, notably Daniel Webster and Stephen A. Douglas, argued openly that popular sovereignty would achieve free soil in any event, and do so without taunting the South. They based this prediction on their belief (or hope) that nature made the new areas unsuitable for slavery and therefore it would be superfluous for Congress also to act against it.[28] Thus a more subtle presupposition of popular sovereignty was that the problem for which it was a solution did not need solving as far as the territories were concerned, but only as far as people's minds about the territories were concerned.

As part of the Compromise of 1850 both the Utah and New Mexico territories were implicitly organized on a popular sovereignty basis at least in the sense that Congress did not recognize or impose either slavery or a restriction on slavery there, nor did it prevent the territorial legislatures from taking whatever actions they wished to take on the subject whenever they

[27] Allen Johnson, "The Genesis of Popular Sovereignty," *Iowa Journal of History and Politics* 3 (1905): 3–19; Milo Milton Quaife, *The Doctrine of Non-Intervention with Slavery in the Territories* (Chicago: Mac C. Chamberlin Co., 1910).

[28] Daniel Webster, *Congressional Globe,* 31 Cong., 1 Sess. (March 7, 1850), pp. 480–81. For Douglas, see below.

wished to take them.[29] Thus one effect of popular sovereignty was that it provided a way to restore the compromise tradition which the moral argument on slavery had threatened to ruin. Its role in this respect has never been clear, and for good reason. Just as political maneuvers of the period after 1846 are generally evaluated in light of the Civil War which they at length produced, so popular sovereignty is almost inescapably evaluated in terms of the violent turmoil that pervaded Kansas for several years after that territory was organized on the basis of popular sovereignty. That is, the role of popular sovereignty in the crisis that began in 1854 has ever since distorted its role in the very different crisis of 1850.

The purpose and achievement of organizing Utah and New Mexico on a popular-sovereignty basis was to put the question of slavery in those territories outside of Congress and therefore permanently outside the concerns of national politics. This object was achieved. Although the reason the history of the sectional conflict abruptly forgets New Mexico and Utah after September 1850 may be that another area, Nebraska, fulfilled the battleground function that would otherwise have taken place farther west, it is nevertheless true that history forgets about the Mexican cession after 1850. Although the connections between the Compromise of 1850 and the events of 1854 are real enough and cannot be ignored, the obvious point needs to be made that people in 1850 did not see their laws as the fatal turn on the way to Kansas-Nebraska but rather another—indeed, they hoped, the *final*—step along the traditional road of compromise.

The rejection of 36°30′ extension and the focus on popular sovereignty in the 1850 legislation obscure the important resemblances between the Compromises of 1820 and 1850. The first of these continued and for the first time even institution-

29 U.S., *Statutes at Large,* 9:446–58; Robert R. Russel, "What Was the Compromise of 1850?" *Journal of Southern History* 22 (1956): 292–309.

alized the custom of sectional balance. The second may be understood as an application of the principle of balance to new geographical realities. California carried free territory farther south than ever before. As if to compensate slaveholders, the remaining territory of the Mexican cession carried potential slave territory farther north than ever before—to 42° north latitude. The new configuration (a more or less vertical rather than horizontal line), and the new mechanisms by which it was achieved (prohibition by the people of California rather than by Congress and accessibility to slavery by a new type of Congressional silence rather than by traditional Congressional silence) should not obscure the fact that rough geographical balance was maintained. The problem with the Compromise of 1850 was not that it did not work. The laws that constituted it worked as well as their sponsors could ever have realistically hoped.[30] The problem with the Compromise was that the man who, more than any other, achieved the passage of the legislation either never understood or allowed himself to forget the true nature of what he had accomplished.

Stephen A. Douglas later asserted that the Compromise of 1850 had been the point at which the sons had broken with traditional federal policy on slavery. He was one of the very few people who believed that "the only conclusion that can be fairly and honestly drawn" from an analysis of the early territorial laws was that "it was the policy of the fathers of the Republic to prescribe a line of demarkation between free territories and slave-holding territories by a natural or a geographical line." For the sake of calm, Douglas had been willing for a time to extend the line through the Mexican cession to the Pacific. But he admitted the policy had no other appeal for him.

[30] See Holman Hamilton, *Prologue to Conflict: The Crisis and Compromise of 1850* ([Lexington]: University of Kentucky Press, 1964), pp. 166–90.

I do not like, I never did like, the system of legislation on our part, by which a geographical line, in violation of the laws of nature, and climate, and soil, and of the laws of God, should be run to establish institutions for a people [regardless of their wishes].[31]

That popular sovereignty played a role in the 1850 laws permitted him, albeit inaccurately, to imply that the policy of the fathers had been repudiated in that year by people like Henry Clay and Daniel Webster.[32] He understood the territorial arrangements of the Compromise as a commitment to popular sovereignty, when what they really were was a victory for moderation. He confused his own desires with those of the nation generally. He took it for granted that the spirit of the Compromise was the spirit of Young America, and that everyone shared his wish to put the sectional conflict aside in order to proceed with the realization of his expansive dreams. His error soon became clear.

No one knew better than Douglas himself that the Compromise of 1850 was to a great extent his own achievement. At the age of thirty-seven he had rescued the Union. Although it could not be known then, the Compromise turned out to be his greatest triumph. In looking for greater ones he now started down the road toward his own isolation. He hoped that this historic act would be followed by his election, at the age of thirty-nine, to the presidency in 1852. He attempted to win the Democratic nomination, and for a time it appeared that he could not be stopped. Against his wishes some of his more enthusiastic supporters explicitly cast him as the champion of Young America in a contest with the "old fogies" of

[31] *Congressional Globe,* 33 Cong., 1 Sess. (January 30, 1854), pp. 276, 279.
[32] Harry V. Jaffa and Robert W. Johannsen, eds., *In the Name of the People: Speeches and Writings of Lincoln and Douglas in the Ohio Campaign of 1859* (Columbus: Ohio State University Press, 1959), pp. 159–61.

his party and the decrepit and discredited policies of the past. (He objected to their analysis not because he thought it was incorrect, but because he thought they were tactless to proclaim it.) The fogies, however, managed to prevent his nomination.[33] This defeat of Douglas and Young America was no aberration. His upward momentum had been permanently arrested.

Stephen A. Douglas's association with Illinois and the West makes it easy to forget that he was a New Englander with roots almost as deep in the Puritan heritage as those of the characters in *The House of the Seven Gables*. Since 1640—for six generations—his ancestors had lived in New England.[34] In one respect both his initiation into the Puritan tradition and his break with this line were early and traumatic. When Stephen was two months old his father, while holding the infant and sitting beside a fireplace, suddenly died. During this transaction Stephen was apparently toppled into the fire, from which a neighbor rescued him at once; he experienced a phoenixlike rebirth, so to say, and this time without a father.[35] Douglas wrote years later that he and his mother were soon taken in, in two senses evidently, by an uncle—"an industrious, economical, clever old bachelor" (the adjectives in that order do not accumulate to a praising effect) who "wanted some one to keep house for him." There is a suggestion here of the exploitation of his mother, and more than a suggestion in connection with his own eventual farm labor. Douglas considered

---

[33] Johannsen, *Stephen A. Douglas*, p. 369; Roy F. Nichols, "The Kansas-Nebraska Act: A Century of Historiography," *Mississippi Valley Historical Review* 43 (1956): 199.

[34] Johannsen, *Stephen A. Douglas*, p. 6.

[35] "I have often been told that he was holding me in his arms when he departed this world." Douglas, "Autobiographical Sketch, September 1, 1838," in Robert W. Johannsen, ed., *The Letters of Stephen A. Douglas* (Urbana: University of Illinois Press, 1961), p. 57; idem, *Stephen A. Douglas*, p. 876.

this new father "rather a hard master, and unwilling to give me those opportunities of improvement and education which I thought I was entitled to." Evidently from a very early age his leading desire was to get away. "I therefore determined upon leaving my home . . . [to] see what I could do for myself in the wide world among strangers."[36]

Thus began in desire, and soon afterward in fact, the wanderings that took him first just a few miles away and then halfway across the country. When he was fifteen he took his first job, not too far from home, as a cabinetmaker. He enjoyed it so thoroughly that he might have stayed at it permanently, he said, but his employer's demands went beyond duties in the shop. He insisted "upon my performing some menial services in the house. I was willing to do anything connected with the shop but could not consent to perform the duties of a servant in the house." For the second time he connected housekeeping with exploitation, and domesticity with constraint. Getting away from the domestic scene was not to be easy. Not until five more years had passed (not until 1833, when he was twenty) did Douglas make the real break from his family and for the West. Traveling alone, "without having any particular place of destination in view," he ended up in Illinois—settling in 1834 in the town of Jacksonville, named for the hero president.[37]

Throughout Douglas's youth Andrew Jackson was a dazzling presence in American life, and Douglas could probably not remember a time when Old Hickory was not his chief hero. Douglas was not yet two years old when the battle of New Orleans ended in an American victory, making Jackson nationally famous. Douglas was fifteen when Jackson was elected president. The boy's politics were forever "fixed" during the campaign, he later recalled, as he and his friends de-

[36] Douglas, "Autobiographical Sketch," p. 57.
[37] Ibid., pp. 57–59.

veloped into "warm advocates of Gen. Jackson's claims."[38]
When Douglas, by now a man, settled in Illinois, Jackson was
in his second term as president. Involving himself almost at
once in Illinois politics and the organization of the Democratic
party there, Douglas was soon making speeches in reply to
critics of Jackson's banking policies. When he entered the
House of Representatives in the 1840s, Douglas's first important speech was in praise of Jackson. In 1853 it was Douglas,
now in the Senate and himself nationally famous, who was
the natural choice to speak at the unveiling of the famous
statue of Jackson in Lafayette Square in Washington.[39] The
identification of the two men, at least in the public mind,
seemed complete.

In the quarter century of Douglas's political prominence he
made himself spokesman for the spirit of Jacksonism, for the
Democratic party, and for the Young America cast of mind
I have already discussed. He identified himself with a decen-
tralized majoritarian democracy that aimed for equality among
white males; with the aggressive, acquisitive, sometimes bel-
ligerent spirit of manifest destiny, which sought national glory
through various kinds of demonstrations of the superiority of
American institutions over all other ones, but primarily by national expansion (to the end of his days he believed that North
America had been providentially set apart as an asylum for
the oppressed of the rest of the world, which meant, among
other things, that the United States must and would eventually
become congruent with the continent. "I do not care whether
you like it or not; you cannot help it! It is the decree of Providence"[40]); with the interests of the building West; with tech-

---

[38] Ibid., p. 58.

[39] Johannsen, *Stephen A. Douglas,* pp. 129–30, 381. Douglas met Jackson
at the Hermitage in 1844. Ibid., pp. 139, 889. For Douglas on Jackson, see
Congressional Globe, 28 Cong., 1 Sess. (January 6, 1844), appendix, pp. 43–46.

[40] Jaffa and Johannsen, *In the Name of the People,* p. 150.

nological modernity ("no man can keep up with the spirit of this age who travels on anything slower than the locomotive, and fails to receive intelligence by lightning"[41]); and with the present as opposed to the decrepit past.[42] He was in short the best spokesman for the predominant national mood of the 1840s. But by 1854 these ideas—and he as their spokesman— were vaguely out of fashion, although hardly without influence.

As chairman of the Committee on Territories in the Senate, he was centrally involved in providing basic civil institutions for the vast territories the United States acquired in the 1840s. It was from this context, and not that of the sectional conflict over slavery in the territories, that Douglas came to his fateful project to organize Nebraska, "that fair field, large as a conti- nent" (said another senator), lying between the Missouri River and the Rocky Mountains and stretching north from just above Texas to the Canadian border.[43] Seen against the background of a career apparently headed endlessly upward and the develop- ment of a nation apparently headed endlessly outward, Doug- las's purposes are clear and coherent. After 1850, Nebraska was the largest area within the national boundaries not yet organized into territorial form. There was no civil regime, a lack that created mounting inconveniences. By the early 1850s people in large numbers were beginning to settle in the area. Others were passing through it to more western realms. Organization would facilitate Douglas's desire to link the settled East and

[41] Douglas to J. H. Crane, D. M. Johnson, and L. J. Eastin, December 17, 1853, in Johannsen, *Letters of Douglas,* p. 270.

[42] "Europe is antiquated, decrepit, tottering on the verge of dissolution," he said in 1853. "Here everything is fresh, blooming, expanding, and advancing." *Congressional Globe,* 32 Cong., 3 Sess. (March 16, 1853), appendix, p. 273.

[43] Benjamin F. Wade, ibid., 33 Cong., 1 Sess. (February 6, 1854), p. 339. The following discussion of the Kansas-Nebraska Act builds upon the com- plementary accounts provided by Johannsen, *Stephen A. Douglas,* pp. 390–464; Nichols, "The Kansas-Nebraska Act"; Potter, *Impending Crisis,* pp. 145–76; and Gerald M. Capers, *Stephen A. Douglas: Defender of the Union* (Boston: Little, Brown and Co., 1959), pp. 87–112.

the settling West by a transcontinental railroad, an accompanying telegraph line, and a chain of communities through Nebraska itself.[44] Among other beneficial results, these projects would enhance the position in east-west commerce of Chicago, which Douglas, for pecuniary and other less tangible reasons, wanted to make the economic heart of the nation. Man and city would assist each other to rise to great power in American life.

The process of organizing the Nebraska territory revealed most of Douglas's strengths and weaknesses as a political leader. As a floor tactician he was unmatched in American politics in his generation, and his later claim that he alone passed the Kansas-Nebraska Act is barely an exaggeration. Although it is not a modest claim, it is a revealingly narrow one. He liked building and organizing for their own sake, and he sometimes, as in this instance, gave the impression that he was more interested in legislating than in legislation. In a maneuver that illuminates both his mentality and the excesses of the 1840s, Douglas at one point early in 1849 had seemed willing to go along with any plan that would organize the Mexican cession. "All I ask is action," he said. "I will cheerfully vote for any bill approved by a majority of the Senate."[45] This approach to politics was an advertisement of vulnerability, for it suggested his availability as a tool to be used by people who did care about the substance of plans. As Kansas-Nebraska revealed, for all of his vigor and cleverness, he could be outmaneuvered. It was not that in this case or any other Douglas was without vision—Young America notions were nothing if not visionary. But with all his expansive dreams and tactical brilliance, he had no eye for the middle distance.

Douglas had been attempting ever since he entered Congress

[44] Douglas to Crane, Johnson, and Eastin, in Johannsen, *Letters of Douglas,* pp. 270–71.

[45] *Congressional Globe,* 30 Cong., 2 Sess. (February 17, 1849), p. 551.

to secure organization for the Nebraska area, but other concerns with higher priorities—such as resolving the sectional conflict over lands farther west—pushed his project aside. When at last in the early 1850s a path began to open for him, it soon became clear that what would ordinarily have been a routine legislative matter had now itself become caught up in the sectional conflict. Two major obstacles stood in Douglas's way. The first involved the great question of a railroad to the Pacific Ocean. It was beyond discussion that in order for such a railroad to be built, the federal government would have to support it through massive land grants and other subsidies. Because of the grandiose nature of the project Congress was unwilling to support more than one route, certainly not more than one at a time. But because of sectional and lesser geographical rivalries, Congress was unable to reach agreement on the course the railroad should follow. Southerners realized that the organization of Nebraska would improve the chances of a northern route at the expense of their own. The second obstacle was slavery. As part of the Missouri Compromise of 1820, Congress had prohibited slavery "forever" in that part of the Louisiana Purchase lying above 36°30′ north latitude—in almost exactly the area, that is, that Douglas now proposed to organize.[46] Southerners knew that to organize Nebraska in accordance with that prohibition would be to strengthen the North and the free-soil movement. Therefore, they had no particular reason to assist Douglas's dream, and two very sound ones to resist it. Yet Southern support appeared to be crucial if Nebraska was to be organized.

To put Douglas in precisely this box is perhaps to make the door out of it seem more obvious than it was at the time. In any case, by the end of 1853 he evidently realized that he was in a position to give up something he had but did not want in

---

[46] See note 19, above.

order to get something that he wanted but did not have. He could give up the Missouri Compromise prohibition in order to gain territorial organization and, he expected, eventually the railroad. He was willing to abandon the Missouri restriction not because he wanted to see slavery spread into Nebraska (he had in fact no such desire), but because he did not believe that the Missouri restriction was necessary to keep slavery out. As a practical matter the restriction seemed to him superfluous and therefore expendable. Douglas considered the question of slavery in the territories generally as an abstraction and (for that reason) a distraction. This was particularly true with respect to Nebraska. "Every intelligent man knows that it is a matter of no practical importance, so far as the question of slavery is concerned," he said in 1854. "The laws of climate, and production, and of physical geography . . . have excluded slavery from that country."[47] Every intelligent man may indeed have known what Douglas believed, but it is safe to say that he was one of the very few intelligent men in the North who would have claimed that this analysis covered the ground of the Nebraska problem.

It is not clear exactly when or how Douglas came to the realization that his plan would work in an immediate, strictly legislative sense. But he presented to the Senate in January 1854 and then shepherded through both houses of Congress and into the willing hands of President Franklin Pierce a bill that through successive versions moved from contradicting while ignoring the Missouri Compromise to explicitly repealing it. Douglas began by attempting to introduce popular sovereignty into Nebraska without removing the Missouri restriction. This contradiction simply led some Northerners to fear that the effect of the language in the bill might be to repeal the restric-

[47] Douglas to the editor of the Concord [New Hampshire] *State Capitol Reporter*, February 16, 1854, in Johannsen, *Letters of Douglas*, p. 289.

tion, and some Southerners to fear that it might not. Under pressure to be more specific, Douglas moved the bill to its final form, which stated that the people of the territories (the area was now divided into two parts—Kansas and Nebraska) were "perfectly free to form and regulate their domestic institutions in their own way." It declared "inoperative and void" that portion of the Missouri Enabling Act of March 6, 1820 that had barred slavery "forever" north of 36°30'. When President Pierce signed the bill into law on May 30, 1854, "forever" had been redefined to mean 34 years, two months, and 24 days.[48]

The Kansas-Nebraska Act was a prosaic but fateful piece of legislation fully meriting the fascinated attention that historians have always given it.[49] In terms of process, it inflicted for the first time a great wound on the compromise tradition. Lincoln surely was reflecting a prevalent fear when he asked not long after the bill was passed: "Who after this will ever trust in a national compromise?"[50] Further, the abrupt and indirect way in which Douglas proceeded gave great impetus to tendencies, by no means new, to think of slavery politics in terms of conspiracy. In terms of institutions, the law accelerated the division of political parties along sectional lines, thereby weakening a crucial obstacle in the way of disunion. In terms of personalities, it transformed the careers of countless individuals —most notably for history those of Douglas and Lincoln. Douglas was placed on the defensive at once, and he remained there for the rest of his life. He emerged from this fracas with the image of an evil, ambitious, would-be tyrant—a reputation that dogged him to the last of his days.[51] As paths were closed

---

[48] The Kansas-Nebraska Act is in U.S., *Statutes at Large,* 10:277–90.

[49] On this, see Nichols, "The Kansas-Nebraska Act."

[50] Roy P. Basler, ed., *The Collected Works of Abraham Lincoln,* 8 vols. (New Brunswick, N.J.: Rutgers University Press, 1953), 2:272.

[51] Potter, *Impending Crisis,* p. 168.

to Douglas, paths were opened to Lincoln, and these two developments were reciprocal. Douglas is as famous as he is now because of his rivalry with Lincoln; Lincoln became famous because of his rivalry with Douglas. As a newspaper declared in
1859, "without Douglas Lincoln would be nothing."[52] With
him, he managed to become everything. Taken together, these
results of the Kansas-Nebraska Act reveal a great deal about
the events of 1860 and 1861, when the Republicans, a sectional
party, elected Lincoln to the presidency and when, as a consequence of that election, there followed secession and civil war
between the sections rather than yet another compromise.

No sooner was it proposed than the Kansas-Nebraska bill
generated pleas for a return to the golden age of the fathers
and a restoration of the founding principles. Even when they
did not agree on what those principles were, nearly all of the
bill's opponents wished, as George Ticknor Curtis did, to
"return . . . to the policy of those who founded the Federal
Government";[53] or as Charles Sumner did, to "return once
more to the original policy of our fathers."[54] "We must return
to our fundamental principles," a magazine exhorted its
readers, "to our primitive spirit, to the noble and manly tone,
which made us giants in our youth, but in the loss of which
we dwindle into dwarfs." Legislation could help, but Kansas-
Nebraska had revealed a decay that no merely legislative
measure could reach. "No single measure of improvement, nor
series of measures, can help us, if we do not recover, along with
them, the old inward health and soundness."[55] The great
outward-bound "nation of futurity" suddenly found itself

[52] Quoted in Jaffa and Johannsen, *In the Name of the People*, p. 22.

[53] Curtis, *Supremacy of Congress*, p. 33.

[54] *Congressional Globe*, 33 Cong., 1 Sess. (February 21, 1854), appendix,
p. 269.

[55] "The Kansas Question," *Putnam's Monthly* 6 (1855): 433.

stopping, so to say, turning around and looking with great intensity into its history. This was scarcely the result Douglas had sought. The irony of his career was even further compounded, however, when the prophet of the expansive future found himself participating in and even encouraging the retreat into the arms of the past.

The psychological meaning of this reaction remains to be explained, but before we leave Douglas it needs to be said that he later revealed by his response to the language of restoration that he knew he had broken some fundamental link to the beginning, if not exactly how or which one. He never really understood, and it is important to stress, that it was the fact of repeal of the Missouri Compromise and not popular sovereignty that was perceived to be the great assault on the authority of tradition and that led to appeals of the sort just quoted. It might seem that popular sovereignty was inherently patricidal for it presupposed the autonomy of the living. Whatever its theoretical implications, however, the policy was as much in accord with tradition as the Wilmot Proviso and Chief Justice Taney's opinion in *Dred Scott* v. *Sandford* that Congress had no power to prohibit slavery in the territories. Supporters of these various and contradictory positions could and did trace them back to the founders.[56] Popular sovereignty indeed was the essence of what the South before the middle 1850s had always sought and sometimes achieved for the territories.[57] It was the leaving of the matter to local regulations and local conditions that assisted the spread of slavery from the Atlantic tidewater to the Mississippi valley.

---

[56] An early backer of popular sovereignty argued that the fathers first vindicated in the Revolution and then repudiated in the Northwest Ordinance one of the leading principles of democracy—that "every generation have a right to govern themselves in their own way." "Popular Sovereignty and States Rights," *United States Magazine and Democratic Review* 25 (1849): 7.

[57] See Moore, *Missouri Controversy*, pp. 122–23.

Its association first with the overthrow of a free-soil law in 1854 and then ironically with free soil itself by late in the decade (as it became clear that Kansas would never become a slave state) called popular sovereignty into question on all sides. It was attacked by Northerners appalled by the first turn of events, and by Southerners appalled by the second. The Republican party came into existence opposing it as a door that might let slavery into the territories. Taney in the *Dred Scott* case opposed it as a wall that might keep slavery out. Douglas was caught in a vise, but to be attacked by zealots on both sides only strengthened his commitment to his policy and his determination to see it prevail. He was not without resources. To Southerners he promised by implication that popular sovereignty combined with manifest destiny meant a slave empire reaching down toward the equator. To Northerners he offered a brilliant argument casting himself as the true heir and good son of the fathers. The Kansas-Nebraska Act only seemed to repeal tradition. In fact, he argued, the law restored it.

In a republic that liked to think it was unburdened by the past, and in which constitutional law on the subject of slavery in the territories was so murky that a search for precedents could yield whatever one sought, one might expect to find such an advocate of Young America as Douglas defending popular sovereignty on the same ground that the *Democratic Review* had in the late 1840s—that the will of the present should prevail. Douglas did not do this. To be sure, he never stopped arguing for "the right of the people of the Territories to govern themselves in respect to their local affairs and internal polity."[58] But he also felt increasingly constrained to argue that popular sovereignty, in addition to comporting with the principle of self-government, was consistent with, and was in fact, the policy of the fathers.

[58] Jaffa and Johannsen, *In the Name of the People,* p. 58.

Nothing better illustrates the ironic turn that Douglas's career took than the article he published in *Harper's Magazine* in 1859.[59] Working through the summer of that year with materials supplied him by George Bancroft, he created what one of his antagonists acknowledged was "something new" in the world—a scholarly article by a political man in a popular magazine.[60] In this famous piece Douglas attempted to win back to popular sovereignty some of the people who had been willing to use it in 1854, without losing the support of people who had come to tolerate it after it had seemed to lead to the free-soil result Douglas had always predicted in Kansas.

The *Dred Scott* decision in 1857 ruled unconstitutional what Douglas had already destroyed—the Missouri Compromise. But Taney's decision was more a challenge than a boost to popular sovereignty, for he, unlike Douglas, did not see the constitutional aspects of the question of slavery in the territories as a question between federal and local authority, but rather as a question between the rights of property and government authority of any kind. If the Fifth Amendment's protection of property swept aside Congressional attempts to interfere with slave property, would it not also be fatal to any local attempt to do the same? Taney was generally understood to have said as much when, after asserting that for Congress to deprive a citizen of his slaves because he entered a particular territory (something that Congress in fact did not do) conflicted with the due process clause of the Fifth Amendment, he added: "If Congress itself cannot do this . . . it will be admitted, we presume, that it could not authorize a Territorial Government" to do so.[61] By Taney's reasoning it would have been just as proper at this point for him to have said: "If

---

[59] "The Dividing Line Between Federal and Local Authority: Popular Sovereignty in the Territories," reprinted in *ibid.*, pp. 58–125.

[60] Curtis, *Supremacy of Congress*, p. 3.

[61] 19 Howard 451; Don E. Fehrenbacher, *Prelude to Greatness: Lincoln in the 1850's* (Stanford: Stanford University Press, 1962), pp. 126, 133–34.

Congress cannot do this, neither could a Territorial Government." He did not say it, although certainly he would have agreed with the proposition. If he had said it, he would have precluded the *Harper's* article, or at the very least forced it down a quite different track.

As it was, Taney left just enough room for Douglas to insist that despite *Dred Scott* the territories could still effectively and constitutionally keep slavery out. He used Taney's own words to analyze the nature of property and its relationship to a political community. Douglas noted that Taney did not say "that the Constitution establishes slavery in the Territories beyond the power of the people legally to control it."[62] If he had, there would not only be no way to keep slavery out of the territories; there would also be no way to keep it out of the free states—a result no responsible proslavery spokesman sought. If the Constitution establishes slavery, then, since the Constitution is the supreme law of the land, the prohibition of slavery by any community would be a denial of due process. Moreover, it would be the duty of Congress to protect slave property everywhere in the Union if local laws did not. To say that the Constitution *recognizes* property in slaves (which was nowhere denied) was not the same thing as saying that the Constitution *establishes* such property.

Douglas observed that in the Constitution there are powers that Congress may confer but that it may not exercise. Congress may, for example, set up courts of law, but Congress cannot hear or decide law cases. Similarly, Congress may set up territorial governments, and confer powers upon them that Congress itself cannot exercise. No one (certainly not Taney, at any rate) doubted that the powers of Congress can reach into the territories just as they can reach into the states. The question was: what is the dividing line? "The powers which Congress may . . . *confer* but can not *exercise,* are such as relate

62 Jaffa and Johannsen, *In the Name of the People,* p. 102.

to the domestic affairs and internal polity of the Territory, and do not affect the general welfare of the Republic."[63] Douglas, of course, then argued that slavery was just such a local concern that did not affect the general welfare of the Republic. (He did not appear to notice that his whole career—as well as this magazine article—proved the contrary.)

Douglas developed his case by appealing to the language of the Constitution. The fugitive slave clause as much as said that slavery was *established* by state law (it refers to a "person held to service or labor in one State, under the laws thereof"[64] and nowhere else) like any other property. Except for the case of the rendition of fugitives (where the Constitution made an exception), slave property was no different, in the eyes of the document, from any other kind of property—and entitled to no more or less protection. Indeed here was a case exactly of the exception proving the rule. Except for the few specific mentions of slavery in the Constitution, Douglas held, "the federal government has no right to interfere with the question, either to establish, or to prohibit slavery." Certainly the clause in the Constitution dealing with territory did not give the federal government power in that realm. He agreed with the interpretation that made "territory" in Article IV synonymous with "land" rather than "political community." Thus Taney was correct to declare the Missouri Compromise unconstitutional. The local status of slavery had been defined exactly by the fathers in order to satisfy both slaveholding and nonslaveholding interests. Both Southerners and Northerners wanted to isolate slavery from federal power—Southerners, in order to protect against any federal move toward emancipation; Northerners, because they did not want to be responsible for an institution that was alien to them.[65]

It was at this point in his treatise that Douglas turned from

[63] Ibid., pp. 63–65.
[64] U.S., *Constitution,* Art. IV, sec. 2.
[65] Jaffa and Johannsen, *In the Name of the People,* pp. 106, 128, 202.

constitutional interpretation based on language to constitutional interpretation based on history. The fathers were acutely sensitive to this distinction between local and nonlocal concerns because defining it had been central to their lives. Indeed, Douglas wrote, the problem of local rights was the cause of the American Revolution itself. Because of this, he asserted in a famous sentence that marks his capitulation to the past, "Our fathers, when they framed this Government under which we live, understood this question just as well, and even better, than we do now."[66] Nothing about the *Harper's* piece is more striking than the amount of space given to praise and interpretation of the acts of the fathers.

In Douglas's interpretation of colonial history, disputes between the colonies and Britain arose over the question of how much local self-government was permitted to the colonies by the British Constitution. The fathers believed in the principle that "every distinct political community" had the right to make its own laws. This belief did not mean that they desired independence; on the contrary, until 1776 they wanted to remain part of the Empire. They revered the British Constitution. They acknowledged that the British government could make all laws that by their nature concerned the Empire generally. "Their only complaint was that they were not permitted to enjoy the rights and privileges of self-government, in the management of their internal affairs and domestic concerns in accordance with the guaranties of that Constitution."[67] When years of pleading did not win these rights, the colonists went to war for them, and only later did they add independence to their goals.

No subject in this contest—so Douglas read the record—was more important than slavery, which Americans in the colonial

[66] Douglas made this statement in a speech in Columbus, Ohio, on September 7, 1859. The speech continued the argument of the article. Ibid., p. 135.
[67] Ibid., pp. 65–67.

period considered a "domestic question" to be regulated by themselves. For instance, the massive importation of Africans to be slaves, added to the presence of menacing Indians on their frontiers, made Virginians in particular increasingly uneasy. They attempted to slow the importation of Africans by taxation, but the Crown annulled the legislation they enacted. In 1772 the Virginia House of Burgesses warned King George III that the continuation of the inhuman importation of Africans endangered the "very existence of your Majesty's American dominions." Douglas argued that Virginia was more concerned about the forcing of "African slavery upon a dependent Colony without her consent" than she was about any of the other problems that led to the Revolution.[68]

From these protests and claims Douglas inferred that the fathers would not have then turned around and treated their own territories as dependent colonies. "Is it reasonable to suppose," he asked,

> after our fathers had fought the battles of the Revolution in behalf of the right of each Colony to govern itself in respect to its local and domestic concerns, that then they conferred upon Congress the arbitrary sovereign power which they had refused to the British Parliament?[69]

Douglas neglected to consider in this regard a crucial distinction between colonial and territorial status: the former was an end in itself; the latter was a stage in preparation for full participation in the political community. He also neglected, strange to say, the Northwest Ordinance of 1787. He did not mention this basic part of his opponents' historical argument at all in this connection, thereby leaving himself open to the

[68] Ibid., pp. 70–72.
[69] Douglas at Columbus, ibid., p. 132.

charges of disingenuousness that his critics did not fail to make.[70]

In the aftermath of the political trauma of 1850, Stephen A. Douglas pledged in public that he would never make another speech on slavery.[71] By 1859, in Lincoln's words, "his explanations explanatory of explanations explained" on slavery had become "interminable."[72] He seemed preoccupied with the intricacies of the matter to the exclusion of just about everything else. To be sure, in 1859 Douglas was still predicting that "the time is coming" when the United States would annex Central America. "We are bound to extend and spread until we absorb the entire continent of America, including the adjacent islands," he said.[73] He was in effect promising—as if to himself—that soon he and the nation would be able to resume pursuit of the goals from which all had been distracted. But his pledges could not obscure the irony that the man of the present and future rather than the past had ended up arguing with a near-pathetic insistence that *he*, after all, was the good and true son of the fathers and heir to their policies. He had involved himself in the slavery disputes in the first place in order to put aside an obstacle to Young America projects, and then spent most of the rest of his career elaborating upon his solution to the slavery problem. The projects of Young America virtually disappeared.[74]

[70] Curtis, *Supremacy of Congress*, p. 8; Basler, *Works of Lincoln*, 3:415–16.

[71] *Congressional Globe*, 32 Cong., 1 Sess. (December 23, 1851), appendix, p. 68.

[72] Basler, *Works of Lincoln*, 3:405.

[73] Jaffa and Johannsen, *In the Name of the People*, p. 149. See also Johannsen, *Stephen A. Douglas*, pp. 683–84.

[74] Cf. Nichols, "The Kansas-Nebraska Act," p. 212.

5

SENTIMENTAL REGRESSION FROM
POLITICS TO DOMESTICITY

O Time! give back my childhood days,
  Those halcyon days of truth,
And I'll give up my manhood ways,
  And be once more a youth.

G. N. BARBOUR, 1852

Whether or not Stephen A. Douglas was the man chiefly ac-
countable for the destruction of the center in American politics, one of the most conspicuous political developments of the
1850s was the diminishing and near-disappearance of the middle ground in the sectional conflict. To be sure, on the territorial question after 1854 there were yet defenders of the compromise tradition willing to show how that tradition stretched
back to the beginning.[1] They were isolated voices. In their last
years Henry Clay and Daniel Webster had stood nearly alone
as the spokemen of the party of feeling in American politics.

---

[1] [Sidney George Fisher], *The Law of the Territories* (Philadelphia: C. Sherman & Son, 1859); George Ticknor Curtis, *The Just Supremacy of Congress over the Territories* (Boston: A. Williams and Co., 1859).

After they died no one of similar stature moved to replace them on the ground they had dominated for so long. The important voices in politics after they departed—people like William H. Seward, Jefferson Davis, and of course Douglas—were either indifferent or hostile to emotion in politics. "We are utilitarians," Davis once said, "and it is not in keeping with that character to be led away by sentiment."[2]

But it would only compound the mysteries that continue to fascinate scholars of the 1850s to assume that there was no sentimental center or that it was without force in American life. People who valued social calm and order above the rights of the slaveholder, the slaves, or even free labor, tended to be people who by temperament shrank from the unpleasantness of invective and the tumble of political life that grew ever more desperate. They liked to think that their flight from politics was altogether representative, that—as one of their number put it—in the country there was a

> party unknown . . . a party that is quiet, retired, unobtrusive, defensive rather than aggressive, avoiding political activity, hating the base strife of parties and demagogues, . . . animated by loyal and conservative public sentiment. . . . It is inefficient because of the very qualities that make it respectable. It does not go to town meetings, nor . . . is it very busy at the hustings; preferring rather the pleasures of domestic life. . . .[3]

Domestic life: there was the key. In the idealized domestic scene conservatives of this sort found a metaphor and a countervailing model against the excesses of politicians. Moreover, without fully realizing it, they sensed that their own retreat from action meshed with a psychological regression that involved people in realms far beyond politics.

[2] *Congressional Globe*, 31 Cong., 1 Sess. (January 24, 1850), p. 227.
[3] [Fisher], *Law of the Territories*, pp. 85–86.

The irony of the thrashings of Young America was that its attempts to grow up and get away from the fathers generated anxieties and regression to the very past/childhood from which it sought to escape. We have seen versions of this regression in the cases of Holgrave and Douglas, both of whom ended up, so to speak, in the houses of their fathers. Sentimentalists sought to make such emotional retreats general. They sought to return Americans to their childhood, the security of their early homes, and even to the bosom of their mothers. It is as though they had learned one of the lessons Harriet Beecher Stowe meant to teach—the efficacy of feeling—as well as one she did not: that Little Eva posed no threat to the established order.[4] Children were little conservatives. In their lives surely were innocence, security, peace, and love—without worry or agitation, or for that matter hard thought. The irony of this regression to the domestic scene and to childhood lay in the highly sentimental image of childhood that informed and permitted it. In seconding "Burke's appeal to the normal instincts of mankind as the conservative principle of society,"[5] sentimentalists sought to turn from politics to instinct, naively thinking that this was the equivalent of moving from chaos to order.

Of all Douglas's antagonists, surely one of the most underrated then and ever since was Edward Everett, the Massachusetts Whig. Everett was elected to the Senate in 1853 and immediately took rank as one of its most luminous members. He had been a congressman from Massachusetts in the 1820s, governor of Massachusetts in the 1830s, minister to Great Britain in the first Whig administration, and Secretary of State in the second. When he took his seat in the Senate speculation de-

---

[4] Ann Douglas, *The Feminization of American Culture* (New York: Alfred A. Knopf, 1977), p. 4.

[5] Henry T. Tuckerman, *The Rebellion: Its Latent Causes and True Significance* (New York: James G. Gregory, 1861), p. 21.

veloped that he would be the Whig candidate for President in 1856. He dismissed the talk. Perhaps, he thought, if he were "as young as Senator D." he might have a chance. In fact it was apparent to the two men, who were the leaders of the respective centers of their parties, that they might be opposing candidates for the White House in the 1856 election. Whatever the chances of such a confrontation might have been before 1854, the Kansas-Nebraska Act ended them. Not only Douglas's political career, but (much more immediately) Everett's own, as well as the party that might have nominated him for president, were casualties of that law.[6]

There was never any possibility that Everett would support Douglas on Kansas-Nebraska. A member of the Committee on Territories, he opposed the emerging bill both there and later on the floor of the Senate. It was not that the question of slavery expansion or even slavery pressed heavily upon him. Indeed he shared with Douglas and other centrist politicians in both parties the belief that the slavery question was not inherently important enough to jeopardize the Union, and that it must not be made to seem so. At one level, he opposed the bill for the reason that many Northerners did—it represented the breaking of a venerable compact. But just as the Missouri Compromise was incidental to Douglas in proposing the legislation, so it was incidental to Everett in opposing it. Everett saw the legislation and its sponsor as emblematic of everything that had been going wrong with American life for a decade. As his sympathetic biographer acknowledged, he "dreaded any kind of change."[7] Every success of a man like Douglas—every policy, every thought—signaled to a man like Everett that the world he had always known was becoming unrecognizable.

[6] Paul Revere Frothingham, *Edward Everett: Orator and Statesman* (Boston: Houghton Mifflin Co., 1925), p. 342. Except where I indicate otherwise, this is my source for biographical data about Everett. A modern, scholarly biography of the man would be very useful to students of the culture and politics of this period.

[7] Ibid., p. 102.

Douglas embraced immigration and understood it in terms of the liberation of the oppressed. Everett did not oppose immigration, but he was made uneasy by the magnitude of what he called "the tide of immigration from Europe, a phenomenon the parallel of which does not exist in the history of the world, an immigration of three or four hundred thousand . . . pouring into this country every year."[8] Douglas was identified with manifest destiny; Everett opposed the "accession of dead acres," specifically Cuba, which to Douglas was always a kind of grail. Where Douglas saw the glorious vision of expanding democracy, Everett saw "military aggrandizement" and feared the excesses of the imperialistic quest: "vast standing armies, overshadowing navies, colossal military establishments, frightful expenditures, contracts, jobs, [and] corruption which it sickens the heart to contemplate."[9] That Everett identified this prospect with Douglas is clear. Indeed, a central purpose of his first speech in the Senate in 1853, he said privately, was to "administer a gentle rebuke to Judge Douglas's bellicose and annexing propensities."[10] In it he criticized Douglas for regarding "geographical extension as the measure and the index of our country's progress."[11]

But his capacity to oppose Douglas's policies was hindered by his distaste for politics and his unwillingness to contribute to agitation. He once said he had been "haunted . . . through life" by images of what would happen if war broke out between the sections,[12] and he admitted that he would do "almost anything" to preserve the Union.[13] He was thus con-

[8] *Congressional Globe,* 33 Cong., 1 Sess. (February 8, 1854), appendix, p. 159.

[9] Ibid., 32 Cong., 3 Sess. (March 21, 1853), appendix, p. 289.

[10] Quoted in Frothingham, *Edward Everett,* p. 342.

[11] *Congressional Globe,* 32 Cong., 3 Sess. (March 21, 1853), appendix, p. 289.

[12] Edward Everett, *Orations and Speeches on Various Occasions,* 4 vols. (Boston: Little, Brown and Co., 1850–68), 4:652.

[13] *Congressional Globe,* 33 Cong., 1 Sess. (February 8, 1854), appendix, p. 162.

strained from doing more than making a decorous speech against the Kansas-Nebraska legislation. At the decisive moment, quite by accident, Everett missed the vote in which the Senate passed the bill. He was so embarrassed and harassed as a result that he resigned his seat after serving in it for only fifteen months. He returned to his home in Boston in a state of mental depression, physical debility, and political disgrace. He was sixty years old and thought his career was over. In this belief he turned out to be mistaken. Actually, the period of his greatest influence in American life was still ahead of him.

In a filiopietistic age it would be difficult to find a more filiopietistic man—toward his own father, the founders, and the past generally—than Edward Everett. It would be understandable if in his mind he identified—and somewhere in his imagination confused—his father with George Washington, so that feelings for one were transferred to the other. The senior Everett was a clergyman who died in 1802 (when the son was eight), less than three years after the death of Washington. One of the few things that Everett could remember about his father was that he had delivered a eulogy on Washington. He himself became a eulogist and commemorator of the past generally. In private, in his diary, he noted each anniversary of his father's death. In public, in orations and books, he celebrated the character and achievements of the founders. In his first great oration, in 1824, he spoke the theme that would dominate his career:

> Divisions may spring up, ill blood may burn, parties be formed, and interests may seem to clash; but the great bonds of the nation are linked to what is past. The deeds of the great men, to whom this country owes its origin and growth, are a patrimony, I know, of which its children will never deprive themselves.[14]

[14] Everett, *Orations and Speeches*, 1:38–39.

To have heard that oration, a critic wrote in 1850, was "some consolation for being no longer young."[15]

It was as a sentimental orator that Everett made his incalculable impact upon the post-heroic age. "Mr. Everett has met the demand of his generation," the *Southern Quarterly Review* stated in 1851, "by assisting to shape and direct its mighty but vague aspirings."[16] His role in American life was not to invent or express new ideas, but to put conventional wisdom into vivid and memorable symbols—delivered in a memorable way. People evidently went to hear him in order to be deeply moved. N. P. Willis said that he could play "resistlessly" on people's emotions.[17] Assessments of his impact almost always focused on what the *Review* called the "graceful elegance of [his] manner."[18] All his admirers commented on it. Emerson recalled that when Everett taught at Harvard in the early 1820s, students who had no particular interest in what he was talking about nevertheless would go hear him "for the manner."[19] Margaret Fuller was typically more emphatic: it was "the manner, the *manner*, the delicate inflections of voice, the elegant and appropriate gesture, the sense of beauty produced by the whole, which thrilled us all to tears."[20] Music, rather than the more predictable connection to drama, was the analogy to another art form that came most quickly to mind: it was the "music of his speech" that moved people, as his voice ranged "at will

[15] G[eorge] S. H[illard], "Everett's Orations and Speeches," *Christian Examiner* 49 (1850): 396.

[16] "Everett's Orations and Speeches," *Southern Quarterly Review* 19 (1851): 458.

[17] Quoted in "Our Window," *Putnam's Monthly* 10 (1857): 422.

[18] "Everett's Orations and Speeches," *Southern Quarterly Review,* p. 460.

[19] Ralph Waldo Emerson, "Historic Notes of Life and Letters in New England," *The Complete Works of Ralph Waldo Emerson,* 12 vols. (Boston: Houghton Mifflin Co., 1903–4), 10:332.

[20] Quoted in Perry Miller, ed., *The Transcendentalists: An Anthology* (Cambridge, Mass.: Harvard University Press, 1950), p. 20.

between trumpet-tone and an almost feminine pathos."[21] This is of course precisely the kind of person whose moment of opportunity is likely to come when ordinary political language lapses into mere disputatiousness; Everett's influence did not depend on words.

He knew exactly what he was doing, and the connection between music and femininity in the last quotation was very apt. Everett understood the double meaning of the term "mother tongue."

> A charm, which nothing can borrow, and for which there is no substitute, dwells in the simple sound of our mother tongue. Not analyzed, nor reasoned upon, it unites the simplest recollections of early life with the maturest conceptions of the understanding. The heart is willing to open all its avenues to the language in which its infantile caprices were soothed; and, by the curious efficacy of the principle of association, it is this echo from the faint dawn of intelligence, which gives to eloquence much of its manly power, and to poetry much of its divine charm. What a noble prospect presents itself, in this way, for the circulation of thought and sentiment in our country![22]

His later career fulfilled the role this first speech implied he would play. He understood the permanent power that language gave to mothers, and he knew how to imitate them in order to reach the children who still lived in his adult audiences. He seemed to celebrate national progress, but his deeper message was always a verbal applying of brakes: we do not need to be in such a hurry or so excitable; we should not stray far from home or let familial bonds go slack.

[21] Oliver Wendell Holmes, *The Complete Works of Oliver Wendell Holmes*, 14 vols. (Boston: Houghton Mifflin Co., 1909), 11:113; "Everett's Orations and Speeches," *Southern Quarterly Review*, p. 460. See also [C. C. Felton], "Everett's *Orations and Speeches*," *North American Review* 71 (1850): 450.

[22] Everett, *Orations and Speeches*, 1:31–32.

Everett seemed the most incongruous sort of Whig, praising people he found free from

> the unhappy restless desire "to better his condition," as it is called, which, in a few exceptional cases, leads to a brilliant fortune, [but] condemns the majority of men to a life of feverish and generally unsuccessful change.[23]

One critic dismissed Everett as "a lady's orator";[24] an admirer acknowledged with regret that his speeches did not have much to do with "hardihood and self-reliance";[25] and his brother-in-law, Charles Francis Adams, said he was almost as timid as a woman.[26] Whether a trait he knew he could not hide, or one he decided to affect, this was a characteristic Everett exploited with increasing ingenuity as he sought to preserve the Union by linking it through his maternal persona to everyone's remembered mother.

Everett's early oratorical triumphs led to political office, a progression that sometimes perplexed his admirers, who considered him unsuited temperamentally for the workaday give and take of the calling. Frederic Henry Hedge regretted that "a mind like Mr. Everett's,—a gem of such rare water, should be . . . so unprofitably set."[27] Emerson too regretted the turn to politics. "He is not content to be Edward Everett, but would be Daniel Webster. This is his mortal distemper."[28] But Everett's temperament was not like Webster's. He did not enjoy and was not effective at politics, and for all of the political of-

[23] Ibid., 4:93.

[24] *Times* (London), December 4, 1863.

[25] H[illard], "Everett's Orations and Speeches," p. 403.

[26] Charles Francis Adams, *Richard Henry Dana: A Biography,* 2 vols. (Boston: Houghton Mifflin Co., 1891), 2:279.

[27] [Frederic Henry Hedge], "Everett's *Phi Beta Kappa Address,*" *Christian Examiner* 16 (1834): 2.

[28] Edward Waldo Emerson and Waldo Emerson Forbes, eds., *Journals of Ralph Waldo Emerson, with Annotations,* 10 vols. (Boston: Houghton Mifflin Co., 1909–14), 3:471.

fices he held, he never thought of himself as a politician. In those positions his performance was always competent, but it was rarely brilliant and usually brief.

The political arena might not have been suitable for him, but the times were propitious in the larger cultural arena in which he was comfortable. Sentimentalism was back in style in the 1850s;[29] the shift in sensibility that worked to the disadvantage of Douglas worked to the advantage of Everett. Within two years after his ignominious resignation from the Senate, he was able to rediscover his power to reach, and then turn to account, what another writer called the "deep current of feeling" that flowed beneath the surface of "apparently increasing insensibility to the truths and traditions of the past."[30]

The specific situation that permitted this comeback was the plight of Mount Vernon. After George Washington died in 1799, plans were made for the eventual burial of his remains in the national capital in an appropriately monumental structure, but nothing came of them and Washington's body remained where it had been originally buried, at Mount Vernon, his home on the Potomac River in Virginia.[31] Over the years the grave and home gradually turned into a national embarrassment.[32] Washington's heirs, who owned the property, let it drift into an unkempt state. Some of the tourists who visited it were distressed at the disrepair of Washington's house and appalled that "the children of America allow the Father of their

[29] He was quite aware that it had been out of style. See *Orations and Speeches*, 1:xi.

[30] Beverley R. Wellford, Jr., "Address Delivered Before the Ladies' Mount Vernon Association, July 4, 1855," *Southern Literary Messenger* 21 (1855): 565.

[31] Daniel J. Boorstin, *The Americans: The National Experience* (New York: Random House, 1965), pp. 349–51.

[32] John Quincy Adams reminded Congress in 1825 that a quarter-century had gone by since it promised to build a tomb in Washington, D.C. James D. Richardson, ed., *A Compilation of the Messages and Papers of the Presidents*, 10 vols. (Washington, Government Printing Office, 1897), 2:315.

Liberties to sleep in a neglected grave."[33] At least one visitor likened the tomb to a pigsty.[34] In the 1850s, unable to afford to refurbish or even to keep the property, Washington's family decided to put Mount Vernon up for sale. The federal government, to which they turned first, did not act to buy it. Efforts to persuade Congress to purchase Mount Vernon were unsuccessful. There was concern among politicians that once the federal government began to move in this direction there would be no end to it.[35] This seemed to leave only the public market, a prospect that produced an anguished response in many quarters. *"The grave of Washington may be brought into the market!"* exclaimed a Virginian with evidently pained disbelief as it began to seem that Mount Vernon would pass into the hands of "Mammon-worshipping speculators" looking to transform it into a "sort of Slash Cottage resort" offering its patrons bowling, a race track, and a bar.[36]

Alarmed at this prospect, a group of Southern women began a campaign to raise money to purchase the property and restore and preserve it. Their purposes were straightforward—to keep "change" and "progress" at bay, at least from that one plot.[37] When he learned of this effort, Everett joined it and

[33] "Spring Days in Washington," *Southern Literary Messenger* 21 (1855): 337; E. Kennedy, "Mount Vernon—A Pilgrimage," ibid. 18 (1852): 53–57; Lewis D. Campbell, *Congressional Globe,* 33 Cong., 1 Sess. (December 15, 1853), p. 53; H[enry] T. T[uckerman], "The Law of Burial and the Sentiment of Death," *Christian Examiner* 61 (1856): 343. See also "Mount Vernon," *Godey's Lady's Book* 59 (1859): 371.

[34] [Edward Everett], "Faux's Memorable Days in America," *North American Review* 19 (1824): 120.

[35] See, for example, *Congressional Globe,* 33 Cong., 1 Sess. (December 15, 1853), pp. 52–54.

[36] J. Lansing Burrows, "Address Before the Mount Vernon Association, July 4th, 1855," *Southern Literary Messenger* 21 (1855): 515–16; Wellford, "Address," p. 565.

[37] Thomas Nelson Page, *Mount Vernon and Its Preservation, 1858–1910* (New York: Knickerbocker Press, 1910), p. 62; Isaac McLellan, "Woman's

enlarged it into a campaign with a double purpose. Washington's house and Washington's Republic were equally vulnerable, and to the same danger. Both could be made unrecognizable by mammon-worshipping speculators—in other words, ruined by men. It was not entirely an accident that Everett's return to prominence occurred in the cultural context of a celebration of so-called feminine—specifically maternal—values, and an assault on the masculine characteristics that had brought the nation to its present pass. He saw that he could use emotion to link the fate of house and nation. He would have Mount Vernon symbolize the Union, and by helping to preserve the first he would also help to preserve the second. Without much effect in the relatively narrow realm of politics, he would carry to more favorable ground the matters that drove him from the Senate, and there exploit the resurgence of sentimentalism. Further, in solving the crises of the real and metaphorical houses, he would also be resolving his personal crisis.

Everett had prepared an oration on "The Character of Washington," which he now put in the service of the cause. Between 1856 and 1860, when the house (though not the Union) was saved, he traveled back and forth across the nation, personally raising more than a third of the purchase price for Mount Vernon. He delivered the speech a total of 129 times, usually to immense audiences.[38] In New York City in 1856 crowds of people, disappointed to find that all the seats for the oration had been sold in advance, overpowered the doorkeepers and filled the aisles and even the stage to hear him at the new Academy of Music, which was designed to seat 7,000 people.[39]

Appeal," *Southern Literary Messenger* 21 (1855): 453; "Mount Vernon: Inscribed to the 'Southern Matron,' " ibid., p. 762.

[38] Everett's detailed description of his tour is in *Orations and Speeches*, 4:3–17.

[39] New York *Times*, March 4, 1856; New York *Daily Tribune*, March 4, 1856; Frothingham, *Edward Everett*, p. 376.

Richard Henry Dana, Jr., estimated that by the time Everett stopped his efforts, his oration had been heard by more people than any other "since the beginning of time."[40]

The oration that drew, and evidently moved, such crowds was indeed about Washington—Everett proceeded through the familiar details of the hero's life and extracted the familiar lessons from them.[41] In this respect he said nothing that his audiences had not known by heart since childhood, but this was, of course, his purpose. Everyone could remember that safe world, but they had been led out of it step by step, or they had neglected it bit by bit, until now the Republic was in danger. On this question Everett was quite direct and fully serious: George Washington could save the Union. He delivered an incantation:

> O, that his pure example, his potent influence, his parting counsels, could bring us back the blessings of national harmony! O, that from the heavens to which he has ascended, his voice might even now be heard and teach us to unite again in the brotherhood of love . . . ![42]

Everett told Americans that "the Father of his Country cries aloud to us from the sods of Mount Vernon, and calls upon us, East and West, North and South, as the brethren of one great household, to be faithful to the dear-bought inheritance which he did so much to secure to us."[43] Do not let the speculators and jobbers have their way. Certain words in this plea provide a key to the meaning of what he was about: "Father

[40] Richard H. Dana, Jr., *An Address upon the Life and Services of Edward Everett; Delivered before the Municipal Authorities and Citizens of Cambridge, February 22, 1865* (Cambridge, Mass.: Sever and Francis, 1865), p. 53.

[41] Everett, *Orations and Speeches*, 4:18–51.

[42] Ibid., p. 23.

[43] Boston *Daily Advertiser*, July 7, 1858.

... brethren ... household ... inheritance." His strategy for handling the various dangers confronting the Republic was to remind Americans who they were and where they were situated in time: they were the children of Washington, they belonged in his house, and they should come home to it.

Once restored, Mount Vernon would be the destination of pilgrimages. Everett predicted that "the latest generations of the grateful children of America will make [their] pilgrimage to it as to a shrine."[44] That there might be talismanic powers in Washington's home was recognized by other contemporary observers. Proposing that Washington's birthday become a national holiday, Henry T. Tuckerman urged:

> Around his tomb let us annually gather; let eloquence and song, leisure and remembrance, trophies of art, ceremonies of piety, and sentiments of gratitude and admiration, consecrate that day with a unanimity of feeling and of rites, which shall fuse and mould into one pervasive emotion the divided hearts of the country, until the discordant cries of faction are lost in the anthems of benediction and of love, and, before the august spirit of a people's homage, sectional animosity is awed into universal reverence.[45]

Advocating mass pilgrimages to Mount Vernon, J. Lansing Burrows asked: "Would there not be kindled in every heart an intenser love of our native land, a sterner resolve to perpetuate unimpaired the Union which his wisdom and valor aided to cement?" The first people to make such visits should be members of Congress. How could politicians journey there, Burrows wondered, "without feeling rebuked for discord, and opening their repentent arms to embrace each other as brothers beside the tomb of Washington?"[46]

[44] Everett, *Orations and Speeches,* 4:45.

[45] [Henry T. Tuckerman], "Holidays," *North American Review* 84 (1857): 363.

[46] Burrows, "Address," p. 517.

The decay of Mount Vernon, the prospect that it might end up in the real estate market or be torn down like any ordinary house, and the ingratitude that permitted these developments symbolized to many people the downward tendencies of the age. To its champions, the throwing off of the past was the very meaning of progress. To its enemies, the departure from the past meant only that the present had sunk far beneath the ancient standards. "The good old principles of our fathers," according to one example of a common complaint, "are giving place to an adoration of Mammon and the deification of the most grovelling and abominable Utilitarianism— . . . a steam engine is the Magnus Apollo of our Mythology."[47]

It was perfectly natural that the intense consciousness of living in a post-heroic age, with its necessarily deferential attitude toward the heroes and achievements of the beginning, should inspire a comparative sense that almost always showed the second age to moral disadvantage.[48] By the late 1840s, when the verbal effusions about material progress were most prevalent, it had become a rhetorical commonplace to speak of "the earlier and better days of the Republic."[49] Some post-heroic Americans charged their generation with being inferior to the founders, who fought the Revolution "better, alas! than we

[47] [T. C. Reynolds?], "Mr. Simms as a Political Writer," *Southern Literary Messenger* 9 (1843): 755.

[48] See, for example, "Washington and his Writings," *American Quarterly Review* 15 (1834): 275–76; "Characteristics of the Statesman," *Southern Quarterly Review* 6 (1844): 118.

[49] For examples of this phrase or a close variant of it, see R[obert M]. T. H[unter], "The Massachusetts Proposition for Abolishing the Slave Representation as Guarantied by the Constitution," *Southern Literary Messenger* 11 (1845): 451; Joshua R. Giddings, *Congressional Globe*, 29 Cong., 1 Sess. (May 7, 1846), p. 772; Ausburn Birdsall, ibid., 30 Cong., 1 Sess. (July 24, 1848), appendix, p. 794; A. G. Brown, ibid., 31 Cong., 1 Sess. (January 30, 1850), p. 260; Robert M. T. Hunter, ibid., 31 Cong., 1 Sess. (March 25, 1850), appendix, p. 375; Mason W. Tappan, ibid., 35 Cong., 1 Sess. (March 31, 1858), appendix, p. 327; Fulton Anderson, in George H. Reese, ed., *Proceedings of the Virginia State Convention of 1861*, 4 vols. (Richmond: Virginia State Library, 1965), 1:58.

could fight it!"[50] In the 1840s and 1850s phrases such as "degenerate sons" or "degenerate progeny" or "degenerate sons of heroic sires" were ritualistically drawn into criticisms of the present.[51] No one questioned that in many quantifiable ways the nation had advanced since the beginning: it was richer, its people more numerous, its territory wider. But throughout the post-heroic period the point was recurrently made that material progress had not been matched by moral advance; that, on the contrary, the nation had "degenerated." "Our Republic," one typical statement went, "has swollen in population and power; but it has shrunk in character. It is not now what it was at the beginning."[52] "There has been a lamentable degeneration," went another, "from that sublime political morality, which characterized our ancestors."[53]

Spokesmen for Young America liked to boast that their "utilitarian" ideas represented "the spirit of the age." As *Putnam's Monthly* noted in 1857, however, it was by then becoming just as common to hear laments "that our utilitarian spirit, while excellent in many respects, is in many others the bane of the age."[54] With the kind of delayed severity that re-

[50] [William O. Johnson], "The Causes of the American Revolution," *North American Review* 80 (1855): 390.

[51] For examples of uses of these formulaic phrases, see "Civilization: American and European," *American Whig Review* 4 (1846): 31; Henry S. Foote, *Congressional Globe,* 30 Cong., 1 Sess. (January 19, 1848), appendix, p. 122; Charles Brown, ibid., 30 Cong., 2 Sess. (February 7, 1849), appendix, p. 120; "Washington's Early Days," *Putnam's Monthly* 3 (1854): 7. But cf. the insistence by Lorenzo Sabine that "those who insist that we are the degenerate sons of worthy sires" were echoing charges that men of that honored generation had made against themselves. "The charges which are made against the present generation, like the sins which exist among them, are as old as the Revolution." "The Past and the Present of the American People," *North American Review* 66 (1848): 445.

[52] Charles Sumner, *Congressional Globe,* 33 Cong., 1 Sess. (February 21, 1854), appendix, p. 267.

[53] "The Perilous Condition of the Republic," *New-England Magazine* 1 (1831): 283.

[54] "A 'Progressive' Age," *Emerson's Magazine and Putnam's Monthly* 5 (1857): 484.

veals the tendencies under assault to be weak enough to de-
nounce with impunity, writers decried the "flashy imbecility of
self-styled 'Young America,'" which mindlessly mistook an
"age of traffic" and "grovelling utilitarianism" for one of un-
exampled progress.[55] Many sentimentalists agreed with the
assertion that Americans disregarded the past and failed to
perceive their existence as a "link in an eternal chain reaching
'before and after,'" and they regretted that this was so.[56] Looking backward from the crisis of 1861 Henry T. Tuckerman concluded that his generation "fully justified De Tocqueville's
theory that devotion to the immediate is the characteristic of
republics."[57] Tuckerman had observed correctly several years
earlier that "it is the cant of the day to repudiate the past."[58]
As he and other sentimentalists did not by any means lose their
voice, it became the countercant of the day to lament the
repudiation. A Whig journal complained, for instance, about
the prevailing American "disposition to reject the experience
and authority of others."[59] Never was there a generation
"which made so little use of the past as ours," Andrew P. Pea-
body wrote. "The perpetually recurring phrase 'of the day' is
almost necessary to commend opinions . . . to serious regard."[60] "The future is almost exclusively regarded, and the
past contemned."[61] A Boston orator deplored "the irreverent
tendency of the time—our careless indifference to the associations and memory of the past."[62]

[55] [Johnson], "Causes of the American Revolution," p. 392; [Andrew Preston Peabody], "The Intellectual Aspect of the Age," *North American Review*
64 (1847): 278, 279.

[56] [Tuckerman], "Law of Burial," p. 340.

[57] Tuckerman, *Rebellion*, p. 21.

[58] [Tuckerman], "American Society," *North American Review* 81 (1855):
30.

[59] "Civilization: American and European," p. 42.

[60] [Andrew Preston Peabody], "Arnold and Merivale: *The History of
Rome*," *North American Review* 72 (1851): 443.

[61] [Tuckerman], "Law of Burial," p. 339.

[62] Boston *Daily Advertiser*, July 7, 1858.

Concerns about degeneration continued to focus particularly on twin pursuits—wealth and power—which were thought to have been virtually unknown to a generation whose ambition was bounded by love and virtue.[63] The selflessness of the fathers' lives, so well and so recently lived and now so vividly presented to the memories of their posterity, stood as an inescapable rebuke to the soft comforts of the present. The observations that politics attracted only second-rate men and that public figures no longer measured up to the standards of statesmanship set by the founders were now made almost as a matter of course in references to the revolutionary era.[64] In 1840, pronouncing a "decline of public virtue," Abel Upshur observed with regret that "we have, no longer, Washingtons among us."[65] The "microscopic realities of today" were incessantly compared to Washington, and almost always to their disadvantage. As late as the time of Andrew Jackson, who was the last president to have experienced the Revolution, there could still be found American leaders of heroic stature, but since his departure, "what a graduated line of still diminishing shadows have glided successively through the portals of the White House! From Van Buren to Tyler, from Tyler to Polk, from Polk to Fillmore, from Fillmore to Pierce!"[66] After quoting an unnamed foreign writer's remark that " 'Few things have more surprised the world than the deterioration of the political men of America,' " *Putnam's Monthly* commented in 1855:

[63] See, for example, "The Country in 1950, or the Conservatism of Slavery," *Southern Literary Messenger* 22 (1856): 433.

[64] See, for examples, [Charles Francis Adams], "The Madison Papers," *North American Review* 53 (1841): 78–79; "The Federal Administrations of Washington and the Elder Adams," *Southern Literary Messenger* 13 (1847): 563; Henry W. Hilliard, *Congressional Globe,* 30 Cong., 1 Sess. (March 30, 1848), pp. 565–66.

[65] Quoted in "Judge Abel P. Upshur, Secretary of the Navy of the United States," *Southern Literary Messenger* 7 (1841): 871.

[66] [Edmund Quincy], "Where will it End?" *Atlantic Monthly* 1 (1857): 245.

"What other conclusion could be drawn, when the chair of Washington and Jefferson has come to be occupied by a Tyler and a Pierce?"[67]

The great danger in this falling off was that it might prove contagious. *Putnam's* interpreted the passage of the Kansas-Nebraska Act in these terms to its readers and, as was characteristic of such statements, rendered its charge in comparative language. The magazine claimed that politicians were "infusing gradually [their] own much-worn spirit into the very body of the community," with the result that Americans were becoming "deadened almost to the heroic examples of their fathers."[68] A year later the magazine concluded that the founding principles "no longer touch our hearts. . . . Great deeds are not done among us."[69] These rhetorical conventions represent the end point of a process that began in the 1830s in the mental confusion and questioning we have already considered. By the late 1840s and early 1850s these puzzlements had resolved themselves into two conflicting tendencies. Change was interpreted by some people as progress, by others as decline. Gradually assessments grew less qualified and more exaggerated until they took final form as opposing boasts or wails that were endlessly (and often mindlessly) repeated.

Although the content of the threnodies did not change noticeably over the years, after 1850 an unmistakable (although paradoxical) note of optimism began to appear in some of them. To many Americans who judged the passing scene according to the putative standards of the ordered world of the beginning, the late 1840s had seemed characterized by "the universal prevalence of the anarchical spirit."[70] The upheavals in

67 "The Kansas Question," *Putnam's Monthly* 6 (1855): 431. See also "The Progress of our Political Virtues," ibid. 5 (1855): 197–204, esp. 198.

68 "Our Parties and Politics," ibid. 4 (1854): 240.

69 "The Kansas Question," p. 431.

70 "California Gold and European Revolution," *Southern Quarterly Review* 17 (1850): 277.

Europe, added to the Mexican War and the reports of disorder and violence in California as grasping men sought gold, seemed to reflect the triumph of chaos east and west. Then the Union threatened to fly apart under similarly centrifugal pressures. As it turned out, however, the worst fears of conservatives were not realized. The revolutions of 1848 in Europe cast up reactionary regimes. In California, "the riotous lawlessness of vagabonds and villains" gave way to the "institution of an orderly and quiet government."[71] The nation did not come apart as a result of its acquisitions from Mexico but instead apparently managed to absorb them. Conservatives took heart from these developments. Order, which had seemed fragile and on the defensive in the late 1840s, began to seem inevitable by the early 1850s. Expecting understandably (but as it happened incorrectly) that these developments would benefit the Whigs, the *American Whig Review* published in 1852 an article titled "The World a Slow Coach after all," which proclaimed with obvious relief that "men naturally prefer custom before change."[72] Distilling the lessons of these varied upheavals into a formula, a conservative orator in 1858 declared: "Anarchy may rule the hour, but the excess of anarchy compels the re-establishment of government."[73]

One sign of the new optimism of the sentimentalists was the shrewd way in which they increasingly exploited the prevailing popular cults of domesticity on the one hand and George Washington on the other—and, in the process of exploiting, merged the two. By the late 1840s the domestic "sphere" (as it was everywhere known) was competing with, and then in the 1850s surpassing, "nature" as the locus of paradise on earth. As early, indeed, as 1839, George Frederick Simmons denied

---

[71] John S. Holmes, Boston *Daily Advertiser*, July 7, 1858.

[72] "The World a Slow Coach after all," *American Whig Review* 16 (1852): 332–39; the quotation is at p. 333.

[73] Boston *Daily Advertiser*, July 7, 1858.

that "any appearances of nature are more exciting to the imagination, or gratifying to the taste than the choice scenes of domestic life."[74] Nature began to lose its paradisiacal image as it gradually lost its association with maternal love.[75] As nature seemed progressively less nurturing and less gentle—"careless of the single life,"[76] as one writer put it—its symbolic role of mother was assumed by the home, which, at least ideally, could be counted on always to provide shelter and security as though it were an extension of the embracing presence of the figure who dominated it.

Probably no one before Lincoln took more effective political advantage of this cult than Harriet Beecher Stowe in *Uncle Tom's Cabin,* the most popular novel of the 1850s. The center of happiness in the world she created is in the home—in the parlor, by the hearth, or in the kitchen. Employing the contrapuntal technique that was one of her most effective devices to arouse compassion, Stowe at one point shifted directly from a scene of horror—the suicide of a slave woman whose child has just been taken from her—to a quite different situation: "A quiet scene now rises before us. A large, roomy, neatly-painted kitchen, its yellow floor glossy and smooth . . . glossy green wood chairs, old and firm . . ." and thus on she wrote, sustaining an image of warm security. Conveying first horror and then happiness, Stowe reminded her presumably domesticated readers that the black race was almost completely barred from the family life they took for granted.[77] Proslavery literati

74 G[eorge] F[rederick] S[immons], "Prospects of Art in this Country," *Christian Examiner* 25 (1839): 311–12.

75 Cf. John Higham, *From Boundlessness to Consolidation: The Transformation of American Culture, 1848–1860* (Ann Arbor: William E. Clements Library, 1969), pp. 2–3.

76 [Charles Eliot Norton], "The Advantages of Defeat," *Atlantic Monthly* 8 (1861): 364. See also Ralph Waldo Emerson, "Fate," *Complete Works,* 6:6.

77 Harriet Beecher Stowe, *Uncle Tom's Cabin; or, Life Among the Lowly,* ed. Kenneth S. Lynn (Cambridge, Mass.: Harvard University Press, Belknap Press, 1962), p. 139. *Putnam's Monthly* implied in 1854 that Mrs. Stowe had taken to confusing her home with the nation and suggested good-naturedly

attempted to meet her on her own metaphorical ground, arguing that it was precisely the comforts of a secure home life that distinguished the situation of the slaves from that of free labor in the North.[78]

Indeed, politicians of all types and publicists for many causes moved to take advantage of this cult, identifying their projects with what Daniel Webster once called "the transcendent sweets of domestic life."[79] Supporters of proposed homestead legislation in the 1850s, for example, drew an explicit, direct connection between domesticity and political and social peace. Pointing to the immigrants whose increasing numbers in eastern cities generated nativism and apprehensions of increased social unrest, they argued that homesteads in the west would palliate the situation in two ways: first, by drawing the immigrants out of the swelling cities; and second, by transforming them into conservatives, an ineluctable and immediate consequence of home ownership and immersion in the domestic scene. Not only would the danger of class struggle thereby be reduced, a New York congressman argued, but any political danger to the Union would be lessened too, for the law would give to "every man a homestead to fight for, and a domestic hearth to incite his courage, should the foeman ever dare invade our soil."[80] In 1858, when this remark was made, who could this foeman be? Andrew Johnson, for one, clearly seemed to have the Union in mind that year in his own argument for passage of the homestead bill. "The country as it is," he began obliquely, required that

that she needed to be told "that her own domestic circle is not America." "Editorial Notes—American Literature," *Putnam's Monthly* 4 (1854): 340.

[78] See Jeanette R. Tandy, "Pro-Slavery Propaganda in American Fiction," *South Atlantic Quarterly* 21 (1922): 41–50, 170–78.

[79] Daniel Webster, *The Writings and Speeches of Daniel Webster*, 18 vols. (Boston: Little, Brown and Co., 1903), 1:226.

[80] John Kelly, *Congressional Globe,* 35 Cong., 1 Sess. (May 25, 1858), appendix, p. 434.

the great mass of the people should be interested [in it] and who are more interested in the welfare of their country than those who have homes? . . . Our true policy is to build up the middle class. . . . When you are involved in war, in insurrection, or rebellion, or danger of any kind, they are the men who are to sustain you. . . . You will have a population of men having homes, having wives and children to care for, who will defend their hearthstones when invaded. What a sacred thing it is to a man to feel that he has a hearthstone to defend.[81]

One of the reasons that political language borrowed so readily from the preexisting imagery of domesticity was that politicians increasingly sensed that the problem of the Union was a problem of emotion, which placed it at least potentially within woman's "sphere." Of course, women themselves, as they were the first to say, were in no position to resolve, or even speak out on, substantive policy disputes. "In the present clouded state of the political atmosphere," Kate Berry advised the readers of *Godey's* in 1851, a woman should "withdraw as much as possible from the threatening storm, and shut her ears from the din of party strife."[82] In the same year Elizabeth Wetherell wrote that the most patriotic thing a woman could do in the present situation was to stay home.[83] Nevertheless, quelling passions among men in sectional politics was no less woman's work than quelling the passions of quarreling children in the home. A man involved in the Mount Vernon project assured women that soothing "sectional feelings and sectional asperities, and reviving . . . fraternal sentiments" was a cause worthy of "the most womanly attributes of women, and to

81 Ibid., 35 Cong., 1 Sess. (May 20, 1858), pp. 2267–68.

82 Kate Berry, "How Can an American Woman Serve Her Country?" *Godey's Lady's Book* 43 (1851): 365.

83 Barbara Welter, "The Cult of True Womanhood, 1820–1860," *American Quarterly* 18 (1966): 172.

which she may appropriately consecrate her highest and her holiest efforts."[84] But how could this be done if woman must remain within her sphere? It could be done by extending the boundaries of the home, so to say, until they were congruent with the boundaries of the nation; or (what amounted to the same thing) they could pull men back psychologically to the home.

Everywhere it was said that women were gentle, conciliatory, patient, quiescent, and forgiving; and everywhere it was also said that these qualities affected the men who existed in their presence. For years Americans had agreed that "the domestic fireside is the great guardian of society against the excesses of human passions,"[85] and now Americans were facing an excess of human passion such as they had not had to face before. Whatever their specific political goals, sentimentalists were hardly suggesting that women should rule, but rather that what they categorized as feminine values and traits should now prevail over masculine ones.[86] In other words, they were saying that if the Union was endangered by aggressive, materialistic, utilitarian *men,* then not women but men imitating women could save the Union simply by ceasing to do what they were doing.

That women could affect politics by changing men, and that they could do so without leaving home, is the theme of one of the most powerful sections in *Uncle Tom's Cabin.* In her chapter on the Bird family, Mrs. Stowe sets sentimental domesticity against the so-called rationality of masculine politics, a confrontation that ends up with the triumph of heart over head. The

---

[84] Wellford, "Address," p. 565.

[85] *The Young Ladies' Class Book,* quoted in Welter, "Cult of True Womanhood," p. 162.

[86] On this point Henry T. Tuckerman was explicit: "The most vital interests of humanity are fostered by a receptive, not an aggressive temper." "Modern Impudence," *Christian Examiner* 65 (1858): 430.

setting is the family's Cincinnati home, where the "light of the cheerful fire shone on the rug and carpet of a cosey parlor" and to which John Bird, a state senator, has just returned for some "good home living" after a session of the legislature that, with his support, has passed a law forbidding people to assist fugitive slaves. Mary Bird is the standard inhabitant of woman's sphere—her family is "her entire world" and she "wouldn't give a fip for all your politics, generally," but she is outraged that the law would command people to act against their humane feelings. Bird patronizingly tells her that the law is "not a matter of private feeling,—there are great public interests involved." She rejects his argument, not on the basis of the quality of his reasoning, but because he reasons at all in such a matter. "I hate reasoning, John,—especially reasoning on such subjects," she tells him. "There's a way you political folks have of coming round and round a plain right thing; and you don't believe in it yourselves."[87]

No sooner does she say this than she is proven correct, for who should now appear at their kitchen door but Eliza, having just crossed on the ice. The great issue of the day thus enters woman's sphere. Of course the Birds help Eliza to make good her escape, and the way that Mrs. Stowe sets this up involves the emotions of her readers by reaching out to the common American experience of the death of a child. Explaining why she has fled from a master she admits was "kind" to her, Eliza asks Mrs. Bird (and all America) whether she has ever lost a child. It transpires that it has been only a month "since a darling child of the family had been laid in the grave." "Then you will feel for me," says Eliza to all readers of the book who knew that experience. Her son was about to be sold away from her—not because her master was cruel but because he was in debt. Indeed the Birds do feel for her, and, at the sena-

---

[87] Stowe, *Uncle Tom's Cabin*, pp. 82–85.

tor's suggestion, give to her child the clothes of their dead one.[88]

The charge against men here is not that they cannot feel, but that they use politics and language to alienate themselves from their feelings. Senator Bird is an eloquent and persuasive man; indeed he

> had not been exceeded by any of his brethren at Washington, in the sort of eloquence which has won for them immortal renown! How sublimely he had . . . scouted all sentimental weakness of those who would put the welfare of a few miserable fugitives before great state interests!

But "his idea of a fugitive was only an idea of the letters that spell the word," thereby making it easy for him to talk himself and others into supporting the legislation. When he finally encounters a fugitive—when the word becomes one with the thing—the powerful structure of his mind cannot prevail against the flood from his heart.[89]

Because of the aura of radicalism that immediately surrounded *Uncle Tom's Cabin* and the passions the book aroused, it has been easy to overlook the profoundly conservative implications of Mrs. Stowe's sentimental politics. Their nature is revealed by her proslavery opponents' exact imitation of her methods to achieve opposite results. It is revealed moreover in the way that, in the matter at hand, the cult of domesticity was exploited with great effect by Americans whose first priority was neither to free or keep the slave but to save the Union. Mrs. Stowe, Everett, and (as we will see) Lincoln all at length understood that the essence of what we call the crisis of the Union was not a conflict between one group that wanted to preserve a particular way of life or value

88 Ibid., pp. 85–94.
89 Ibid., p. 93.

and another group that wanted to destroy it. The conflict was one in which many groups competed—all of them conservatives who sought to preserve cherished values and traditions that had come into conflict with other cherished values and traditions. There is, to be sure, a case to be made that the conflict between the sections was or became a revolution, but it was a revolution without revolutionaries.

The second cult that the sentimentalists used to maximum advantage, that of George Washington, seemed to reach a peak in the 1850s. "The name of Washington is constantly on our lips," Walt Whitman said in 1858 without a trace of irony. "His portrait hangs from every wall, and he is almost canonized in the affections of our people."[90] (Even in fiction: a portrait of Washington hangs on the wall over the fireplace in Uncle Tom's cabin, suggesting one source of the slave's saintly virtues and strength.[91]) A magazine reported that "all that can now be recalled, relating even indirectly to our earliest President, commands such interest and attention."[92] New biographies of Washington appeared, although there were many already in print. Both Edward Everett and Washington Irving published lives of the founder during the decade, and Crosby, Nichols and Company brought out E. Cecil's *Life of George Washington,* intended for children, in 1858. After *Graham's* began to serialize J. T. Headley's biography of Washington in 1854, the magazine received a flood of new subscriptions, "for which we were scarcely prepared."[93]

As Edward Everett traveled about the country, he found

[90] Walt Whitman, *I Sit and Look Out: Editorials from the Brooklyn Daily Times,* ed. Emory Holloway and Vernolian Schwarz (New York: Columbia University Press, 1932), p. 59.

[91] Stowe, *Uncle Tom's Cabin,* p. 25.

[92] "The Boston Ladies' Reception of Washington," *Putnam's Monthly* 9 (1857): 154.

[93] "Business Matters," *Graham's Magazine* 44 (1854): 346.

that beneath the recurrent political crises there lay a foundation of deep emotion that united Americans far more than politics divided them, that despite "the bitter dissensions of the day . . . this one great sentiment—veneration for the name of Washington—is planted down in the very depths of the American heart." Everywhere in the Union the name of Washington "touched the same sympathetic chord," and called up the same affections and memories. That being the case, how could there ever be disunion? Americans might, to be sure, "have their sectional loves and hatreds, but before the dear name of Washington, they are absorbed and forgotten."[94] Others appeared to share his optimism. John J. Crittenden said in 1852 that the memory of Washington still "exercises a great influence over the hearts of all true Americans. . . . In times of trouble and peril all our hearts naturally turn to him."[95] For this reason even Henry T. Tuckerman, a writer who ranks among the leaders of American pessimists in the 1850s, concluded that not all of the results of political turmoil were negative. "The fanaticism of party strife," he declared, "has awakened the wise and loyal to a consciousness of the inestimable value of that great example and canonized name, as a bond of union, a conciliating memory, and a glorious watchword."[96] This example stood as a rebuke to modern politicians. Washington was removed as far as possible from the world of politics by his admirers, who pointed out that he was chosen for office not in a caucus or convention, but "in the hearts of the people."[97]

It is a sign of the prevalence of this sentimental way of thinking about Washington that the fact that he was after all a rebel played so small a part in his popular image, despite

[94] Boston *Daily Advertiser*, July 7, 1858. See also Everett, *Orations and Speeches*, 4:235.

[95] Quoted in Mrs. Chapman Coleman, ed., *The Life of John J. Crittenden, With Selections from His Correspondence and Speeches*, 2 vols. (Philadelphia: J. B. Lippincott Co., 1871), 2:27.

[96] [Tuckerman], "Holidays," p. 363.

[97] Everett, *Orations and Speeches*, 4:23.

reminders of the type John C. Calhoun made in his last speech to the Senate in 1850.[98] The conservative and renunciatory qualities of Washington dominated versions of his character to the point that by the middle of the century his cult in many ways had overlapped that of domesticity. Tuckerman, for example, asserted that the virtues that had produced triumph in the Revolution—virtues such as "unselfish devotion and patient self-respect"—were "the great reconciling principles of . . . domestic life" as well as of historical action.[99] As if registering a shift in emphasis (as well as perhaps criticizing Andrew Jackson), a magazine stated in 1829 that the

> character of George Washington, pre-eminent as it is for those civil and military talents which were peculiarly his . . . was not less exalted in the private walks of life, and distinguished for all those domestic endearments which were daily exemplified in the bosom of his family.[100]

Indeed of all aspects of Washington's character, the ones that came to be most celebrated were those associated with his love of "domestic felicity."[101] Paradoxically, although he was "the first man of [his] age," and probably of any age, "his great desire was to occupy a private station."[102] Patriotic duty sometimes required Washington to leave home, but everyone knew (for he

[98] "The Union [cannot] be saved by invoking the name of the illustrious Southerner whose mortal remains repose on the western bank of the Potomac. He was one of us—a slaveholder and a planter. We have studied his history, and find nothing in it to justify submission to wrong. On the contrary, his great fame rests on the solid foundation that, while he was careful to avoid doing wrong to others, he was prompt and decided in repelling wrong." *Congressional Globe,* 31 Cong., 1 Sess. (March 4, 1850), p. 454.

[99] [Henry T. Tuckerman], "The Character of Washington," *North American Review* 83 (1856): 29.

[100] "Mount Vernon," *Casket* 4 (1829): 505.

[101] Everett, *Orations and Speeches,* 4:20.

[102] Robert F. Stockton, in William Hincks and F. H. Smith, eds., *Washington's Birthday: Congressional Banquet in Honor of George Washington, and the Principles of Washington* (Washington: Buell & Blanchard, 1852), p. 4.

said it often) that he would rather be a private citizen at Mount Vernon than be anyplace else in, or emperor of, the world. "From beneath that humble roof went forth the intrepid and unselfish warrior . . . ; to that he returned happiest when his work was done."[103] Washington could have "made himself emperor of the United States. Why did he not do it?" asked a writer as he prepared to suggest that it was Washington's love of domesticity that saved Americans from monarchy. "There can be no doubt that a love of home and native soil, and of the shade of retirement was one of the master passions of his mind."[104]

Edward Everett on his tour took advantage of these themes by suggesting that, like Washington, he also had abandoned the realm of politics, or rather transcended it. More than three years after the Mount Vernon series had begun, and while it was still continuing, he evidently had no difficulty making the claim that since leaving the Senate he had "abstained from all participation in political action of any kind." He derided politics, political ambition, political issues, and political parties. He knew how unsatisfying it all was, and had therefore turned to the "more congenial" and certainly "more useful occupation [of] seeking to rally the affections of my countrymen, North and South."[105] His intent here is clear: the whole purpose of his effort for Mount Vernon was to plead with the nation to imitate him (as he imitated Washington) in his flight from the man's world of politics to the maternal sphere of domesticity.

The celebration of maternal values extended ultimately to the fathers themselves as, in the 1850s particularly, people began to comment on the feminine qualities in their characters. "Jefferson in some respects resembled woman," a writer noted without aversion in 1858. "Like woman, he was constant

---

103 Everett, *Orations and Speeches*, 4:45.
104 "Where Are We?" *Southern Literary Messenger* 19 (1853): 237.
105 Everett, *Orations and Speeches*, 4:235.

rather than passionate; he had her refinement, disliking rude company and coarse pleasures,—her love of luxury, and fondness for things whose beauty consists in part in their delicacy and fragility."[106] In the case of Washington, some accounts of the father of his country seemed prepared to transform him into the *mother* of his country. *Putnam's Monthly* suggested in 1854 that Washington's countenance grew more womanly as he grew older.[107] According to one description of his appearance on the balcony of Federal Hall in New York to take the presidential oath in 1789, Washington first "bows to the people; and, then, sinks, exhausted, into a chair. The fearless soldier of the Monongahela, is a woman, in that presence." There was of course a lesson here. "Then, only, is our nature perfected, when the strong man is blended, in it, with the loving woman."[108] In the middle 1850s, a Virginian lecturing both on Washington and on mothers combined his subjects in a blurring sentimental haze, conveying the impression that the power of the memory of the first did not differ from that of the second. "In the most insensate soul," he suggested,

> there are treasured associations and memories, which forgotten amid the wild tumult of angry passion, awaken at the whisper of a mother's name to beat in every pulsation of the heart and thrill through every fibre of the frame. There is a sentiment of holy veneration in the soul of the child to its mother, which he must sound the lowest depths of human infamy who may forget or disregard.[109]

106 [William Dorsheimer], "Thomas Jefferson," *Atlantic Monthly* 2 (1858): 800.

107 "Washington's Early Days," *Putnam's Monthly* 3 (1854): 4.

108 George Washington Doane, *One World; One Washington: The Oration, in the City Hall, Burlington, on Washington's Birth-day, 1859; By Request of the Lady Managers of the Mount Vernon Association, and Many Citizens of Burlington* (Burlington, N.J.: Ladies' Mount Vernon Association, 1859), pp. 19–20.

109 Wellford, "Address," p. 564.

What is probably the most famous speech on the achievement of the founders employed a phrase commonly used to describe the act of giving birth: "our fathers brought forth."[110]

The point of the convergence of the celebration of domesticity and the celebration of Washington to the point that Washington was made to resemble a mother almost as much as a father was not so much to emasculate men as to infantilize Americans generally. The home that the Union-saving sentimentalists evoked was not, after all, the home of modern reality, but of memory. If "return home" was a metaphor for the political restoration of the beginning of the Republic, it was also a metaphor for psychological regression to the simultaneous beginning of the self.

Changes in "national mood," even though we witness and experience them in our own lives, are among the most difficult developments for historians to account for, or even to describe. In the case at hand, one can scarcely avoid perceiving a great psychological change among the American people generally between about 1848 and 1855—a change barely indicated by recalling in a summary way a series of related developments: the passing of the "Young America" vogue; the waning of the expansionistic consensus; the new interest in "feminine" values, in childhood, and in the home; and the eclipsing of attacks on "the past" by various pleas to return to it. The "past" had been very obviously on the defensive in the 1840s; now, as in the 1820s, it was again an object of widespread veneration, or at least respect. "There may be something beneficent, after all, in this looking back to old times," a writer acknowledged in 1853. "There is, indeed, a certain pathos in the 'past,' which has a charm for most feelings."[111]

[110] Roy P. Basler, ed., *The Collected Works of Abraham Lincoln*, 8 vols. (New Brunswick, N.J.: Rutgers University Press, 1953), 7:23.

[111] William Dowe, "George Washington," *Graham's Magazine* 43 (1853): 37.

Many Americans sought in various ways, as we have seen, to make sense of, and in some cases exploit, their perception that a widespread desire to "return" to the national beginning by restoring the founding principles was as characteristic of the 1850s as a desire to get out and away seemed to characterize the mood of the 1840s. In terms of political institutions, the desire for return manifested itself in the appearance of both the Republicans and the nativist Know-Nothings. Both claimed that the nation was being changed beyond recognition by insidious forces; both called for a return to the purity of the beginning. Like the Republican struggle to restore the Missouri Compromise, the campaign for Mount Vernon was part of the encompassing effort, which had begun over Kansas-Nebraska, to restore the authority of the past and rescue the nation from its degeneration from the standards of the fathers.

Washington's home was a "relic of a noble manly age"[112] now gone—the American beginning—and the call for the restoration of Mount Vernon and pilgrimages to it reflected a more encompassing desire for a journey backward in time to what one writer called "our golden age."[113] But the "past" that Washington's home symbolized was more than the national beginning; it was also the childhood and youth of the post-heroic generation. Appeals to return to the past, or restore the relics and established institutions and policies of the past, took their emotional charge from their appeal to even deeper desires to return to the beginning of the self.[114] It is not

[112] Burrows, "Address," p. 517.

[113] [Joseph Cook], "Conversational Opinions of the Leaders of Secession: A Monograph," *Atlantic Monthly* 10 (1862): 622.

[114] A contemporary analysis of the Know-Nothings suggested, for example, that part of their appeal lay in the power of their ritual to recall and imitate the play of children. "Secret Societies—The Know Nothings," *Putnam's Monthly* 5 (1855): 88–97, esp. 92. The *Southern Literary Messenger* asserted that among adult readers books "such as might be thought to please children, or a half-civilized people, are now the fashion of the day." "We do not want to be roused from this dream of life, that holds captive all our powers." "The Days We Live In," *Southern Literary Messenger* 20 (1854): 759.

an accident that heightened nostalgia for the American beginning coincided with the prevalence of an intense longing
for childhood, and that both desires seemed to grow with the
crisis of the Union.

G. N. Barbour's poem, "An Appeal to Time," illustrates the
personal side of this pervasive wish. Published in 1852, it
began:

> O TIME! give back my childhood days,
>   So fraught with joyous glee;
> With all my boyish pranks and ways—
>   Oh! give them back to me.

It went on to ask:

> Let mother smile upon me now,
>   To see my childish joy;
> Let father kiss my little brow,
>   And call me "darling boy."

And it ended with this plea and promise:

> O Time! give back my childhood days,
>   Those halcyon days of truth,
> And I'll give up my manhood ways,
>   And be once more a youth.[115]

In 1860 the *Saturday Evening Post* published Elizabeth Akers's
poem, "Rock Me To Sleep," which began:

> Backward, turn backward, O Time, in your flight,
>   Make me a child again just for to-night![116]

[115] G. N. Barbour, "An Appeal to Time," *Godey's Lady's Book* 45 (1852): 151.

[116] Elizabeth Akers, *The Sunset Song and other Verses* (Boston: Lee and Shepard, 1902), p. 311.

The piece became very popular at once, made a celebrity of its author, and was set to music by several composers.[117] Such appeals evidently reflected the wishes of many people in the 1850s who sought to recover both the early Republic and their early lives, and thought of both together in the remembered image of the latter.

In this connection the case of Everett is particularly striking, not only because of his almost inescapable presence, but also because he anticipated the psychoanalytic description of the phenomena of transference and regression as he sought the role of therapist to an age gone off course. He knew that in certain ways people do not get far from their childhood; that they do not leave it behind so much as they cover it over with successive layers of mature experience and thought. He encouraged regression—lifting these layers and going back down into childhood.[118] In doing this, he was by no means alone.

[117] "During the Civil War it was printed on leaflets and scattered by thousands in the army." Ibid., p. 309.

[118] Regression is defined in psychoanalysis as "the *re-emergence* of modes of mental functioning which were characteristic of the psychic activity of the individual during earlier periods of development." Jacob A. Arlow and Charles Brenner, *Psychoanalytic Concepts and the Structural Theory* (New York: International Universities Press, 1964), p. 71. Freud wrote that "every earlier stage of development persists alongside the later stage which has arisen from it. . . . The primitive stages can always be re-established." Sigmund Freud, "Thoughts for the Times on War and Death," *The Standard Edition of the Complete Psychological Works of Sigmund Freud,* ed. and trans. James Strachey, 24 vols. (London: Hogarth Press and the Institute of Psycho-Analysis, 1953–73), 14:285–86. In asserting that a longing for a part-imagined, part-remembered childhood was both widespread in the 1850s and politically significant, I do not mean to argue that regressive desires characterized the mentality of all Americans, or even of any Americans in all respects, at that time. Obviously, as is true with all great political crises in history, large numbers of people managed to escape altogether the anxieties that inspired these wishes. Moreover, people who did not escape them would not necessarily have faced any difficulty functioning normally in other realms. Regression need not connote illness or even abnormality; it can be partial and temporary. Therapists

In the 1850s not only Everett's but the metaphorical language of the sentimentalists generally facilitated and encouraged regression by giving sharp focus and definition to inchoate desires that were widely shared. The emotional connections they drew between present political anxieties and childhood experiences helped to illuminate the road back—a road that, as they suspected and Freud confirmed, was already paved. When Abraham Lincoln spoke at the close of his First Inaugural of the mystic chords of memory, he used the word *chords* to mean strings in two different senses, which he combined. He talked of chords in the sense of the strings of a musical instrument of the emotions—which would "yet swell the chorus of the Union, when again touched, as surely they will be, by the better angels of our nature." But he was also talking about *cords* of memory —strings, "bonds of affection" that linked "every battle-field, and patriot grave, to every living heart and hearthstone, all over this broad land."[119] Memory was a string both to bind and to be played, and sentimentalists used it in both senses.

The sentimentalists who encouraged regression had in mind a social goal—to restore the Republic to its early virtue—that they sought to achieve psychologically, by restoring the individual to *its* early virtue. Both the Republic and individual members of the post-heroic cohort were better earlier than they

have long been familiar with people like the businessman, for example, who might describe "his efficient and successful activities in a highly complex business or profession, while he behaves with us so often as if he were passive, helpless, and childlike." Martin H. Stein, "The Problem of Character Theory," *Journal of the American Psychoanalytic Association* 17 (1969): 695.

[119] Basler, *Works of Lincoln,* 4:271. This was conventional sentimental language, and was suggested to Lincoln by William H. Seward. Cf. a writer's comments on the effects of the poems of Felicia Hemans on Horace Greeley: "These touched a new chord in his heart." "Horace Greeley," *Putnam's Monthly* 6 (1855): 79. Also, Daniel Webster, according to a contemporary, "felt that all the primal instincts of patriotism—all the chords of the heart— bound men to their own state, and not to the common country." George S. Hillard, quoted in S. P. Lyman, *The Public and Private Life of Daniel Webster: Including Most of His Great Speeches, Letters from Marshfield, &c., &c.,* 2 vols. (Philadelphia: John E. Potter and Co., 1852), 2:212.

were in the 1850s in the sense that the earlier world was simpler and (so it seemed) characterized by fraternal regard. This world was not lost, and could be regained, because it was still there in what one writer called "the wide empire of memory."[120]

The technique of the sentimentalists was based on the then-prevailing concept, itself a precursor of psychoanalysis, that the mind worked mechanically by associations and that it could grasp and fix a new idea if the idea resembled what was already known. Similarly, an abstraction could be made emotionally significant if it could be associated with objects already close and important to the mind. People could be made to feel, for instance, that the problem of the Union was actually their own personal problem and that they had a stake in the way it was resolved. Association theory, which like much of the rest of psychological thought was based on an analogy to physics, took the mechanistic view that thought ran along channels carved out by associated memories. In a sense it amounted to a psychological equivalent of the legal concept of precedent. Like the law, the mind refers to and builds upon its previous workings. Taking the view that the imagination was essentially passive and mechanistic, the theory held not only that words had the power to evoke images in the person who heard them, but that these images were the result of the manipulation and linking of other, remembered images, and that these words could also evoke the emotion attached to the original image. Applying this theory to their own needs, sentimentalists acted on the belief that certain common words evoked common images and common emotions, and that these emotions could be mobilized in the service of political or social causes. Daniel Webster once said, for example, that "all experience evinces that human sentiments are strongly influenced by associations,"[121] and the content of his oratory argues that he meant it. Conservatives who were unable or unwilling to seek and

[120] "Declaration of Independence," *Casket* 7 (1832): 50.
[121] Webster, *Writings and Speeches,* 2:70.

wield power through politics were quite aware that they could still call upon "the power of association—one of the subtlest, strongest forces that can stir the human heart and life."[122]

The psychological function of the cult of domesticity in politics was to provide a vivid model for the organization and manipulation of the regressive tendencies that were everywhere evident. By subtly comparing themselves (and behind themselves, the founders) to mothers, the sentimentalists reminded Americans of the childhood home they had only physically left. The domestic categories they applied to political and social life and the emotions they sought to awake and transfer from one realm to the other reflected their assumption that the memories they had in mind existed in a common storehouse. Just to use the word "home" was to touch the magic chord and release the memories and perhaps the tears. "Home! How many associations of life and joy are there in that one word!"[123]

> *Home.* . . . Perhaps there is no other word in language that clusters within it so many and so stirring meanings,—that calls into play, and powerfully excites, so many feelings. . . . "Home,"—murmur but its name, and memories start around it that put fire into the brain, and affections that almost suffocate or break the heart. . . . "Home,"—what does it not stand for, of strongest, of most moving associations!—for childhood's grief and gladness . . . for a father's embrace, or for his death-bed,—for a mother's kiss, or for her grave.[124]

The purpose of regression, of a fancied retreat within the security of the remembered domestic scene, was, of course, to flee from the prospect of the competition, contentiousness, and

[122] John S. Holmes, Boston *Daily Advertiser,* July 7, 1858.

[123] F[rederick] A[ugustus] F[arley], "Household Education," *Christian Examiner* 46 (1849): 443.

[124] [Henry Giles], "Economies," ibid., p. 241.

even violence that might rage without—and would indeed rage if Americans continued to follow the business-as-usual path of its degenerated adult male leadership. Nothing could be more secure than the home, and nothing could be more innocent than childhood[125]—or so it was taken for granted. "What is so beautiful as childhood?" asked a writer in *Graham's Magazine* in 1841. "Where can we find such purity and frankness, such an absence of all selfishness, as in the love of children?"[126] A poetaster's lines in *Godey's Lady's Book* were scarcely different from those of countless others who played the theme:

> Infancy, blest infancy, that ne'er knew
> A thought less bright than rosy morn.[127]

But the ironic result of regression was that, instead of thwarting, it encouraged aggression, and indeed made it possible by providing a vivid image of violence and by stating the conditions under which violence might occur. Hardly the least of the contributions of the sentimentalists to the crisis of the Union was the compelling image of fratricide they created as the dreaded alternative to the domestic placidity they hoped to restore. In warning against violence, however, the sentimentalists did not realize that they were playing into the hands of the deepest fantasies of the people they sought to calm. In at least two respects the flight to childhood was naive and even dangerous. For one thing, regression holds out the promise of removing rivals. From a world characterized by the competition of brothers for the exclusive possession of an estate, Americans were encouraged to retreat psychically to a world in which

[125] The readers of one magazine were urged to "raise [themselves] to the level of children's innocence." "Claims of the Beautiful Arts," *United States Magazine and Democratic Review* 3 (1838): 261.

[126] "Brother and Sister," *Graham's Magazine* 19 (1841): 145.

[127] Virginius Hutchen, "An Apostrophe to Memory," *Godey's Lady's Book* 43 (1851): 178.

possession of the mother had been probably exclusive, and in which compromise was irrelevant. The Union-saving sentimentalists seemed to reject the political world after 1854, partly because they feared that politics could not any longer achieve compromises that were meaningful or that could work. They urged Americans to seek emotional reunion "before the tomb of Washington" and to develop new ways of cooperating with one another that ran deeper than politics. But the regression they encouraged did not involve selfless love so much as it did a wish for a time when exclusivity was possible and when the great mother territory did not need to be shared.

For another thing, the equating of childhood with innocence (an equation reinforced by the analogous belief that the early Republic was virtuous) was a peculiar conceit of a period that was post-Calvinist and pre-Freudian. The post-heroic cohort's predecessors a century earlier did not—and their successors a century later would not—share it. But the image that Americans of this period had of childhood (though not always of the actual children who existed at their knees) prevented them from seeing that children (the lasting childish part of themselves which regression liberated in distorted form) worked up and reveled in fantasies of violence. They had either forgotten or never understood that a childhood lived just this side of the Revolution had probably unavoidably been a breeding ground for fratricidal fantasies, and that to return to childhood was to call these fantasies back again. But such was the case: the sentimental flight from the dangerous and fearsome patricidal tendencies they attributed to Young America liberated something that turned out to be much worse: the fratricidal impulses of the post-heroic generation. We cannot, of course, know what might have happened at the end of the 1850s if a man like Emerson had succeeded in organizing culture, and if a man like Douglas had succeeded in organizing politics, on the basis of the autonomy of their generation. If patricide in this sense had been permitted to occur, fratricide might have been avoided. But of course what I have been arguing is that it was naive of Emerson and Douglas ever to have thought that they could have gotten away with it.

6

THE LITERATURE OF
FRATRICIDE: CIVIL WAR AS
MEMORY AND PROSPECT

The age seeks exaggeration,—delights in storms and
monsters. This taste appears in the prevailing tendencies of the drama, and of romantic literature, as
well as of the periodical press.

Christian Examiner, 1839

But for the prophecy the history would not be.

BRONSON ALCOTT, 1840

The metaphor of the house divided, which comes from the
New Testament,[1] became a commonplace early in the crisis of
the Union when sentimentalists insisted that there was only
one alternative to fraternal affection among Americans. "If a
house be divided against itself, it will fall," Daniel Webster
declared in 1851, "and crush everybody in it."[2] Among people

---

[1] Matt. 12:25, Mark 3:25, Luke 11:17.

[2] Daniel Webster, *The Writings and Speeches of Daniel Webster,* 18 vols.
(Boston: Little, Brown and Co., 1903), 4:244. "A nation divided against it-
self cannot stand." Sam Houston, *Congressional Globe,* 31 Cong., 1 Sess.
(February 8, 1850), appendix, p. 102; Don E. Fehrenbacher, *Prelude to Great-*

for whom the preservation of the Union was the highest political priority, it was a convention of speech throughout the postheroic age that peaceable disunion was not possible. "It would be done in blood."[3] In other words, there could be no disunion without war "of the deadliest and bloodiest type, in which a man's foes should be those of his own household."[4] "The hand of brother will be raised against brother, and our country will run with rivers of blood."[5] The Union-saving sentimentalists exactly counterpoised their exhortations to fraternal love with imagery of fratricidal terror. The prospect of civil war was drummed into the national consciousness and made vivid and real by the people who feared it the most. By 1860 the idea that these stark alternatives were the only choices before the nation amounted to a conviction from which few Northerners dissented.

On a conscious (or at least explicit) level it was everywhere agreed that fratricide was the worst fate that could befall the Republic, a convention of rhetoric that permitted indulgence in graphic detail of predictions of the course a fratricidal conflict would take if it were not avoided. For a characteristic example of the direction such fantasies took, we may examine one that was spoken in the House of Representatives early in 1860 by Elijah Babbitt, a Republican from Pennsylvania. His scenario began with the prediction that postsecession Southern-

ness: *Lincoln in the 1850's* (Stanford: Stanford University Press, 1962), pp. 183–84.

[3] Elijah Babbitt, *Congressional Globe,* 36 Cong., 1 Sess. (January 20, 1860), p. 546.

[4] Edward Everett, *Orations and Speeches on Various Occasions,* 4 vols. (Boston: Little, Brown and Co., 1850–68), 4:240.

[5] Garnett B. Adrain, *Congressional Globe,* 36 Cong., 1 Sess. (December 13, 1859), p. 136. See also "Our Country," *American Whig Review* 1 (1845): 276; Richard S. Donnell, *Congressional Globe,* 30 Cong., 2 Sess. (February 19, 1849), appendix, pp. 238–39; Sam Houston, ibid., 31 Cong., 1 Sess. (February 8, 1850), appendix, p. 99; Lewis Cass, ibid. (February 11, 1850), p. 331; John W. Noell, ibid., 36 Cong., 1 Sess. (December 12, 1859), p. 118.

ers, no longer having a legal means of retrieving fugitive slaves, would pursue them across the border into the United States. His prophecy then became quite vivid:

> You would pursue them across the line, and there would be resistance, bloodshed, retaliations, burnings, and arsons; and all sections of this Union would then inevitably be drawn into a bloody war, and the land be deluged in fraternal blood. It is just as inevitable as that water will find its own level. Feuds which exist between members of the same families, where they do exist, are the most bitter of all feuds. Wars . . . between . . . the same people, are the most bloody, the most savage, and the longest continued, of any wars that take place in this world. All history attests the fact. Along this line of a thousand miles—a line, perhaps, which might run just by this Capitol—contending armies would continually fight, and desolate both sides of the line by fire and the sword. No family could live near it. The country would soon return back to its original state of uncultivated nature, to its own primeval forests. No man would desire to live, or could live here; but the wolf and the panther, which long years ago prowled in this then unbroken wilderness, would return to their former home. The howl of the wolf and the scream of the panther would again be heard along the banks of the Potomac—yes, and peradventure breed their young in the deserted Halls of this Capitol. It would be a retrogression of two hundred years in civilization backward towards barbarism. . . . The industry of the country would die out, and the whole land would become a howling wilderness. Ay, sir, and another indubitable consequence would be, that the peculiar institution of the South, slavery . . . would die out. It could not live after the dissolution of this Union.[6]

Although vivid, this warning was but a variation on a settled convention. Other versions differed from Babbitt's, but usually

[6] Ibid. (January 20, 1860), p. 546.

only in detail. Where he saw two contending sections, others saw fragmentation extending to the point of petty, mutually hostile military principalities, or even beyond that to anarchistic end points that resisted precise imagery. Where he saw a return to the barbarism of nature, others saw the rise of the barbarism of tyranny and the reuniting of the nation under the hand of a military despot.[7] But all versions saw a progression from separation to fratricidal war to utter ruin. None could envision a separation resolved short of war, or a war halted short of destruction.[8] Thus the sentimentalists' great gift to history and historiography was their concept of the inevitability, under certain circumstances, of civil war.

The house-divided image helps us understand why peaceable reunion of the states, though in theory no less possible than civil war, did not follow secession, in 1861 or ever. So identified had the ideas of secession and civil war become, that many people assumed after secession occurred that civil war could not be far behind. This is a great irony, of course, for the purpose behind the rhetorical connection was not to ensure that civil war would follow secession, but that people would be so intimidated by the prospect of civil war that they would not attempt secession. It did not work, and the only role sentimentalist imagery could play after secession was to make civil war seem unavoidable.

Still, it would be a mistake to satisfy ourselves that the imagery of the house divided served only the function of warning. For one thing, it is highly stylized; the qualities of

[7] Henry Clay, *Congressional Globe,* 31 Cong., 1 Sess. (February 6, 1850), appendix, p. 127; Lewis Cass, ibid. (February 11, 1850), p. 331.

[8] Horace Mann, ibid. (February 15, 1850), appendix, p. 221; Isaac P. Walker, ibid. (March 8, 1850), appendix, p. 285; Everett, *Orations and Speeches,* 4:50. Some Southerners insisted on the other hand that disunion need not and would not be followed by civil war. See, for instance, Jeremiah Clemens, *Congressional Globe,* 31 Cong., 1 Sess. (February 20, 1850), p. 398; Sydenham Moore, ibid., 36 Cong., 1 Sess. (December 8, 1859), p. 72; "The Prospect before Us," *Southern Quarterly Review* 19 (1851): 537–38.

ritual and convention which are so apparent worked against the dynamic of a warning, which would seem to require more spontaneity in order to be effective. Just as the Southern threat of secession became "shopworn" over time as it assumed the status of an incantation,[9] so the Northern counterthreat of civil war grew less effective as it grew more insistent. For another thing, the fantasies of civil war are conspicuously devoid of technological content. To note this is not to assert the obvious fact that they did not envision the American Civil War of 1861–65 with all the advances in the development of machines and munitions that accompanied it. It is to assert that only incidentally were they concerned with machines and munitions at all. The matter is one of scale and orientation: the images are personal and they are primeval rather than futuristic. Babbitt does not see machines taking over the world, but rather panthers and wolves, while industry dies out. Such images sought to do more than warn; they were meant to have an aesthetic appeal in their own right.

The imagery that Elijah Babbitt summarized so vividly was older than the conflict between the sections over slavery and, though it was invoked most often in that context, bore no necessary relation to it. As early as 1800 Daniel Webster, then a student in college, foresaw civil war between one part of the Union and another, but hoped that the "manes" of the deceased Washington would help keep the Republic united.[10] Mason L. Weems wrote that disunion was Washington's greatest dread, and insisted that it could "never take place without civil war."[11] Indeed, so familiar was the idea of disunion even in his time that Weems worried that it had "worn off half

[9] David M. Potter, *Lincoln and His Party in the Secession Crisis* (New Haven: Yale University Press, 1942), pp. 1–19.

[10] Webster to James Hervey Bingham, February 5, 1800, in Charles M. Wiltse, ed., *The Papers of Daniel Webster, Correspondence* (Hanover, N.H.: University Press of New England, 1974–), 1:28.

[11] Mason L. Weems, *The Life of Washington,* ed. Marcus Cunliffe (Cambridge, Mass.: Harvard University Press, Belknap Press, 1962), p. 219.

its horrors,"—whereupon he sought to revivify them, envisioning at length "a whole nation suddenly filled with terror" as young men go off to war.[12]

He focuses first on the homes they leave behind, loud with the shrieks, groans, and lamentations of disrupted and devastated families. "But all this is but the beginning of sorrows," Weems writes, by way of introducing a carnage he describes almost lovingly. Two armies meet with "all the bitterness and exterminating spirit of a family quarrel." Such is their passion that they battle until one side is slaughtered. "When brethren turn their swords into each other's bowels, war degenerates into murder, and battles into butcheries." The atrocities of fratricide do not exhaust the passion for vengeance; the surviving brothers next turn to invade homes, joyously plundering and killing. But even this is not the end, for now an angry God will punish the abuse of liberty by taking it back and sending in its place

> some proud tyrant, who, looking on our country but as his estate, and ourselves as his cattle, shall waste our wealth on the pomps of his court, or the salaries of his officers; destroy our sons in his ambitious wars, and beggar us with exactions. . . . But, O ye favoured countrymen of Washington! . . . The arm that wrought your political salvation is still stretched out to save; then hear his voice and live! Hear the voice of the Divine Founder of your republic: "Little children love one another." [13]

When Weems and the countless other people who sounded the same ideas over the next sixty years spoke so vividly of civil war, they were not only warning and predicting, they

12 Ibid., pp. 217, 219.

13 Ibid., pp. 220–22. Weems does sometimes seem to forget the difference, but later words in the passage make clear that the Divine Founder quoted here is not Washington.

were also dramatizing shared "memories." Weems was explicit about this: "as was the case in the last war"—the Revolution—is a passage that precedes part of his warning.[14] Indeed, the image of fratricide emerged in American culture not in the context of speculation about the future but in the context of historical explanation. Fratricide may have been a terrifying prospect in the post-heroic period, but it was also something that in some sense had already occurred. Thus regression to childhood involved, among other things, the calling up of a *memory* of *imagined* fratricidal conflict, for it was just before the birth of the post-heroic generation, so its members believed, that the fathers saved the house and the family in a fratricidal war, and it was during their childhood that they could hardly avoid hearing about and imagining the adventures they had missed.

In the nineteenth century it was quite common to describe and characterize the American Revolution as primarily a civil conflict. James Fenimore Cooper, in the last of the four romances he wrote about it, called the contest a "civil war" which saw "husband divided against wife—son against father —brother against sister."[15] Daniel Webster also called the Revolution a "civil war" that Americans fought "on their own soil and at their own doors."[16] Perhaps no one did more to fix this image than Weems, who in his biography of Washington treated not only the conflict he feared but also the one he remembered as a "great civil war." He recounts a dream he claims Washington's mother had when her son was a boy. Their house caught fire. Young George put it out, and then urged that it be restored with newer and better materials. This

[14] Ibid., p. 221.

[15] James Fenimore Cooper, *Wyandotté; or, The Hutted Knoll, The Works of James Fenimore Cooper*, 33 vols. (New York: G. P. Putnam's Sons, [1895–1900]), 21:120–21.

[16] Webster, *Writings and Speeches*, 1:244.

was "certainly a very curious dream," Weems acknowledges on the way to explicating it. The fire stands for "civil war" and the new roof for the Union, which, "by guarding alike the welfare of all, ought by all to be so heartily beloved as to *endure for ever.*" The house itself was built earlier—we do not know when—and now needed only to be saved, restored, and, in the process, improved.[17]

William Gilmore Simms was yet another prominent author who wrote of the Revolution as "fierce civil warfare . . . when neighbours were arrayed against one another, and when, on one side, negroes and Indians formed allies, contributing . . . additional forms of terror."[18] He knew that the focal point of modern interest in the war was the guerrilla-domestic (what he and the period generally called the "partisan") quality of a great part of the military struggle. In part this was a response to the particular events of the Revolution. "The war,—the partisan conflicts excepted,—presented few striking instances of strategic excellence, or audacious valor," a Southern journal observed.

> It was a war waged languidly on both sides; and would have been almost without interest, but for the civil conflicts of the country. In these alone, may be found any very striking materials for such histories as belong to the romantic periods of European progress.[19]

That this kind of thinking was ahistorical is beside the point. The fascination with guerrilla warfare amounted to a desire that did not depend on—indeed triumphed over—fact. One

[17] Weems, *Life of Washington*, pp. 57–58.

[18] W[illiam] Gilmore Simms, *The Partisan: A Romance of the Revolution* (New York: W. J. Widdleton, 1870), p. 53.

[19] "Headley's Life of Cromwell," *Southern Quarterly Review* 14 (1848): 521.

writer who recognized that in military terms the war did not meet romantic requirements suggested some changes in it.

> Washington's war was the noblest basis of a commonwealth; and since the beginning of the world no nation ever had so splendid an origin. . . . Still, we confess, when we consider what is due to the important picturesque of these things—or, rather, due from *that* to the future sentiment of a nation—we feel inclined to make some change in the course of the war. We would . . . have Washington defeated, decisively, by over-powering odds, like Aristomenes, Bruce, Vasa and the rest, and driven into the fastnesses of the Alleghenies, where he should live for some time, in a prowling condition, on wild animals and Indian corn, with a price upon his head, and surrounded by a few ever-faithful adherents—his adventures being too much enveloped in secrecy for an exact historic account, and amply suiting all the requirements of tradition—till the rallying of the Eastern States and the crowding of backwoodsmen to his standard, should enable him to march out again, scatter a number of detachments, and fall upon Howe with determination, defeating him with great slaughter, in the renowned and beautiful valley of the Mohawk. This, certainly, would be an improvement.[20]

Other writers, less aware perhaps of the distinction between history and desire, merely wrote out their fantasies as though they were facts. Guerrilla warfare was simply more interesting than warfare of a more formal sort, and the Revolution had to be adjusted retroactively to meet this standard.

> The annals of border war . . . are always tinged with romance; without the pomp and circumstance attending the movement of armies, border warfare is ever the most bloody; our own was peculiarly so; . . . those who flourished in the

[20] "American Arts and American Arms," *Graham's Magazine* 44 (1854): 88.

double honor of traitor and fratricide, were always striking
valiant blows upon weak adversaries, and fighting desperate
battles with women and children.[21]

Now we are closer to the point: partisan warfare was more interesting than any other kind because it involved the whole
family and enveloped the home.

James Russell Lowell once observed that "the mythic instinct
erelong begins to shape things as they ought to have been,
rather than as they were," and he cited American understanding of the Revolution to illustrate the point.[22] Indeed, Americans did tend to avoid thinking of their Revolution in terms of
a formal conflict between armies. Francis C. Gray wrote that
"it was not, like most wars, a contest between cabinets or
armies, a mere trial of military or diplomatic skill. . . . It does
not indeed excite attention by accounts of very numerous
armies or remarkably bloody battles."[23] People did not talk of
soldiers marching off to war as much as they did of "the
husband, the father, the brother, the son, gone forth on the
errand of peril and death."[24] The war was important and
memorable because it was personal. "The passions of the contest operated directly and intensely on every man."[25] "Even
those who were engaged in the most arduous operations," John
Knapp wrote, were at the same time caught up in "the various
fortunes, and often romantic adventures of heart-formed con-
nexions." European soldiers might march off to their wars in
well-drilled groups and separate themselves from "all domestic
interest and feelings," but "the American soldiery retained in
the fort and field every concern and sympathy of the fireside

21 "Literary Notices," *New-England Magazine* 1 (1831): 448.

22 [James Russell Lowell], "The Rebellion: its Causes and Consequences,"
North American Review 99 (1864): 246.

23 [Francis C. Gray], "Botta's American Revolution," ibid. 13 (1821): 173.

24 Everett, *Orations and Speeches*, 1:556.

25 [Gray], "Botta's American Revolution," p. 174.

and neighbourhood."[26] This was so, at least in part, because
fort was often fireside, and field was often neighborhood.

If the Revolution was close to the childhood of the members
of the post-heroic generation in terms of people they knew, it
was also close in terms of where it was fought. To nineteenth-
century Americans the locus of the Revolution was quite literally near the home. "War itself often found its way to the fireside and severed the strongest and tenderest ties."[27] C. C. Felton
said in 1850 that the lesson of the Revolution was the need to
be prepared to die in defense—literally—of hearth and home.[28]
Another writer in the 1850s claimed that Americans counted
"the terror of households" along with other tribulations of the
Revolution as being among "the greatest treasures of the nation's memory."[29] In an anniversary oration he delivered on
the battle of Lexington, Edward Everett lingered on such domestic terrors, describing the fate in that conflict of a man
named Harrington.

> He fell in front of his own house, on the north of the Com-
> mon. His wife, at the window, saw him fall, and then start
> up, the blood gushing from his breast. He stretched out his
> hands towards her, as if for assistance, and fell again. Rising
> once more on his hands and knees, he crawled across the road
> towards his dwelling. She ran to meet him at the door, but it
> was to see him expire at her feet.[30]

Like Harrington's wife, American women found themselves
involved in the war because it came to them. "Our matrons
and sisters were exposed to the dangers and often heard the

---

[26] [John Knapp], "National Poetry," *North American Review* 8 (1818):
173.

[27] [Gray], "Botta's American Revolution," p. 174.

[28] [C. C. Felton], "Everett's *Orations and Speeches,*" ibid. 71 (1850): 446.

[29] "American Arts and American Arms," p. 87.

[30] Everett, *Orations and Speeches,* 1:555.

tumult of the contest," John Knapp wrote in 1818. "The march of armies was by their own doors, and the battle field not seldom on their patrimonial hills and plains."[31] In a book that received much attention in the 1850s, Elizabeth F. Ellet argued that women in their domestic role played a central part in the outcome of the war. She conceded that men were more conspicuous actors in the conflict, but "what could they have done but for the home-sentiment to which they appealed, and which sustained them in the hour of trial and success?"[32] Ellet argued, moreover, that the chronic quality of the festering crises with Britain provided the foundation for women's crucial historical role. The Revolution was the culmination of more than a decade of recurrent disputes, and during that time the possibility of rebellion became increasingly foreseeable.

> There was time for the nurture, in the domestic sanctuary, of that love of civil liberty, which afterwards kindled into a flame. . . . The talk of matrons, in American homes, was of the people's wrongs, and the tyranny that oppressed them, till the sons who had grown to manhood, with . . . views enlarged to comprehend their invaded rights, stood up prepared to defend them. . . . Patriotic mothers nursed the infancy of freedom.[33]

A critic praising Ellet's book hoped that it would lead other historians to "trace the workings of the politician up, from the feelings engendered by the fireside, and show us how naturally it is that the domestic nature informs and influences the decision, the courage, and the enterprise of the patriot."[34]

[31] [Knapp], "National Poetry," p. 173.

[32] Elizabeth F. Ellet, *The Women of the American Revolution,* 3 vols. (New York: Baker and Scribner, 1850), 1:13.

[33] Ibid., p. 14.

[34] "Ellet's Women of the Revolution," *Southern Quarterly Review* 17 (1850): 314; see also "Review of New Books," *Graham's Magazine* 37 (1850): 325.

The guerrilla and domestic images of the Revolution and of war in general were the most compelling of all possible representations of violence to the post-heroic generation because they linked up to the kinds of unconscious fantasies that must have inhabited their imaginations since infancy. Regression to childlike patterns of thought tended to liberate and highlight these fantasies as well as the gentle affections the sentimentalists recalled as the basis of the emotional world of the past. It is no accident that the language of the crisis of the Union was pervaded with the primal vocabulary of children, and by this I do not mean only talk of fathers, mothers, and houses, but also the vocabulary of violence and dangerous creatures like monsters. "Nations, like man himself, have ends or ideals of existence, which constitute the inmost ground or essence of their being, and when they depart from these, they either degrade themselves into some lower form, or grow into monsters."[35] To Stephen A. Douglas, who was the target of this remark, the nation was like a growing boy. He could never appreciate that others saw it growing out of control into something that was much more grotesque.[36]

Children happen to be anxious, frustrated, aggressive, violent little people—violent in their acts and in their desires. As Anthony Storr has written, "if small babies possessed the physical strength and co-ordination of adolescents we should indeed live in a destructive world."[37] That their ignorance of "reality" leads them to invent fantasies as violent as their thrashings is, according to Erik Erikson, one of "the best documented phenomena in psychoanalytic literature."[38] It also

[35] "The Kansas Question," *Putnam's Monthly* 6 (1855): 433.

[36] Roy P. Basler, ed., *The Collected Works of Abraham Lincoln,* 8 vols. (New Brunswick, N.J.: Rutgers University Press, 1953), 3:55.

[37] Anthony Storr, *Human Destructiveness* (New York: Basic Books, 1972), p. 47.

[38] Erik H. Erikson, *Young Man Luther: A Study in Psychoanalysis and History* (New York: W. W. Norton & Co., 1958), p. 113.

comports with common sense and, for many people, with their own fragmented memories of the way they once saw the world. We forget when we place an infant snug in his crib that to him—not yet mobile and therefore powerless—the walls of the crib might as well be almost as far away as the edge of the universe, and that the shapes that move around him might seem threatening rather than benign, and might just as well be God as parents. The child in objective terms may be secure indeed, but we cannot assume he knows this; his emotions may be closer to anxiety than contentment. The psychic life of children is filled with fantasies of being pursued, ripped apart, and eaten by wolves or dragons.[39] Nor are such fears confined to infants. According to a study published in 1977 by the Foundation for Child Development, interviews with more than 2,200 children between the ages of seven and eleven revealed that two-thirds of them feared that "somebody bad" might come into their houses.[40] Children tend to respond to such imagined threats by retaliation in the form of the invention of fantasies of violence they would like to inflict.

Although children have murderous desires in all directions, parricidal and fratricidal urges dominate because the respective family members—especially the mother, in the experience of most people—are close at hand and the source of real and imagined insults. From her observation of small children, Melanie Klein concluded not only that such fantasies are a "regular component of [their] mental life" but that "the real objects behind those imaginary, terrifying figures are the child's own parents, and that those dreadful shapes in some way or other reflect the features of its father and mother, however distorted and phantastic the resemblance may be." She

[39] Melanie Klein, *Contributions to Psycho-Analysis, 1921–1945* (London: Hogarth Press and the Institute of Psycho-Analysis, 1950), pp. 267–77.

[40] Richard Flaste, "Survey Finds That Most Children Are Happy at Home but Fear World," New York *Times*, March 2, 1977.

also found that the objects of childish aggression are the same people. "When the child's aggressive instincts are at their height it never tires of tearing and cutting up, breaking, wetting and burning all sorts of things like paper, matches, boxes, small toys, all of which represent its parents and brothers and sisters."[41] If Klein was correct, each person carries with him in life the memories of a past that was violent in fact and fantasy. In our case these fantasies conspicuously resemble the imagery with which a simultaneous history was remembered.

To exploit these theories in connection with the subject at hand, let us turn to literature and specifically to the historical romance. During the post-heroic age the image of fratricidal civil war to structure both the history of the Revolution and the possibility of another war was shaped and standardized, even institutionalized, in the literary genre of the romance (and to a lesser degree in the melodrama). The genre was more romantic than historical—dependent more on the conventions of fiction than the actualities of history—for any glance at one of them reveals a realm where memory and expectation (whether fear or desire) become almost indistinguishable. They contain the same archetypal fantasies and images we find in the orations and the cautionary biographies about revolutionary figures, but are even more rewarding to investigation because they are more sustained and more complex in development.

As its name suggests, there is an anomalous quality to the historical romance, for it purports to merge the antagonistic entities of what happened with (to quote Clara Reeve's definition of the romance) "what never happened nor is likely to happen."[42] The ground on which the two were in effect compromised was the domestic scene, which if it did not re-

[41] Klein, *Contributions to Psycho-Analysis*, pp. 268, 274.
[42] Quoted in René Wellek and Austin Warren, *Theory of Literature*, 3rd ed. (New York: Harcourt, Brace & World, Harvest Books, [1962]), p. 216.

solve at least veiled the problem of plausibility by permitting the development of events within the confines and customs of everyday life. The historical romance, indeed, facilitated the tendency of the age to merge (and by merging confuse) political history with family life, because the conventions of the novel shaped stories in the same personal, domestic, and emotional way that Americans structured their own worlds. The house provided the setting and the family provided the structure for their plots, with the result that history was shaped by these conventions more than the other way around. Thus the real source of what happens in a romance is desire. Responsible to plausibility but not really to fact, it enjoyed broad freedom to create the past or at least to emphasize certain aspects of the past in accordance with the way things should have been and might yet be.

Several American historical romances gave the sanction of history to fratricidal fantasies and desires. A child growing up in the early nineteenth century could have vaguely sensed a congruence between the nature of the greatest deeds in history and his own nature, thereby validating what would otherwise be a source of anxiety and guilt. Here and nowhere else did the actions of the fathers comport with the desire for action on the part of the sons. The fathers had saved the house and restored it through fratricide. If need be, could not their sons do the same?

To modern readers, nineteenth-century historical romances sometimes seem like adult reworkings of a child's fantasies, a similarity that helps us understand why praise was intended when a critic said of Walter Scott, the greatest and most influential of the historical romancers, that he told a story "just as an excited child would tell it."[43] They are childlike (for one

[43] John McVickar, quoted in Perry Miller, *The Raven and the Whale: The War of Words and Wits in the Era of Poe and Melville* (New York: Harcourt, Brace and Co., 1956), p. 28. Romances were also disparaged—for being

thing) in that they are not subtle. Good and evil are clearly defined according to received standards and they are separated by a sharp line—not a gray realm of moral ambiguity. There was no popular sovereignty in the territory *they* controlled. Because they were public and widely disseminated, romances could serve as models for collective regression. Their admirers claimed that they could "restore" both the historical past and the childhood of the self.

> We love to be transported back to the heroic age of adventure, and to hold converse with the choice and master spirits of a stirring age. Sated as we are with the commonplace events and characters of our own time . . . we are willing to resign ourselves with all the simplicity and freshness of boyhood, to a well told tale of ancient chivalry.[44]

"For so long a season after youth has flown forever," another critic wrote similarly of romances in 1849, "they bring back pleasing glimpses of its better hopes, its summer fancies, its skies without a cloud, its songs without a murmur. Romance is, in fact, one of youth's most legitimate restorers. It brings back all its first, glowing and most generous conceptions—when the heart was least selfish,—when the affections were most fond."[45] It was no accident that Scott and the historical romances were championed by social conservatives (Rufus Choate, for one, thought they could save the Union),[46] and

childlike, for the blurring damage they did to the line between truth and fantasy, and for their alleged tendency to "unfit children for the dull duties of real life, and make them act too much for stage effect." "Books for Children," *Christian Examiner* 5 (1828): 403. See also "Novel-Reading," *Putnam's Monthly* 10 (1857): 384–87, esp. 384.

[44] "The Hawks of Hawk Hollow," *American Quarterly Review* 18 (1835): 445.

[45] "Modern Prose Fiction," *Southern Quarterly Review* 15 (1849): 53.

[46] Samuel Gilman Brown, ed., *The Works of Rufus Choate with a Memoir of His Life*, 2 vols. (Boston: Little, Brown and Co., 1862), 1: 343–44.

that the objections to the unsettling effects of novels gradually faded before the supposed conservative power of restorative fiction.

We will concern ourselves in particular here with three American historical romances written during the post-heroic age. Two of them concern the Revolution; the third resembles them in certain ways, except that its fantasies attach not to the war that was but to the war that could be.

No work better caught and structured the sentimentalist fantasy of the American Revolution than *The Spy,* James Fenimore Cooper's archetypal American historical romance. Published in 1821, it was not only one of the very first such works to appear in the United States; it was also one of the best liked. It "at once attained popularity, and it has kept it," *Graham's* noted in 1849 on the occasion of yet another new edition.[47] A critic in the 1850s recalled that *The Spy* had been a "revelation . . . it proved that American society and history yielded abundant material for the most inviting form of romance."[48] Before it appeared, doubts existed that a successful historical romance could be written about America. "Should it be attempted," Daniel Jackson wrote in 1811, "the theatre must be erected on the field of the revolution, an era not sufficiently remote . . . to be arrayed in the vesture of fiction."[49] In general, Americans then still appeared to believe that they had no past,

47 "Review of New Books," *Graham's Magazine* 35 (1849): 132.

48 "American Literary Celebrities," ibid. 43 (1853): 144; [George S. Hillard], "James Fenimore Cooper," *Atlantic Monthly* 9 (1862): 54.

49 Quoted in Benjamin T. Spencer, *The Quest for Nationality: An American Literary Campaign* (Syracuse: Syracuse University Press, 1957), pp. 43–44. Cooper also challenged, but with less success, the notion that George Washington did not belong in works of romantic fiction. See [Walter Channing], "Reflections on the Literary Delinquency of America," *North American Review* 2 (1815): 39; [Edward Everett], "Sparks's *Life and Writings of Washington*," ibid. 47 (1838): 378; "Notices of New Works," *Southern Literary Messenger* 29 (1859): 475.

"no 'dark ages,' no mythology, no time beyond which the memory of man doth not run,"[50]—no time, that is, except one this critic did not have in mind: the time of one's own early childhood. Here was one past that did lie at least largely beyond the reach of memory, and what the memory could not produce, Cooper's imagination was prepared to supply, giving body and progression to pervasive but fragmentary fantasies.

Cooper reduces the Revolution to personal scale from the beginning of his work by making it the story of the divided, tormented Wharton family of New York City. The head of the family, a vague figure known to the reader only as Mr. Wharton, is a Loyalist by sentiment, but his higher priority is self-preservation. He believes that if he can avoid identification with either side during the Revolution, he will be able to avoid the confiscation of his property no matter who wins it. Accordingly he moves to no man's land in Westchester County, well outside of the city. There he sets up his house, a domicile peopled with female relations of various ages and opposing loyalties, who provide order, warmth, and security, in sharp contrast to the political chaos that prevails without.

It is the home and the nearby terrain that provide the setting for Cooper's romance and his interpretation of the Revolution. Wharton's determination to avoid the war has ironically but predictably put him directly in its path. Indeed, as the story begins, the war arrives at his very door—in the person of George Washington, who is seeking refuge from a storm. (The Whartons never learn the identity of their illustrious but highly cautious guest. When asked his name, he introduces himself as "Mr. Harper." Thus Washington's first quoted declaration in the book is a lie. But he cannot do it easily: "a faint tinge gathered on his features" as he pronounces the

[50] "Documentary History of the American Revolution," *American Quarterly Review* 18 (1835): 83.

pseudonym.[51]) While Washington is there, Wharton is visited also by his son, Henry, a captain in the British army, who has taken the great risk of passing through American lines in disguise in order to pay his filial respects. Aware of the ruse, Washington gently warns the young man that he chances arrest as a spy. After Washington departs this is just what occurs. While still at home, and still wearing his disguise, Henry Wharton is arrested as a spy by an American officer, Major Peyton Dunwoodie, who in addition to being his captor happens to be his cousin, his best friend, and the fiancé of his sister, Frances, the rebel heroine. Handed over to a military tribunal, Wharton is tried and summarily condemned to death.

When he then learns of Henry's plight, Washington is presented with a dilemma. Only he has the power legally to spare the young man, whom he remembers affectionately and knows to be innocent. Yet for obvious reasons he will not personally interfere with the established forms of military law. Washington, as commander-in-chief, would preside over the convicted spy's execution. Washington, as benevolent father, would spare the son. Sentiment triumphs over law. Washington assigns to his trusted spy, Harvey Birch (the title figure of the romance), the task of rescuing Wharton, a difficult operation that appears to require continued supervision by Washington and that consumes the greater part of the book. Thus Cooper sets up a situation in which Washington, supposed to be directing the fighting of a war, is forced to exert time and effort to thwart his own subordinates and the law in order to save from tragedy a family that is opposed to him politically and that has brought its imminent fate on itself by the avarice and cowardice of the father and the imprudence of the son.

Throughout the romance the focus of Cooper's fantasy of the

[51] James Fenimore Cooper, *The Spy: A Tale of the Neutral Ground, Works*, 6:6.

Revolution remains on the besieged home. War is the monster outside attempting to penetrate and destroy the domestic sanctuary, and the underlying question the book presents is whether it will be able to do so. The interplay of violence and domesticity marks the romance from the beginning when Washington appears alone in the wilderness in a fierce storm, and then retreats indoors, into the apparent sanctuary of the home which sits at the heart of chaos. Domestic routine—and the system of manners whereby outsiders are integrated into domestic routine—continues as the war goes on around the Wharton home. After one skirmish during which the house sequentially functions as fort, hospital, and prison, the Wharton women, as if to assert that not even the most calamitous events on a historical scale can affect the nature of life in their "sphere," give a banquet, which is carried out "with proper attention to all points of etiquette and precedence."[52] The captive Henry Wharton is present; so are his captors, who are treated as guests.

But the violence of the wilderness Washington flees, and the peace of the home he enters, are both deceptive. In a short time the storm subsides, and Cooper indicates this is meant to signify the war at the level of the contest with Britain. The dissipating clouds in the eastern sky are compared to "the retreating masses of a discomfited army . . . while in the west the sun had broken forth and shed his parting radiance on the scene below." "How grand! how awfully sublime!" Washington exclaims to himself. "May such a quiet speedily await the struggle in which my country is engaged."[53] May politics follow the example of nature. But it is at this point, as nature puts on a benign dress, that the sanctuary of the home is exposed as superficial, for it is now in greater danger than ever. The task before Washington is to bring the harmony of sublime

[52] Ibid., p. 167.
[53] Ibid., p. 45.

nature to the home—it is the task, paradoxically, of domesticating domesticity. The senior Wharton, whose moral standards suit the wilderness to which he moves, has compromised the sanctuary of the home by placing it in the way of violence. His son compounds the hazard by his filial errand. Partisan bands, more highwaymen than warriors, roam the area, and anarchy prevails. Ultimately the house is invaded and set on fire by the "Skinners," the partisan group that claims to support the rebel cause. Americans, not the British, destroy the Whartons' American home, and the bitter battle that rages within it as it burns is fought between American partisans and American regulars, not between the Americans and the British. Still, the Wharton women only at length, and then reluctantly, acknowledge "a dreadful confusion in the house," whereupon they resolve to intervene with the certainty that "our presence will quell the tumult." They manage to stop nothing. The battle and the fire run their course until the American regulars rout the American partisans and the house burns until only the ashes remain as "dreary memorials of the content and security that had so lately reigned within."[54]

Fratricide and domestic destruction are the themes of *The Spy,* but finally these disasters are prevented. Peyton Dunwoodie captures and is barely stopped from killing Henry Wharton who, though fighting for the British, is, much more importantly, an American and set to be his brother by marriage. Brother would kill brother, but Washington prevents it. The father saves the family. When Washington enters the Wharton home, he assumes symbolically the role of parent. After an acquaintance of no more than a few minutes he gazes, for example, at Frances Wharton "with a smile of almost paternal softness."[55] Though she does not know who he

54 Ibid., pp. 275, 280.
55 Ibid., p. 9.

is, the nature of Washington's character cannot be hidden, and Frances responds with more filial affection for Washington than she displays toward her real father, who with the rest of the family settles into a state of childlike dependency. At the end of the story Washington tells Frances that she is his "child" and that "all who dwell in this broad land are my children." Nothing else he could have told her would have moved her more.

> As he spoke, with a solemnity that touched Frances to the heart, he laid his hand impressively upon her head. The guileless girl turned her face towards him, and the hood . . . falling back, exposed her lovely features to the moonbeams. A tear was glistening on either cheek, and her mild blue eyes were gazing upon him in reverence.

Washington leans over and presses "a paternal kiss upon her forehead."[56] Never revealing his identity to the young woman, he leaves her forever, disappearing into the wilderness from which he came. The transfigured Frances glides across the field in the moonlight toward her home, which she knows is now a safe haven. The family quarrel is over, and the Revolution, its public counterpart, will soon be over too.

Cooper presents Washington as the saving father, but his is an ambivalent portrait nonetheless. The physical act of rescue is performed by Harvey Birch; he rescues one of the Wharton sisters from the burning house, and liberates the condemned Henry at next to the last minute. Birch is Washington's agent— not only in the sense of spying for him, but in the broader sense of executing his wishes. In one way, then, the character of Birch merges with the character of Washington. Both have saved the Wharton family from tragedy, and neither could have done it alone—although Washington takes all the credit

[56] Ibid., pp. 380–81.

for the act when he tells Frances that she is his child. The young woman understands and accepts the metaphor. It is at this point—at the point of claimed immortality—that Cooper reveals how Washington and Birch are separated by barriers as sturdy as the bond of common effort that ties them together. It is impossible that Harvey Birch, for all the gratitude that is due him, could claim even a metaphorical bond to the people he has saved. He is a detested spy thought to be motivated not by patriotism but by profit. Which is to say that in terms of deeds he belongs very much to the age of the fathers, but in terms of renown he has a bond not with that age but with the post-heroic one. Cooper makes this suggestion in a confrontation between Birch and Washington, in which he reverses the standard apportioning of selfishness and selflessness in history that the sons were accustomed to make. The criticism of Washington is oblique and isolated, but it is unmistakable and amounts to a devastating portrait of self-interest.

Near the close of the war Washington summons Birch and attempts to pay him gold for his past services and for his future silence. Birch recoils in disgust from the money. Washington obtusely interprets the disgust as a reaction not to the idea of gold but to the paltry amount, and he apologizes for not being able to offer more. "Does your excellency think that I have exposed my life, and blasted my character, for money?" asks the bewildered Birch. Washington still does not understand. "If not for money, what then?" Birch apparently cannot bring himself to make a direct answer, and counters with a question: "What has brought your excellency into the field? For what do you daily and hourly expose your precious life to battle and the halter?" Birch is of course suggesting patriotism, but Washington instead speaks of fame.

> There are many motives which might govern me, that to you are unknown. Our situations are different: I am known as the

leader of armies—but you must descend into the grave with the reputation of a foe to your native land. Remember that the veil which conceals your true character cannot be raised in years—perhaps never.

Washington persists in his offer; Birch persists in refusing. Finally Washington writes a note attesting to Birch's character, adding as a final example of his lack of understanding that "it may be serviceable to your children." "Children!" Birch exclaims. "Can I give to a family the infamy of my name!" In that cry Birch reveals the depth of the sacrifice he has made, as well as the difference between himself and Washington, a difference in no way lessened by the fact that neither man will ever have actual children of his own.[57]

In the 1850s Herman Melville recalled that Cooper's novels had powerfully affected his mind when he was a boy; soon after making this remark he suggested how. *Israel Potter,* which began to appear in serial form in *Putnam's Monthly* in 1854, is as much a parody of the romance genre as part of it, an opposing answer from Young America to the consciously sincere filiopiety of *The Spy* particularly, and also to *The Pilot,* Cooper's other major work about the Revolution. *Israel Potter* is also a play on the confining filiopiety of the age generally, and an acknowledgment of its power, a stance toward tradition that is signaled at the start: the book is dedicated to "His Highness The Bunker Hill Monument." Not for nothing would Melville call his hero a plebeian Oedipus.[58] Yet so completely did he seem to remain within the boundaries of the conventions both of filiopiety and the historical romance that

[57] Ibid., pp. 419–21.
[58] Herman Melville, *Israel Potter: His Fifty Years of Exile, The Works of Herman Melville, Standard Edition,* 16 vols. (London: Constable and Co., 1922–24), 11:214.

few critics caught the patricidal energy that moves the book.

Like Harvey Birch, the title figure in this story is an inconspicuous but important participant in some of the most crucial events of the war, often acting as the secret agent of a founding hero whose room for maneuver is constricted by his fame. Like Birch (and like Robin Molineux, for that matter) he is less historical than he is the timeless, representative Yankee, by turns farmer, peddler, surveyor, who is carried about (and in this case abroad—to England) by vast historical forces. Not for half a century, not until the symbolically important month of July 1826 does Israel Potter manage to return to the United States. He is by then utterly obscure—as if to confirm what many members of the generation seemed to sense—that this was the time the heroic age ended and the post-heroic age began.

That Potter might become a patricide is twice suggested and twice retracted early in the book. By nature self-reliant, he continually comes into conflict with people who expect deference. When his father on arbitrary grounds orders him to stop seeing a particular young woman, Israel disobeys him. "Ere on just principles throwing off the yoke of his king, Israel, on equally excusable grounds, emancipated himself from his sire."[59] But this rift turns out to be superficial and temporary. Israel loses the woman in any case and makes peace with his father, emulating him by settling down as a farmer. There he might have remained forever but for the Revolution, which finds him at his plow and carries him through a series of misadventures to England where, as a fugitive, he attempts to avoid calling attention to himself by taking work as a gardener.

But the skills of the Yankee are irrepressible. So accomplished does he become at this occupation that before long he is employed in the gardens of King George III, who often

[59] Ibid., p. 7.

walks near him on his constitutionals. Israel senses a chance to affect the course of history and again we are prepared for at least an attempt at patricide. "Seeing the monarch unguarded before him; remembering that the war was imputed more to the self-will of the king than to the willingness of parliament or the nation; and calling to mind all his own sufferings growing out of that war," Israel begins to imagine himself as a "regicide." But then he falls into conversation with the monarch and finds him utterly benign, not at all the tyrannical monster of the last stages of colonial propaganda. The paternal claims of the monarch are easily cast aside. When Israel (politely he thinks) calls the king "Sir," George asks, "Why do ye sir me?—eh? I'm your king." "Sir," Israel responds, "I have no king." Far from angering the monarch, this personal acting out of the Declaration of Independence almost charms him; certainly it wins his respect. The two develop the more modern, republican bond of employer and employee. Israel's thoughts of murder give way almost to affection.[60] Having come to terms with his father, Israel has now come to terms with the head of his parent country. Who then will play villain to the democratic protagonist? Who hangs most heavily over his head? The answer, it turns out, is Benjamin Franklin. Young Israel can deal with his father and the king; both give him room to grow. But young Israel cannot deal with his (its) immortal revolutionary father.

Pushed again into the war, Israel becomes a spy assigned to carry messages to Franklin, who is living in Paris while attempting to arrange an alliance between the rebellious colonies and France. But like Washington, who seems to put the Revolution aside in order to save the Whartons, Franklin lets the alliance wait while he turns his full paternalistic attention to Israel. He takes this self-reliant young man, who has success-

[60] Ibid., pp. 37–38.

fully negotiated certain Oedipal hurdles, and attempts both to domesticate and to reduce him to childlike dependence again. Just as the founders came down to post-heroic Americans as the embodiment of catechetical virtue, so Franklin plays the paternal role by suggesting, even imposing, rules by which Israel should live. The old man's conversations with Israel consist almost entirely of unsolicited advice on small matters, such as the dangers of "over-gratitude," and the foolishness of high-heeled boots, a new fashion so pervasive he thinks it might take a pamphlet to end it. Franklin becomes the father as "maxim-monger," and within a few minutes of meeting Israel issues the following aphorisms:

> The chief art of life, is to learn how best to remedy mistakes.
> . . . At the prospect of pleasure never be elated; but, without depression, respect the omens of ill. . . . In pecuniary matters always be exact as a second-hand. . . . Never joke at funerals, or during business transactions. . . . Never eat pastry. . . . Business before pleasure.[61]

Franklin also represents sexual repression, telling Israel (who has requested no aid because he sees an opportunity rather than a problem) that he will protect him from the wiles of an attractive chambermaid who has been hovering about.[62]

Melville's way of dealing with this oppression involves transforming Franklin from father to brother, thereby making him vulnerable to fratricidal impulses. He suggests that Franklin's scriptural counterpart is "the patriarch Jacob." Jacob was indeed the father of all Israel. But he was also known—and surely this was the parallel that inspired Melville—as the clever, hypocritical bargainer who tricked his brother Esau out of his share of their common inheritance.[63] Both Franklin ("depend

[61] Ibid., pp. 62, 53–58.

[62] Ibid., pp. 68–69.

[63] Ibid., p. 59; Perry Miller, *Nature's Nation* (Cambridge, Mass.: Harvard University Press, Belknap Press, 1967), pp. 223–24.

upon it, he's sly, sly, sly") and Jacob, Melville observes, were "keen observers of the main chance."[64] With his allusion to *Genesis* Melville has set up a contest between brothers, each of whom represents much more than himself. The struggle between Jacob and Esau began in their mother's womb. "And Jehovah said unto her, two nations are in thy womb. And two people shall be separated from thy bowels: And the one people shall be stronger than the other people; and the elder shall serve the younger."[65] Surely Melville knew that the developing sectional contest was sometimes likened to the struggle between Jacob and Esau.[66]

Israel soon begins to suspect that he is being robbed of his manhood. "Every time he comes in he robs me, with an air all the time, too, as if he were making me presents. . . . Why [does he] not let me take care of myself?" But just at this point who should show up to help him do just that but John Paul Jones. Melville signals Jones's relationship to Franklin and to Israel at the moment of his first appearance. Israel's attention is diverted from one of Franklin's maxim offerings when, through the jamb of a door that, "like a theatrical screen," separates the heroes from each other, he sees Jones, quite unrepressed, kissing the willing chambermaid.[67] Franklin and Jones are as related—and as different—as the superego and id of a single psyche. Israel, who can see both while they cannot see each other, is the ego who mediates between their demands.

---

[64] Melville, *Israel Potter*, pp. 70, 60.

[65] Genesis 25:23.

[66] "Though Jacob and Esau quarrelled already in the womb, yet, so long as the weaker and more politic brother can get the elder brother's portion, and simple Esau hunts his whales and pierces his untrodden forests, content with his mess of pottage,—honestly abiding by his bargain, though a little puzzled at its terms,—we think that fratricide, or the sincere thought of it, is very far off." [James Russell Lowell], "The Pocket-Celebration of the Fourth," *Atlantic Monthly* 2 (1858): 382.

[67] Melville, *Israel Potter*, pp. 69–71.

Jones was the least paternal of all the fathers, and if he represented anything like repression, the post-heroic generation managed to avoid being aware of it. "The name of Paul Jones has been familiar to our ears from earliest infancy," a critic wrote in 1825, "and such has been its magic, that we have never sought authentic information of his life and actions, without a secret anxiety lest it should trespass upon the poetical corner, he has so long held in our minds, by the romance of his real or supposed adventures."[68] Unlike that "professor of housewifery," the "domestic" Franklin, Jones is "disinherited" and moves in a "wonderful atmosphere of proud [friendlessness] and scornful isolation." He is no one's son, and no one's follower. A "sailor of the universe," he is not committed to the destinies of any particular nation, but rather to the cause of liberty in general.[69] To this point, Melville's Jones recalls Cooper's portrait of the hero in *The Pilot*. In this earlier romance, Jones, who says he is fighting an oppressive parent, is made to represent the antithesis of domestic values. He changes names (from John Paul to John Paul Jones) and changes loyalties (from British to American), claiming to represent the superiority of choices dictated by reason over those dictated by custom and tradition. He acknowledges no ancestors and will leave no progeny. But he has no answer, other than a disdainful smile, to the arguments of a woman (and Cooper) who, in an almost exact anticipation of Mrs. Bird's lecture to her husband in *Uncle Tom's Cabin,* is permitted the last word: "What avail your subtleties and false reasonings against the heart? It is the heart which tells us where our home is, and how to love it." Patriotism is but an extension of family love: "Have not the nations grown from families, as branches spread from the stem?"[70]

[68] *United States Literary Gazette* 3 (1825): 51–52.
[69] Melville, *Israel Potter*, pp. 62, 72, 73.
[70] James Fenimore Cooper, *The Pilot: A Tale of the Sea, Works,* 7:148–49.

Melville's Jones, although he still represents the antithesis of domesticity, is not the man of reason arguing against sentiment. He is rather the man of passion acting against both reason and sentiment. In this reversal Melville seems to try to show Cooper and sentimentalists generally what happens when the door is opened to feeling, the way Franklin opens his door to Jones. He is not, however, refuting—but only supplementing—Cooper's portrait of the rational man making rational choices. Passion and sentiment may be true opposites, but passion and reason are false ones. Not only are they close, but at times they become indistinguishable. Franklin seems to embody all that Western civilization had or could become. Jones comes close enough to Franklinian ideals to be able to converse with the man on his own level. They cooperate to win the rights of man. But Israel quickly apprehends that Jones's civilized qualities are not even skin-deep (since he is tattooed like a "thorough-bred" savage), but only clothing-deep. He resembles a "disinherited Indian chief in European clothes," a "barbarian in broadcloth." He is a frank embodiment of the "primeval savageness which ever slumbers in human kind." The Paris of Franklin, Melville reminds his readers, was soon to become the Paris of the Reign of Terror.[71]

Thus Jones is not the opposite of Franklin but an extension of him. Franklin becomes Jones or, more to the point, Jones gradually slips into and takes over Franklin. Melville dramatizes this first by shifting Israel's employ from Franklin to Jones and then by rendering in great detail one of the great naval battles of all time—between the *Bon Homme Richard* and the *Serapis*. Jones commands the ship named for Franklin; the ship sinks; Jones (and also Israel) survive victorious. Melville finds the violence here fratricidal, "as if the Siamese Twins, oblivious of their fraternal bond, should rage in un-

---

[71] Melville, *Israel Potter*, pp. 72, 81–82.

natural fight." He also finds "something singularly indicatory" in the battle, which he considered unsurpassed for the courage, hatred, and obstinacy it displayed.

> It may involve at once a type, a parallel, and a prophecy. Sharing the same blood with England, and yet her proved foe in two wars—not wholly inclined at bottom to forget an old grudge—intrepid, unprincipled, reckless, predatory, with boundless ambition, civili[z]ed in externals but a savage at heart, America is, or may yet be, the Paul Jones of nations.[72]

He seems to be writing of the predatory imperialism for which spokesmen for Young America like Stephen A. Douglas stood. But what we see most clearly is that, with the help of Jones, Israel has displaced his patricidal desires into the actuality of fratricide. What Melville really seems to be suggesting with his allusions to Jacob and Esau and the Siamese Twins is that manifest destiny is only the safest form of America's proneness to violence and that if it ceases to find an outlet in this external form, it will find it inside the house in an "unnatural fight" that only seems to be oblivious to fraternal bonds but actually fights all the more hideously because of them.

Israel Potter suggests that the distance between fantasy linked to memory and fantasy linked to prophecy was not very great. Another romance of the post-heroic age was more specific than this, suggesting that the war of memory was also the war yet to be. In 1836, the year after William Gilmore Simms published *The Partisan,* a historical romance of southern guerrilla struggles in the Revolution, Nathaniel Beverley Tucker published *The Partisan Leader,* a romance that resembles it in many ways except that it does not even pretend to concern the past. Tucker's romance is a prophecy of disunion and civil war between the North and South.[73]

---

[72] Ibid., pp. 165, 158.

[73] Nathaniel Beverley Tucker, *The Partisan Leader: A Tale of the Future* (Chapel Hill: University of North Carolina Press, 1971). The novel appeared

Tucker came from Virginia, where self-consciousness about the post-heroic quality of the second quarter of the nineteenth century was probably greater than elsewhere in the Union. The home of the greatest of the fathers, Virginia frequently reminded herself—and was reminded by others—that she had ceased to produce great men.[74] Nathaniel Beverley Tucker was one Virginian in particular who had several reasons to be sensitive to this problem. His heritage produced heavy pressures from the start. Born in 1784, the year after the War of Independence ended, he was the son of St. George Tucker, a veteran of the Revolution who had been wounded at Yorktown, a professor of law at the College of William and Mary, and an emancipationist at a time when such sentiments were not only permissible but even fashionable in Virginia.[75] Beverley Tucker's mother had been married earlier to a Randolph, and the flamboyant John Randolph of Roanoke was his half brother. The strong personalities of these relatives overshadowed and dominated Tucker's, and he was unable to match their achievements. Caught in a law practice that did not flourish, humiliated by the recurrent need to turn to his successful father for money, Tucker migrated after the War of 1812 to Missouri, where he acted the part of state builder. Al-

in 1836, bearing the publication date 1856, and listing as its author "Edward William Sidney."

[74] "Virginia . . . by common consent, is to repose on the recollection of what she has done." J. W. Barbour to John J. Crittenden, May 31, 1820, in Mrs. Chapman Coleman, ed., *The Life of John J. Crittenden, With Selections from His Correspondence and Speeches,* 2 vols. (Philadelphia: J. B. Lippincott Co., 1871), 1:48; "Review of President Dew's Address," *Southern Literary Messenger* 3 (1837): 130–35; William Sawyer, *Congressional Globe,* 29 Cong., 1 Sess. (February 3, 1846), p. 303; Benjamin F. Wade, ibid., 33 Cong., 1 Sess. (February 6, 1854), p. 339; "Foote's Sketches of Virginia," *Southern Literary Messenger* 17 (1851): 9; Robert M. T. Hunter, "Inauguration of the Equestrian Statue of Washington: Oration," ibid. 26 (1858): 184; "Great Men, a Misfortune," ibid. 30 (1860): 312.

[75] For biographical information on Tucker, see Percy Winfield Turrentine, "Life and Works of Nathaniel Beverley Tucker" (Ph.D. diss., Harvard University, 1952).

though he was more successful in his career in the West than in Virginia, it appears that his longing for his own state was very strong, making him an illustration of Sydney Smith's exactly contemporaneous definition of nostalgia—the feeling one gets living on the banks of the Missouri.[76] Tucker's father died in 1827, John Randolph in 1833, and in the latter year, as though liberated by these deaths to return home, Tucker went back to Virginia and took his father's position at William and Mary.

Although a quiet supporter of Andrew Jackson before 1832, Tucker fell into a state of complete disillusionment with national politics in general during the nullification crisis, an attitude that had been growing within him for several years. Tucker was alienated by Jackson's forceful opposition to nullification, yet he had no sympathy for Calhoun's elaborate schemes, which he found cumbersome and misdirected mechanisms for dealing with profound economic and constitutional questions. To Tucker the debate over the idea of state nullification of federal law was a debate over the best way to *preserve* the Union. He wanted to destroy it completely. To William Gilmore Simms in 1850 he repeated an insomnious vow he said he had been making daily for thirty years: "I will never give rest to my eyes nor slumber to my eyelids until it is shattered into fragments."[77] Tucker shared his generation's profound reverence for "the principles . . . consecrated by the blood of our fathers" in the Revolution, which he considered the greatest work in history. He shared the prevailing sentimental attitudes about indebtedness ("which can never be cancelled") to the fathers, and the duties frequently to celebrate and constantly to imitate them. The fathers would "live for-

---

[76] Sydney Smith, "America" [1818], *The Works of the Rev. Sydney Smith,* 3 vols. (London: Longman, Brown, Green, and Longmans, 1848), 2:34.

[77] Quoted in William P. Trent, *William Gilmore Simms* (Boston: Houghton Mifflin Co., 1892), p. 183.

ever, in the hearts of their descendants,"[78] but about the Union Tucker made no similar statement. As other filiopietistic Southerners gradually learned to do, when he spoke of preservation for posterity, he spoke of the fathers' principles, example, and character, and he spoke in terms that were personal or abstract rather than specifically institutional.

With other perceptive members of his generation Tucker recognized that filiopiety clashed with ambition. In 1838, the year of Lincoln's Lyceum speech, he told the Young Men's Society of Lynchburg, Virginia, that "the beacon-light which guided . . . our own illustrious Washington, along the path of glory, still shines for us, and to us the same path is still open. To emulate their deeds and rival their renown is the task before us." Having repeated a convention of rhetoric that his audience must have already heard countless times, Tucker then turned sardonically upon the formula:

> Yes, gentlemen! The career of [Washington] is open to us; but it is only as the career of Cyrus was open to Sardanopulus; the career of Titus to Domitian; the career of Trajan to Elagabelus; as the career of every monarch, illustrious for wisdom and virtue, has been open to those scourges of the earth, whose life has been one wanton and tyrannical abuse of powers conferred for the benefit of their fellow men.[79]

Two years earlier, during the presidential campaign of 1836, Tucker was certain that the man who would play Domitian to Washington's Titus was already there. Martin Van Buren was waiting in the political wings, and the only question was whether, by electing him president, the people would become

---

[78] [Nathaniel] Beverley Tucker, "Political Science," *Southern Literary Messenger* 5 (1839): 565.

[79] [Nathaniel] Beverley Tucker, "A Discourse on the Genius of the Federative System of the United States," ibid. 4 (1839): 761.

the victims of his obvious designs. It was this question that led Tucker to write his romance.

The plot of *The Partisan Leader* is set in 1849, thirteen years in the future, by which time the abuses that alarmed Tucker had led in his imagination to despotism. In Tucker's scheme, Van Buren is elected in 1836 (precisely the calamity that the publication of the romance was intended to prevent), and then successively reelected in 1840, 1844, and 1848. Tucker's image of Van Buren comports with and helped developed the Whig caricature of the man that would be used against him with effect in the election of 1840. Far degenerated from his sires, he is an effete figure who complacently presides over the government in a posture of continuous repose, exerting himself only to decorate his spoken comments with languorous gestures by a hand "fair, delicate, small, and richly jewelled."[80] He is supported in power by the commercial and industrializing North, which has over the years usurped control of the federal government, and uses that control to impose exploitative, unconstitutional, indeed tyrannical measures (the protective tariff is the most insidious of these) upon the South.

As the power of Van Buren and the North increases toward despotic heights, that of Virginia declines. "The land of Washington, and Henry, and Mason, of Jefferson, Madison, and Randolph, sunk to the rank of a province." The home of the fathers was now ruled by epigoni whose "chance to be remembered in history depends, like that of Erostratus, on the glories of that temple of liberty which they first desecrated and then destroyed."[81] Finally in 1848, however, Virginia's electoral votes do go elsewhere, and when Van Buren is returned once more to the White House it is now by Northern votes alone. Thus the South must face in fiction the specter that in actuality it would not face until 1860: what it called a sec-

[80] Tucker, *Partisan Leader*, p. 134.
[81] Ibid., p. 39.

tional president. No other Southern state supports Van Buren, for it has become increasingly obvious through his terms that in order to consolidate his position in the North he has been orienting his policies toward the benefit of that section alone.

The fictional response of the Southern states to the election of 1848 is all the more striking for the matter of fact way in which Tucker presents it:

> Under these circumstances, the Southern States had been, at length, forced to see that the day for decisive action had arrived. They therefore determined no longer to abide the obligations of a constitution, the form of which alone remained, and having, by a movement nearly simultaneous, seceded from the Union, they had immediately formed a Southern Confederacy.

Driven from the Union by Northern "rapacity and fanaticism," the South forms its nation on the economic foundation of a commercial treaty with Great Britain. The treaty establishes free trade between them, thereby signaling the commercial isolation and ruin of the North and putting the South in position to be "once more the most flourishing and prosperous country on earth."[82]

One state that does not join the new Confederacy, indeed does not even secede, is Virginia, a failure of nerve that Tucker associates with the state's general decline in the postheroic age. Her hesitation makes the state the focus of all attention. The South attempts to persuade Virginia to join the Confederacy; Van Buren resorts to force to prevent yet another departure. He sends federal troops into Virginia ostensibly to protect against an attack by the Confederacy but actually to hold Virginia in the Union. No one fails to notice that the troops are not stationed on Virginia's border with the Con-

[82] Ibid., pp. 40–41, 65, 66.

federacy, where presumably any invasion would commence, but rather around the state capitol in Richmond, where any move toward secession would have to take place.

Tucker follows the conventions of the romance in creating a family to impose structure, emotional focus, and human scale upon a great historical confrontation, but it is with a certain self-consciousness that he does so. Half apologizing for making critical political decisions turn on romantic love, he explains that "it is in such causes that the spring of great events is found." The patriarch of Tucker's family is Hugh Trevor, a man of character, a fictional composite of the virtues of the revolutionary fathers. "Men pointed him out to their children, and said to them: 'Copy his example, and follow his steps.' "[83] Just as Washington's preoccupation with the Whartons in *The Spy* seems to distract him from, but then becomes, the Revolution, so Van Buren becomes interested in the Trevor family to the exclusion of all other concerns, although here the political reason is apparent. The Trevors are politically the most influential family in Virginia. Van Buren figures quite plausibly that if he can keep the allegiance of the Trevors by flattery, bribery, or threats (the full range of his tools of statecraft), he can keep Virginia in the Union.

This will be a delicate project, for the Trevor house is divided, reflecting the division of the nation. As the fathers were, Hugh Trevor is a staunch supporter of the Union; at least he starts out that way. Gradually in the 1840s he moves into a position of doubt and is beset for a time by a divided mind. He has two sons who are also divided, not internally but against each other. In the parental generation conflict surfaces in the form of ambivalence; in the next generation conflict surfaces in the opposing characters of two brothers.

Owen, the older brother, grows up to be a Yankee. As a youth he had been sent by the admiring patronage of Andrew

83 Ibid., pp. 128, 45.

Jackson to West Point, the starting place of a dazzlingly successful military career. By 1849, the secession year in this fiction, he has risen to the rank of colonel. Underneath the shining plate of success, however, his character has eroded. Influenced by years of living in the North, Owen has become "indifferent to duty, frivolous, self-indulgent, and mercenary." Politically he is what Northern sentimentalists would consider a good son: the Union for him is sacred, and he rejects the idea of state sovereignty. But, his Unionism aside, he actually has no heart, for the tie between his politics and remembered domesticity has been cut cleanly. Owen has no time for "thought of the simple joys of his childhood's home," and he ends up rejecting all that is good in the "manners, habits, institutions, and character of Virginia."[84]

The younger son, Douglas, is different from his brother in every way. He is a youth of great and unremittingly emphasized merits: honorable, generous, brilliant, articulate, frank, discreet, temperate, gentle, chivalrous, assiduous, independent, warm, impervious to flattery, handsome, graceful, brave, and imaginative. To be sure, he too has attended West Point, but his family and home remain the focus of his emotional world. "His heart had never ceased to glow at the name of Virginia, and he returned to her as the wanderer should return to the bosom of his home—to his friends—to his native land."[85]

With these brothers character is, of course, destiny, and the machinations of Van Buren merely cause the Trevor brothers to take the political sides that their natures have preordained. The chief effect of the president's tactlessness is to push their father to resolve his ambivalence in favor of the Confederates. Tucker sets history on its head. Hugh Trevor recognizes the successful imitation of his own virtues concentrated in the heroic decision of the chivalric Douglas; this time father fol-

[84] Ibid., pp. 327, 54, 48.
[85] Ibid., p. 53.

lows son. It is in describing this change of heart that Tucker
adjusts history to conform to his own desires. He uses Trevor
to present his version of a standard Southern way of account-
ing for particular departures from the paternal creed: the fathers indeed created the Union, which has been our own near-
ruin; but they were also rebels, and if they had lived until
now, and could see what we see, they would approve of what
we do and, in time, join us.

It is the loss of the allegiance of all the Trevors but one that
leads Van Buren to order federal troops to Virginia to prevent
the loss of the state, and it is this action that in turn sets off
civil war. Taking the lead of a band of Virginians at last re-
vitalized, Douglas Trevor retreats to the Virginia mountain
wilderness to prepare for the developing battle. His brother
Owen is given the command of the Union army. In describing
the preparations for the brothers' war, and then its beginning,
Tucker manipulates the conventions of the romance as family
conflict is transformed into guerrilla conflict. The brother
whose character is best trained and most correct in a domestic
situation is also the one best prepared to wage partisan war.
His character (as well as that of his army) corrupted by the
Yankee commercial ethos, which stresses comfort as its chief
goal, Owen moves his Union troops ill-prepared to the fray.
The trappings of militarism—the colorful ranks, martial music,
beautiful women waving handkerchiefs—this show masks only
briefly the corrosion of will and stamina that bourgeois life has
worked on Northern character. When the elaborate army of
one brother and the partisan band of the other clash, the result
is the one the reader has been prepared for from the start: the
gallant Douglas defeats the Union troops and captures his
brother Owen. Later, in a turn in the story that is no less
stunning for being anticlimactic, Owen escapes and is killed—
almost by accident, and not by Douglas.

Tucker was evidently unable to imagine a civil war that

was no longer a brothers' war, for shortly after the death of Owen the book abruptly ends. The political conflicts that ostensibly concern it have in no way been resolved. But the family conflict has been settled, for the good son has defeated the bad one. To persist with the story after that would have been pointless from the standpoint of the romance, so Tucker simply stops it. In political terms *The Partisan Leader* sets out to dramatize the restoration of the early world of the Republic, but it succeeds only in dramatizing a fantasy of regression: the restoration of the contemporaneous early world of the self. Allusions to childhood abound in the book. Douglas Trevor never loses touch with his childhood, and his defeated brother is more than once compared to a spoiled child. For Tucker, civil war was an echo and recapitulation of a child's fantasy of fratricide. Once that had been played out he lost not only interest in its political counterpart but the capacity to comprehend it at all.

Tucker's solution to the problem of the fathers was to split the part of their legacy he liked (heroic action for independence) away from the part he rejected (the Union) and to dramatize this separation in the form of a good son who survives and a bad son who is killed. Thus he found a way to destroy the part of the fathers he did not like, but do so paradoxically in the name of the fathers. Fratricide in this scheme was actually displaced patricide. There is no evidence that Abraham Lincoln ever read or even heard of *The Partisan Leader,* but Tucker's formula for moving beyond the fathers while being true to them—an acting out of fratricide in a context of regression—prophesied not only civil war. It also prophesied exactly the way that Lincoln attempted to resolve his own problem with the fathers and at the same time save the Union without separation and violence. It is to this phase of the crisis of the Union that we now turn.

7

ABRAHAM LINCOLN AND THE
MELODRAMA OF THE HOUSE DIVIDED

Aggressive conflict between the generations [can]
be "solved" by . . . finding an enemy outside the
group who could be dominated or killed.

MARTIN WANGH, 1972

The ritualistic custom of sectional compromise, which permitted the acting out of fratricidal wishes while also containing
them, had helped to preserve the Union for more than half
a century before it collapsed with the passage of the Kansas-
Nebraska bill. As though attempting to find another peaceable
way of achieving exactly the same result, Abraham Lincoln between 1854 and 1860 moved to create a substitute ritual. In the
original one, the brothers would begin with extreme demands,
would threaten to divide the house, and then, seeming to heed
the warnings that a house divided must lead to fratricide,
would discover, and then acquiesce in, a middle formula. In
Lincoln's new version all the good brothers would band together to direct their angry passions upon a scapegoat brother
and, by throwing him from power (symbolically killing him),

actively rid themselves of the only danger to their Union at the same time that they psychologically returned to the world of the fathers who had created it. This ritual was ultimately as sentimental as the one it replaced. Unlike the one it replaced, however, it never demonstrated that it had any power to save the Union. On the contrary, it led directly to the result it sought to avoid—civil war.

Even in his lifetime it was well known that Abraham Lincoln was a close and frequent reader of Shakespeare.[1] The interest became almost intense during the Civil War years, when he would sometimes spend hours at a stretch reading from Shakespeare's tragedies—often aloud to the people about him. According to his own testimony and the memories of others, Lincoln was evidently drawn to three passages in particular, for he kept returning to them. The first, from *Hamlet,* was a speech by Claudius, who usurps the throne of Denmark after murdering his brother, the king. Overwhelmed with guilt, he says:

> O, my offence is rank, it smells to heaven;
> It hath the primal eldest curse upon't,
> A brother's murther!

He longs to pray for pardon, but he cannot,

[1] Abraham Lincoln to James H. Hackett, August 17, 1863, in Roy P. Basler, ed., *The Collected Works of Abraham Lincoln,* 8 vols. (New Brunswick, N.J.: Rutgers University Press, 1953), 6:392–93. On Lincoln and Shakespeare, see Don E. Fehrenbacher, "Lincoln and the Weight of Responsibility," *Journal of the Illinois State Historical Society* 68 (1975): 45–56; David Chambers Mearns, *Largely Lincoln* (New York: St. Martin's Press, 1961), pp. 126–33; Roy P. Basler, *A Touchstone for Greatness: Essays, Addresses, and Occasional Pieces about Abraham Lincoln* (Westport, Conn.: Greenwood Press, 1973), pp. 206–27.

> since I am still possess'd
> Of those effects for which I did the murther—
> My crown, mine own ambition, and my queen,

and he does not intend to give them up.[2]

Lincoln told a Shakespearean actor in 1863 that he preferred this soliloquy to the one by Hamlet that begins, "To be or not to be."[3] He told Francis B. Carpenter, an artist, in 1864 that Claudius's speech "always struck me as one of the finest touches of nature in the world." He then proceeded to recite it "with a feeling and appreciation," Carpenter thought, "unsurpassed by anything I ever witnessed upon the stage." After this Lincoln fell into a silence during which his mind made the connection to the second of his favorite passages, the opening speech of *Richard III*. Here the future king speaks of his own ugliness and regrets the "weak piping time of peace" he lives in. Hindered by both from more noble pursuits, "to entertain these fair well-spoken days, I am determined to prove a villain." Lincoln told Carpenter that actors did not deliver the lines with any sign of awareness of the force of the man's ambition.

> Richard, you remember, had been, and was then, plotting the destruction of his brothers, to make room for himself. Outwardly, the most loyal to the newly created king, secretly he could scarcely contain his impatience at the obstacles still in the way of his own elevation. He appears upon the stage . . . burning with repressed hate and jealousy.

At this point, according to Carpenter, Lincoln "unconsciously" assumed the character of Richard and repeated the speech from

[2] Act 3, sc. 3.
[3] Lincoln to Hackett, in Basler, *Works of Lincoln*, 6:392.

memory. The artist was again greatly moved at "the force and power" of Lincoln's acting, and jokingly suggested to him that he had missed his calling.[4] Obviously, what Lincoln was showing him was that he had not missed it at all.

The third passage was from *Macbeth,* Lincoln's favorite among all Shakespeare's plays. "I think nothing equals Macbeth," he once said. "It is wonderful."[5] Another witness to his recitations recalled hearing Lincoln read from the play five days before he was murdered. He was particularly drawn to the scenes in which Macbeth "falls a prey to moral torment." After he replaces Duncan, whom he has slain, as king, Macbeth says:

> Better be with the dead,
> Whom we, to gain our peace, have sent to peace,
> Than on the torture of the mind to lie
> In restless ecstasy. Duncan is in his grave;
> After life's fitful fever he sleeps well.

After reading these lines aloud, Lincoln "paused to expatiate on how exact a picture Shakespeare here gives of a murderer's mind when, the dark deed achieved, its perpetrator already envies his victim's calm sleep. He read the scene over twice."[6] How could Lincoln have been certain that Shakespeare's picture of the murderer's mind was exact?

---

[4] F[rancis] B. Carpenter, *Six Months at the White House with Abraham Lincoln: The Story of a Picture* (New York: Hurd and Houghton, 1867), pp. 49–52. See also John Hay, August 23, 1863: Lincoln "read Shakespeare to me, the end of Henry VI and the beginning of Richard III, till my heavy eyelids caught his considerate notice." Tyler Dennett, ed., *Lincoln and the Civil War in the Diaries and Letters of John Hay* (New York: Dodd, Mead & Co., 1939), p. 82.

[5] Lincoln to Hackett, in Basler, *Works of Lincoln,* 6:392.

[6] Adolphe de Chambrun, *Impressions of Lincoln and the Civil War: A Foreigner's Account,* trans. Aldebert de Chambrun (New York: Random House, 1952), p. 83. The *Macbeth* passage is in Act 3, sc. 2.

Of all Shakespeare's creations, Lincoln was drawn to the plays, characters, and indeed the very scenes that most vividly dramatize fratricidal ambition. In all three of these plays, ambitious and envious men kill members of their own families to reach and keep power. Claudius and Richard kill brothers and Macbeth kills his cousin. Each becomes king as a result. Each reflects powerfully upon his own guilt and alienation from all that is good—and then goes on killing. Lincoln was not only fascinated with these characters. He evidently identified with them. Carpenter's memoir indicates that Lincoln did more than imitate Richard III: he became Richard III, the man he understood to be consumed with "repressed hate and jealousy."

How could Lincoln have identified with the mentality of men consumed with fratricidal guilt? Was there any sense in which he also burned with repressed hate and jealousy and then committed a "brother's murther" in order to get to power? Between 1854 and 1860, the years in which Lincoln sought (using again his own words about Richard) to "make room for himself," it would seem that he was headed in the opposite direction by attempting to avoid fratricide in the form of the civil war that he and many others considered possible. But there was an intensely personal aspect to Lincoln's politics in the 1850s, for there was one man in his way who had to be pushed aside; that man, of course, was Stephen A. Douglas. The rivalry between these two men was one of the most extraordinary in background, as well as one of the most fateful in result, in the history of American politics. Douglas after 1854 represented all that Lincoln opposed, and he sat in the Senate seat that Lincoln coveted in 1858. One reason this rivalry has been so intriguing to historians is the problem of scale it presents. On the one hand, the man who stood in Lincoln's way was not just any American, but probably the most famous politician in the nation. On the other, Lincoln had known

Douglas since the days when both men were equally obscure. He could scarcely have avoided developing powerful feelings about Douglas personally before he found himself opposing Douglas on grounds of political principle.

The two politicians had begun their careers at about the same time in the 1830s—young lawyers in the center of Illinois, serving together in the state legislature, and debating against each other even then. But between the 1830s and the 1850s events carried Douglas to national and even international renown. The prominence Lincoln attained was far narrower in scope. Thus to the obscurity he endured was added the humiliation of Douglas's success. In a private fragment, Lincoln wrote to himself in 1856:

> Twenty-two years ago Judge Douglas and I first became acquainted. We were both young then; he a trifle younger than I. Even then, we were both ambitious; I, perhaps, quite as much so as he. With *me,* the race of ambition has been a failure—a flat failure; with *him* it has been one of splendid success. His name fills the nation; and is not unknown, even, in foreign lands. I affect no contempt for the high eminence he has reached. So reached, that the oppressed of my species, might have shared with me in the elevation, I would rather stand on that eminence, than wear the richest crown that ever pressed a monarch's brow.[7]

In addition to the factors inherent in a contest fought upon major issues for high office, this one contained the emotional charge of a long-sustained and unbalanced rivalry.

Initially it was not to Shakespeare especially but more to the structure and the language of drama generally that Lincoln turned in order to give a single scale to a personal rivalry that had become a public contest involving the very principles on

[7] Basler, *Works of Lincoln,* 2:382–83.

which the nation was founded. He compared his debates with Douglas in 1858 to "the successive acts of a drama" whose audience was not just the attending crowd, or even the nation, but (because of Douglas's fame) the entire world.[8] The analogy is revealing. Lincoln learned his politics at the village level, where affairs were managed through the interaction of a few individuals one knew personally. Anyone who reads the accounts of the way, as president, he dealt with the public to a striking degree on an individual, personal basis is likely to surmise that he never really got beyond the sense, which after all his generation largely shared, that politics was an extension of personal relationships. His ancient habits did adjust to his stature, however, and it is just here that theater provided an opening to the wider world. It was as though he thought of himself as moving from a narrow, private realm to a public stage. He continued always to think of politics as the inter-action of political leaders. To the extent that he could comprehend mass society at all, it seems to have been as an audience that watched the struggles of the great in order to be moved by and choose between them. The people were acted upon, rather than actors, in politics. This is not to say that the audience was either passive or infinitely manipulable. On the contrary, it brought to the drama feelings and opinions that were decidedly fixed and that set the boundaries of political action. In this conception it was more the task of the actors through their speeches to arouse and exploit preexisting feelings than to change them.

It was on this "stage" that Lincoln cornered and "killed" his rival Douglas. As if trying to prevent disunion and fratricidal war, Lincoln between 1854 and 1860 staged a ritual in which the fratricidal emotions of Americans (not excluding the South) could be satisfied by heaping upon this scapegoat re-

[8] Ibid., 3:252–53.

sponsibility for all their problems and then symbolically murdering him. The accumulated tensions of many years might thereby be peaceably relieved. Lincoln's rivalry with Douglas might be interpreted in these terms, but it must be said that the effect did not fully match his apparent intent. Lincoln did manage eventually to cast Douglas aside and rise to power; the good son did defeat the bad one. But the social and psychological purposes of the ritual were not achieved. Not only did the fratricidal play fail to prevent actual fratricide, but Lincoln's pursuit and defeat of Douglas actually contributed to the bringing of fratricidal war.

It might seem that guilt was an inappropriate reaction to a murder that was symbolic and committed with the best of filiopietistic intent. That civil war followed soon upon it was an ironic, for it was an unintended, development that might have occurred had Lincoln not existed. But Lincoln's emotional identification with ambitious men who became conscience-stricken murderers makes more sense when we recall that he did wish to "kill" the fathers, whose memory blocked his own chances for immortality, and that in order to banish this unacceptable desire he projected it onto a mythical patricidal figure whom he must be prepared to slay in order to save the fathers' work. Now the figure at last appeared and was slain according to expectation.[9] But surely no sensitive person could have failed entirely to see that the symbolic murder, which led to power but also to war, was required more by displaced homicidal wishes than by any objective danger Douglas and his friends posed to republican institutions.

From the late 1830s, when he made the Lyceum speech, until 1854, the year of the Kansas-Nebraska Act, Lincoln was on the

[9] "Aggressive conflict between the generations [can] be 'solved' by externalization, that is, by finding an enemy outside the group who could be dominated or killed." Martin Wangh, "Some Unconscious Factors in the Psychogenesis of Recent Student Uprisings," *Psychoanalytic Quarterly* 41 (1972): 221.

edge of the history that was being made. To be sure, he served a term in Congress from 1847 to 1849, but to note it only calls attention to the peripheral role he played in the politics of the time. Unlike Douglas, he was not identified with territorial expansion, real estate speculation, railroad promotion, or the other quests that constituted "the spirit of the age." Outwardly he lived the life of respectable middle-class Whiggery, rising to prominence and prosperity in Springfield, Illinois; marrying well, raising a family, and buying a house at the corner of Eighth and Jackson streets, which he expanded through the years in accordance with his needs and rising status. Every outward sign indicated that the national political situation would keep his life on that course. He seemed resigned to this, declaring in 1852 that "the nation has passed its perils, and is free, prosperous, and powerful."[10]

The events of 1854 and afterward changed the course of Lincoln's life. They gave him a role to play that comported with—and allowed him to exploit—his filiopiety, his ambition, and his prophecy of the emergence of the bad son. They gave him an opportunity to mediate between the conflicting desires of Americans—toward the restoration of the security of childhood on the one hand and the achievement of democratic manhood on the other. They put him in position to attempt to resolve simultaneously the crisis of the Union, the post-heroic problem, and his own psychological dilemma. He succeeded ultimately in all of these efforts, although not in the way that he intended.

By inspiring the creation of the Republican party, the Kansas-Nebraska Act gave Lincoln a vehicle to ride to power. In their opposition to the extension of slavery and in their policies generally, the Republicans appealed to the diverse psychological needs of the American people in a way that the Whigs—and for that matter the post-Jackson Democrats—

[10] Basler, *Works of Lincoln*, 2:122.

had never been able to do. The Whigs had presented themselves as the party of preservation. The Republicans presented themselves as the party of restoration. They claimed to stand "precisely on the ground upon which . . . Washington and Jefferson stood."[11] They sought to "roll back the governments of the nation and the States to the principles and policy of our revolutionary fathers."[12] Like preservation, restoration denotes conservative goals. Unlike preservation, restoration requires activist means. As we have seen, preservation and action seemed to many Americans to be incompatible desires. Republicans now argued that they were complementary.

A debate that occurred in 1858 between Rufus Choate, a sentimentalist who had moved from the moribund Whigs to become a Buchanan Democrat, and James Russell Lowell, a Young America spokesman who had joined the Republican camp, illustrates the matter. Countering an assertion made by Choate that the new party was guilty of irreverence for the past, Lowell repeated the by-then familiar party line that "the object of the Republicans is to bring back the policy and practice of the Republic to some nearer agreement with the traditions of the fathers." But the lesson Lowell found in those traditions was hardly the sentimental one of "forbearance, submission, and waiting for God's good time." Rather the "tradition is rebellion," he claimed, bringing into conjunction two words that sentimentalists saw as opposites. The past to which the Republicans would return was not the domesticated past of conservative fantasy, but one resembling the masculine past Emerson summoned to mind when he gazed at

[11] Lyman Trumbull, *Congressional Globe,* 36 Cong., 1 Sess. (December 7, 1859), p. 39.

[12] E. P. Walton, ibid., 35 Cong., 1 Sess. (March 31, 1858), appendix, p. 331. On the early Republican party generally, see Eric Foner, *Free Soil, Free Labor, Free Men: The Ideology of the Republican Party before the Civil War* (New York: Oxford University Press, 1970).

the portrait of Washington. "That is the America which the Fathers conceived, and it is that to which the children look forward." The difference Lowell saw between the sentimental- ists and the Republicans was that for the former the Revolution was to be remembered. For the latter it was a set of principles that the sons must act out and translate into policy.[13]

Thus, to put the matter in more personal terms, the Republi- cans presented a formula that taught people how to be both men and good sons. The dictates of filiopiety required that the nation, now in great danger, be saved. In the process the needs of ambition could simultaneously be fulfilled. The object of the Republicans was regeneration—to give birth in accordance with tradition. Since giving birth had been the act of the fathers that had originally marked off the generations, the act that had made their fame both possible and perma- nent, and since the sons had worried that they could never play a similar role, the Republicans offered nothing less than the resolution of a central dilemma of the age. Manhood and fulfilled ambition for this generation could be achieved by saving the nation and restoring it to the original republican purity from which it had departed—by giving it, to anticipate here, "a new birth of freedom."

Of all Republicans, Lincoln was in the best position, in terms of his own political beliefs, his personality, and his geographi- cal location, to exploit the opportunities that generated the party. Richard Hofstadter once showed how Lincoln was able simultaneously to appeal to people who were hostile to slavery (he said it was wrong and must someday die) and to people

---

[13] Rufus Choate, Boston *Daily Advertiser*, July 7, 1858; [James Russell Lowell], "The Pocket-Celebration of the Fourth," *Atlantic Monthly* 2 (1858): 378–79. See also [idem], "The Election in November," ibid. 6 (1860): 499– 500. Lowell's formulation was precisely the same as the one secession-minded Southerners were reaching at the same time: rebellion and tradition were not antagonistic but synonymous.

who were hostile to blacks (he said he opposed their becoming socially or politically equal to whites) by insisting with regard to slavery and implying with regard to blacks that the territories not be ruined by either.[14] Lincoln was similarly able to appeal to Young America types who wanted action and manhood, and to sentimentalists who wanted the restoration of, and regression to, a supposedly more secure past. It is true that he sometimes disparaged both casts of mind. He derided Young America for its "great passion—a perfect rage—for the *'new.' "*[15] He believed the sentimentalists overestimated or at least talked too much about the danger to the Union. He regretted their willingness to make almost any concession to avoid the conflict they feared, thereby "reversing the divine rule, and calling, not the sinners, but the righteous to repentence—such as invocations to Washington, imploring men to unsay what Washington said, and undo what Washington did." Certainly he counted himself among the Union savers. "But when I go to Union saving, I must believe . . . that the means I employ has some adaptation to the end."[16] Sentimentalist encouragement of regression alone was not an effective means because it represented the search for security and order that Lincoln believed contributed to a climate hospitable to a tyrant. Sentimentalists tended only to prolong the crisis. Moreover, Lincoln always insisted that it was not enough merely to save the Union; it must be "worthy of the saving."[17]

Yet, if he identified with neither, in many ways Lincoln's character combined traits that the two mentalities considered antagonistic. He was the masculine, rugged rail-splitter of the

[14] Richard Hofstadter, *The American Political Tradition and the Men Who Made It* (New York: Alfred A. Knopf, 1948), pp. 106–19.

[15] Basler, *Works of Lincoln,* 3:357.

[16] Ibid., p. 550; 2:270.

[17] Ibid., 2:276.

West and (to some people) he would become the bearded patriarch. But the beard was offset by the shawl, and Herndon's picture of Lincoln going to market wearing that garment, carrying a basket and with children in tow, casts up a domesticated image indeed.[18] Horace White said that Lincoln's nature was "one of almost child-like sweetness,"[19] and Seward observed that he had "a curious vein of sentiment running through his thought which is his most valuable mental attribute."[20] Francis Parkman also noticed these qualities, although not with favor. According to one of Parkman's contemporaries, Lincoln failed to meet his standard that men should be masculine and women feminine. "This wish always to keep the two types, mutually complementary, separate and apart, lay at the bottom of his putting Washington so much higher than Lincoln as a hero; for the womanly tenderness of Lincoln seemed to him out of place."[21] But as the changing image of Washington suggests, many people in the 1850s welcomed a blending of "the two types." If Lincoln had consciously set out to fit his persona to the androgynous tendencies of the time, he could scarcely have done better than he did.

In his words and personality he merged the cult of domesticity with the mainly Republican theory that a conspiracy existed to extend slavery, a process that modified both cult and theory. People like Harriet Beecher Stowe and Edward Everett were counterpolitical sentimentalists uncomfortable with ideology. People like Salmon P. Chase and, much of the

---

[18] Emanuel Hertz, ed., *The Hidden Lincoln: From the Letters and Papers of William H. Herndon* (New York: Viking Press, 1938), pp. 414–15.

[19] Horace White, Introduction to William H. Herndon and Jesse W. Weik, *Abraham Lincoln: The True Story of a Great Life*, 2 vols. (New York: D. Appleton and Co., 1892), 1:xxiii.

[20] Quoted in Glyndon G. Van Deusen, *William Henry Seward* (New York: Oxford University Press, 1967), p. 251.

[21] Henry Dwight Sedgwick, *Francis Parkman* (Boston: Houghton Mifflin Co., 1904), pp. 310–11.

time, William Henry Seward were political ideologues uncomfortable with sentiment. Lincoln was at ease with both.
Originating little, he borrowed from, adapted, and mixed both
strains to express his own understanding of the danger to the
nation and how to end it forever. As if sensing the regressive
desires present among members of his generation, he encouraged them by creating a public fantasy that corresponded not
only with the reality of political developments and his own
needs, but also with the child's fantasy of the monster coming
into the house—a monumental case of "regression in the
service of the ego." That is, unlike the sentimentalists who
cast up images of terror as warnings, Lincoln seemed to understand that they could be used to reach and to work through
adult problems. By a ritualistic working out of what we may
call the fantasy of the besieged house, Americans could exploit their regressive urges to get beyond the problems that had
set them on that course in the first place.[22]

Lincoln agreed with other Republicans that the Kansas-
Nebraska Act represented a repudiation of the slavery policy
of the fathers, which he insisted had remained essentially intact
until the mounting of this assault. His own version of the
fathers' record on slavery was that they generally abhorred it
and placed it on the road to eventual extinction. They made
to the institution only such concessions (protecting it in the
Constitution, permitting it in some territories) as necessity
(the need to create and preserve the Union, or the existence of
slavery already in a given area) dictated. It was the duty of the
sons, Lincoln went on to say, to follow both parts of the
fathers' policy. Although the abolitionists might deplore it,
they must follow the fathers in upholding the arrangements

[22] Cf. D. W. Winnicott, *Through Paediatrics to Psycho-Analysis* (New York:
Basic Books, 1975), pp. 278–94.

they made to protect slavery in the states that chose to have it. Although slaveholders and advocates of popular sovereignty, among others, might deplore it, they must also follow the fathers in pursuit of their ultimate goal. This meant, in practical terms, that they must keep slavery out of areas into which it had not already spread.[23]

Until 1854, according to Lincoln, the policy of the fathers had been successfully working in two different ways. First, it was achieving its goal. The "public mind" assumed that slavery was "in course of ultimate extinction." The second result followed from the first. Because the public mind so assumed, "all was peace and quiet. . . . A long course of peace and prosperity seemed to lie before us." The Kansas-Nebraska Act marked a great and mistaken departure from this course, a departure that defined the task of Lincoln and all other good sons: slavery must be placed again where the fathers left it. But the Kansas-Nebraska Act was not just a case of bad judgment, although it was that. Nor was it only an example of degeneration from "the high republican faith of our ancestors," although it was that too.[24] In addition to both, and much more to be feared than either, the Kansas-Nebraska legislation was an insidious act that could be explained only as a deliberate assault on republican institutions.

Opponents of the Kansas-Nebraska bill argued from the start that it was the brainchild of a "slave power conspiracy" which sought to extend the sway of the despotic institution.[25]

[23] Lincoln's views on the fathers and slavery pervade his speeches and other writings from 1854 to 1860. In particular see Basler, *Works of Lincoln*, 2:230–31, 235, 240–41, 248–50, 266–67, 274, 405–7, 452, 492, 501, 514, 520, 551; 3:18, 77–78, 276, 307, 464–66, 522–35.

[24] Ibid., 3:439; 2:270, 242.

[25] See the "Appeal of the Independent Democrats," in J. W. Schuckers, *The Life and Public Services of Salmon Portland Chase, United States Senator and Governor of Ohio; Secretary of the Treasury, and Chief-Justice of the United States* (New York: D. Appleton and Co., 1874), pp. 140–47.

Lincoln, too, eventually adopted a conspiratorial explanation for the law, but it is important to realize that his version of conspiracy differed in important respects from the prevailing one, which focused on the machinations of the slaveholding class. He asserted that a cabal of mainly Northern Democrats, which dominated the federal government and counted Stephen A. Douglas, Franklin Pierce, James Buchanan, and Roger B. Taney among its leaders, was plotting to transform slavery from an institution that was transitory, sectional, and limited to blacks, into one that would become perpetual, national, and perhaps even biracial. The Kansas-Nebraska Act was the first blow. When the nation after three years got more or less used to that, the cabal delivered the second: the opinion of the Supreme Court in the *Dred Scott* decision, which stated that Congress could not bar slavery from the territories. The third and worst blow, Lincoln said in 1858, *"is* probably coming, and will soon be upon us." He expected that once the American people had learned to live with the *Dred Scott* decision, the Supreme Court would then move to strike down the antislavery constitutions of the free states, thereby making slavery in effect a national institution.[26]

In legalistic terms, the case for the existence of a conspiracy began with the construction of what Lincoln considered to be superfluous language in the Kansas-Nebraska Act. The law stated that its "true intent and meaning" was "not to legislate slavery into any Territory or State, nor to exclude it therefrom, but to leave the people thereof perfectly free to form and regulate their domestic institutions in their own way, subject only to the Constitution of the United States."[27] Lincoln asserted that the reference to "State" in this clause was suspicious since no state was the object of the legislation, and in any case the

[26] Basler, *Works of Lincoln*, 2:375, 385, 453, 461–69, 518, 525–26, 541; 3:18, 95; 4:16. The quotation is from 2:467.

[27] U.S., *Statutes at Large*, 10:283.

power of states over slavery had never before been seriously questioned. The second superfluous passage was "subject only to the Constitution," since no one could have doubted it. Lincoln saw the entire section of the law as the herald of eventual Supreme Court decisions interpreting the Constitution to say that the people in neither territories *nor states* were free to prohibit slavery.[28]

Popular sovereignty, according to Lincoln, was a superficially appealing phrase that was actually a hideous misnomer, for it was designed to provide an ideological curtain behind which the plotters schemed. Contrary to its claims, popular sovereignty had nothing to do with government by the consent of the governed, which Lincoln always considered to be the "leading principle . . . of American republicanism."[29] It pointed instead toward tyranny. The application of the doctrine to the problem of slavery in the territories demonstrated the point. People who wished to carry slaves into the territories did not propose to ask their consent either to be slaves or to go to the territories.

Lincoln's conspiracy theory, which was central in his political thought at perhaps the crucial point in his career, has usually been an object of puzzlement and even embarrassment to scholars, because it seems to have so little to do with the events it purported to explain.[30] His analysis virtually ignored

[28] Basler, *Works of Lincoln,* 2:466–67. As late as December 1860, Lincoln was still fearful of "an early Supreme court decision, holding our free-state constitutions to be unconstitutional." Lincoln to John D. Defrees, December 18, 1860, in ibid., 4:155.

[29] Ibid., 2:266.

[30] J. G. Randall, *Lincoln the President,* 4 vols. (New York: Dodd, Mead & Co., 1945–55), 1:107–8; Allan Nevins, *The Emergence of Lincoln,* 2 vols. (New York: Charles Scribner's Sons, 1950), 1:361–63. But see Harry V. Jaffa, *Crisis of the House Divided: An Interpretation of the Issues in the Lincoln-Douglas Debates* (New York: Doubleday & Co., 1959), pp. 275–301; and Don E. Fehrenbacher, *Prelude to Greatness: Lincoln in the 1850's* (Stanford: Stanford University Press, 1962), pp. 79–82.

and by implication ruled out two other dangerous possibilities that loomed much more obviously and were far more often stressed by nearly everyone else. First, of course, was the fear of disunion and subsequent civil war that we have already considered. The second usually receives far less attention for the simple reason that, unlike the first, it was not eventually realized. This was the possibility that acquiescence in popular sovereignty would revive expansionist pressures, leading the South (or the "slave power" in some formulations) to demand the acquisition of new territories—Cuba for example—hospitable to slavery. This was an obvious prospect and a prevalent concern throughout the 1850s. Douglas himself made the possibility credible with his repeated insistence that further territorial expansion to the south was certain. He thereby left himself open to the charge, which some of his opponents did not fail to push, that he was a lackey in the service of an expansionist slavocracy.

These prevailing formulations of danger stressed the sectional nature of the crisis. Lincoln's analysis did not. Indeed, of all the major actors in the politics of the 1850s, Lincoln was the least inclined to interpret the recurrent crises in sectional terms. Born in a slave state and married to a woman born and raised in a slave state, he always had great empathy for the South. He seemed to go out of his way to stress that geography and economics, rather than a superior character, distinguished the Northern record on slavery from that of the Southern. "We are not better . . . than they." He said that the people of the South were "just what we would be in their situation" and that there were no more "tyrants . . . in the slave States than in the free."[31] He also avoided appearing to take seriously the danger of secession. Several times after 1854 he dismissed, occasionally with derision, the possibility of disunion. "All this

[31] Basler, *Works of Lincoln,* 4:3; 2:255, 264.

talk about the dissolution of the Union is humbug—nothing but folly," he said at one point. "The people of the South," he said at another, "have too much of good sense, and good temper, to attempt the ruin of the government, rather than see it administered as it was . . . by the men who made it." Even after secession had occurred, he insisted in public that "the crisis is . . . artificial" and he evidently underestimated the danger of war between the sections until the American Civil War itself was actually upon him.[32]

For all that, Lincoln was not oblivious to the possibility of disunion and civil war, although like many Northerners he tended to take the double prospect less seriously with each passing year that it was threatened but never came to pass. He said in 1854 that the failure to restore the Missouri restriction would signify the end of the compromise spirit "which first gave us the constitution, and which has thrice saved the Union." Without that spirit, the sections would rapidly become polarized. It was easy to envision "the South flushed with triumph and tempted to excesses; the North, betrayed, as they believe, brooding on wrong and burning for revenge. One side will provoke; the other resent. The one will taunt, the other defy; one [aggresses], the other retaliates"—and so events would move, to their oft-predicted calamitous end.[33] In 1855 Lincoln seemed at least briefly to despair that the slavery problem could ever be resolved peaceably. He came to think that "there is no peaceful extinction of slavery in prospect for us"—a prediction that, if not the same thing as an expectation of civil war, is certainly consistent with such an expectation and

[32] Ibid., 2:354–55; 4:95, 238. "Mr. Lincoln entered Washington the victim of a grave delusion. . . . He fully believed that there would be no civil war,— no serious effort to consummate Disunion. . . . I infer that Mr. Lincoln did not fully realize that we were to have a great civil war till the Bull Run disaster." Horace Greeley, *Recollections of a Busy Life* (New York: J. B. Ford & Co., 1868), pp. 404–5.

[33] Basler, *Works of Lincoln*, 2:272.

with few others.[34] Lincoln was not unaware, either, of the possibility of renewed expansion. It is true that not until after his election as president in 1860 did he show much interest in the prospect that popular sovereignty could lead to the acquisition of new territory for slavery. But at that point this seemed to surpass the danger of the northward spread of slavery in his thinking about the effects of Douglas's doctrines.[35]

If Lincoln understood these dangers, why did he neglect to stress them? A plausible answer is that they did not share one crucial factor with his analysis of passing events. Regardless of the connection it did or did not bear to the politics of the 1850s, Lincoln's interpretation comported with his preexisting needs and ideas and the others did not. He had been disposed throughout his adult life to expect a certain kind of crisis. The Kansas-Nebraska Act brought events into phase with his expectations. He clearly sensed this: his charges against Douglas accorded precisely with the dangers predicted in the Lyceum speech. It was, after all, "Douglas and his friends" who moved the slavery question "from the position in which our fathers originally placed it."[36] This move was not made in good faith. By his policies and his arguments for them, which were "the van-guard—the miners, and sappers—of returning despotism,"[37] Douglas had proven himself to be an enemy of the true meaning of the Revolution. The bad son of the Lyceum prophecy had at last appeared to make his assault upon the fathers' institutions.

[34] Lincoln to George Robertson, August 15, 1855, in ibid., p. 318. But the letter in which he said this reveals that he had already formulated the question ("Can we, as a nation, continue together *permanently* . . . half slave, and half free?") that he would answer in the House Divided speech without even considering the possibility of civil war.

[35] Ibid., 4:154, 155, 172.

[36] Ibid., 3:117.

[37] Lincoln to Henry L. Pierce and others, April 6, 1859, in ibid., p. 375.

Stephen A. Douglas—a man Lincoln knew even before he made the prophecy, and a proven spokesman for the majoritarian ethos: this was a potential despot? He may not seem particularly tyrannical or even dangerous to us, but we must recall that the despot's role, a projection of Lincoln's own wishes, existed and needed to be played. The emotional charge from within shaped what Lincoln came to see in Douglas as much as or more than Douglas's actions or character shaped Lincoln's attitude toward him. Douglas needed to do little more than pass across Lincoln's established field of vision in order to be recognized as the long-threatened danger and cast into the well-delineated image. A rough congruence sufficed. There was one difference between Douglas and the tyrant of prophecy, and it made Douglas all the more dangerous: his methods were covert. The imagined figure, we recall, would tear down the fathers' temple of liberty. Douglas "shirks the responsibility of pulling the house down, but he digs under it that it may fall of its own weight."[38] It was his burrowing method that made Douglas, who seemed so genial and even jolly, so fearsome in fact. He was "the most dangerous enemy of liberty, because the most insidious one."[39] That Douglas did not seem to present a threat to republican institutions was no obstacle to conspiracy theories. Conspirators, of course, go out of their way to hide their real purposes, which suggests, paradoxically, that Douglas could have avoided Lincoln's charge only by agreeing with it.

Like the possible success of the tyrant in Lincoln's prophecy, so now the results of the conspiratorial effort would depend heavily on a gathering indifference to the principles and safeguards of liberty. Douglas's famous claim of indifference to whether or not slavery spread was a cloak that covered *"real*

---

[38] Ibid., p. 205.
[39] Lincoln to Samuel Galloway, July 28, 1859, in ibid., p. 394.

zeal" for the expansion of the blight. The strategy behind popular sovereignty was the "debauching of public sentiment"—to
wear down the love of liberty and make people indifferent
to it by blurring the distinction between liberty and despotism.
Popular sovereignty was "calculated to break down the very
idea of a free government, even for white men, and to undermine the very foundations of a free society." People who
became indifferent to the principle of liberty in one context
were on the way to indifference to liberty generally, which
opened the way to tyranny.[40]

Douglas's interpretation of the Declaration of Independence was meant to assist this downward process. He took the
position that when the fathers had written "all men are created
equal," they had in mind only the equality of Americans and
Englishmen and were not referring to American blacks, most
of whom they continued to hold as slaves.[41] To Lincoln,
who interpreted the words "all men" to mean *"all* men," the
passage was the statement of an ideal. Movement toward the
ideal was the very purpose of a free society. Moreover, the
principle of equality was placed in the founding document
as an obstacle in the path of later would-be tyrants, "a stum-
bling block to those who in after times might seek to turn a free
people back into the hateful paths of despotism." Douglas
knew this, which meant that one of his first needs was to
trivialize the passage.[42]

Douglas shrewdly attacked liberty at its most vulnerable
point and its most vulnerable time. He and other enemies of
liberty understood (as Lincoln had prophesied in the Lyceum
speech) that prosperity dulled sensitivity to encroachments
upon political rights—particularly abstract, piecemeal, and
seemingly distant encroachments upon the rights of others.

[40] Ibid., 2:255; 3:469; 4:16.
[41] Ibid., 3:113.
[42] Ibid., 2:405–7.

Lincoln worried that "now when we have grown fat," Americans would be unable to appreciate—let alone act against—the dangers they faced.[43] Douglas and others like him began with blacks and with the remote territories because they thought they could count on a racist society to acquiesce in a move that did not obviously, directly, and immediately affect them.

Sufficient numbers of white Americans could not be roused to a sustained resistive effort by telling them that the issue in the territories was whether or not a small number of slaves might go there, nor even by telling them that the question of the extension of slavery into the territories was the skirmish line in the encompassing struggle over the future of black slavery in the entire Republic. They could be aroused only if they were made to feel that their own liberty and prosperity were at stake. It was precisely here that Lincoln reworked the slave power conspiracy idea to fit his own structure of thought. Concede one exception to the meaning of the Declaration of Independence, he argued, and there would no longer be any barrier to others. "It does not stop with the negro," he warned. "Is the white man quite certain that the tyrant demon will not turn upon him too?" Successful in their immediate quest, Douglas and his friends would soon besiege the white man's house.

> Our defense is in the preservation of the spirit which prizes liberty. . . . Destroy this spirit, and you have planted the seeds of despotism around your own doors. Familiarize yourselves with the chains of bondage, and you are preparing your own limbs to wear them. Accustomed to trample on the rights of those around you, you have lost the genius of your own independence, and become the fit subjects of the first cunning tyrant who rises.[44]

[43] Lincoln to Robertson, in ibid., p. 318.
[44] Ibid., pp. 500, 553; 3:95.

Nowhere did Lincoln more effectively vivify this set of perceptions and fears than in the famous opening passage of the House Divided speech of 1858. More than that, his words at this point revealed his strategy for involving the people generally in his own struggle. "We are now far into the *fifth* year," he began,

> since a policy was initiated, with the *avowed* object, and *confident* promise, of putting an end to slavery agitation.
>
> Under the operation of that policy, that agitation has not only, *not ceased,* but has *constantly augmented.*
>
> In *my* opinion, it *will* not cease, until a *crisis* shall have been reached, and passed.
>
> "A house divided against itself cannot stand."
>
> I believe this government cannot endure, permanently half *slave* and half *free.*
>
> I do not expect the Union to be *dissolved*—I do not expect the house to *fall*—but I *do* expect it will cease to be divided. It will become *all* one thing, or *all* the other.
>
> Either the *opponents* of slavery, will arrest the further spread of it, and place it where the public mind shall rest in the belief that it is in course of ultimate extinction; or its *advocates* will push it forward, till it shall become alike lawful in *all* the States, *old* as well as *new*—*North* as well as *South.*
>
> Have we no *tendency* to the latter condition?[45]

The passage says that the agitation that began with the Kansas-Nebraska Act in 1854 will not continue indefinitely. It will move toward a crisis that will be resolved in one of two ways. Either slavery will thrive and become legal everywhere, or the spread of slavery will be halted, leading to a consensus that the institution is on the way to eventual disappearance. The present tendency of events is toward the former result.

[45] Ibid., 2:461–62. On the speech generally, see the analysis in Fehrenbacher, *Prelude to Greatness,* pp. 70–95.

Once the crisis is resolved, agitation will cease. The course of events will seem so firmly set that there will be no cause for agitation to continue. The quoted passage is more pessimistic than otherwise, but the tenor of the entire speech is actually optimistic, reflecting Lincoln's confidence in the outcome of the conflict. "The result is not doubtful," he says in closing. *"Wise councils* may *accelerate* or *mistakes delay* it, but, sooner or later the victory is *sure* to come."[46] That is, good and evil are engaged in a desperate struggle. There will be suspense about the outcome for a time, but good will triumph in the end. This formulation is unmistakably melodramatic, as was the ritual it implied. In order to make his ideas available to the public and involve it in his own concerns, Lincoln dramatized the demons of his mind according to the dictates of popular culture.

Thus Douglas in many ways resembled the villains of melodrama, who smilingly attempted to get people within their clutching powers by cloaking their evil motives under sacred principles. Lincoln cast himself into the representative role of the good son who attempted to do no more than defend the fathers' house against usurpation by tyranny. In exploiting the popularity of melodrama in this way he was hardly unique. The lines between drama and oratory were never clearly fixed in the nineteenth century.[47] Some of the most popular plays contain long set speeches that were indistinguishable from oratory. Some politicians, who after all had as much need to hold popular attention as playwrights did, cast complex politi-

---

[46] Basler, *Works of Lincoln,* 2:468–69.

[47] Thus, for example, "The lyceum is the American theatre." "Lectures and Lecturers," *Putnam's Monthly* 9 (1857): 317. See also "Percival's Poems," *Southern Quarterly Review* 5 (1844): 213. Henry T. Tuckerman wrote that "orations constitute our literary staple by the same law that causes letters and comedies to attain such perfection in France, domestic novels in England, and the lyrical drama in Italy." "Edward Everett," *Graham's Magazine* 38 (1851): 74.

cal and constitutional questions into the stock situations and
stock language of popular theater.[48]

In his important study of ancient Greek drama, Gerald Else
has argued that the genre of tragedy developed out of oratory
as the result of an attempt to revivify the epic tradition, which
was losing its hold on a society given over to the making of
money. In successive steps, Solon, Thespis, and Aeschylus invented the new form to keep the people of Athens in emotional contact with their ancient myths.[49] I have been arguing
here that American orators and other writers experienced similar apprehensions and made similar efforts to keep Americans
in emotional contact with their own already mythic origins.
In the American case the attempt to restore the past through
art did not lead to the invention of a new genre but to the exploitation of an existing one. In their effort to involve the
American people emotionally in their own restorationist desires, American politicians increasingly tended verbally to structure the crisis according to the conventions of melodrama. Indeed, it is only a slight exaggeration to say that by the end of
the 1850s, the crisis of the Union not only imitated, but had
become, a work of art, with the paradoxical result that as the
crisis grew more serious its seriousness grew more difficult to
measure. For the crisis grew to resemble drama at a time when
drama was itself far gone into what the age referred to nega-
tively as theatricality. "Nobody now, on entering one of our
theatres, expects to see the mirror held up to nature, or society," a critic observed with regret in 1856. Attacking "the
false and the forced" on the stage, he continued: "All men do
not growl and frown their emotions in private life; but upon

---

[48] Almost all of my statements about nineteenth-century American drama
owe something to David Grimsted, *Melodrama Unveiled: American Theater and
Culture, 1800–1850* (Chicago: University of Chicago Press, 1968), which is
an excellent book in all scholarly respects, and witty besides.

[49] Gerald F. Else, *The Origin and Early Form of Greek Tragedy* (Cambridge, Mass.: Harvard University Press, 1965).

the stage, they all must do so. All women do not gasp and shriek their joy or sorrow by the domestic hearth; but upon the stage they all must do so."[50]

Emerging early in the nineteenth century, melodrama was tragedy that had been reworked (some would say debased) by sentimentality. It grabbed and held the attention of its audience by developing ordinary situations into a series of sensational incidents linked together by sentimental dialogue. The juxtaposition of the plausible and the implausible permitted the audience the luxury of sympathetic feelings unrestrained by the reality of personal responsibility or danger. Freed from any burden of involvement, they could be moved to weep delicious (and surely communing) tears for misfortunes that, although perfectly recognizable, were not theirs.

Plots of melodramatic plays typically involve a dastardly assault on familial ties or the sanctity of the home. All evil in the world is embodied in a stock villain whose malevolence, highlighted by his strenuous pretenses to virtue, is obvious throughout to everyone but his should-be antagonists. He praises the values of his victims in order to put them off guard. But he always fails ultimately, when the hero blocks, though barely in time, his wicked designs. Melodrama is a celebration both of virtue, which can be counted on to prevail, and of its audience, which is assumed to possess already the values represented by the protagonist. That the outcome is known in advance does nothing to diminish either suspense or the emotional nature of the course to the result. Indeed, it is the very certainty that the threatened calamity will not materialize that permits the temporary sway (and surely the vicarious enjoyment) of evil and danger. At the same time this certainty implies that evil, although the focus of everyone's concern, is not to be taken too seriously. Melodrama

[50] "The World of New York," *Putnam's Monthly* 7 (1856): 446.

strikes an implied bargain with its audience based on the premise of escape from the real world; part of the suspense it engineers is the suspension of reality itself. Play and audience agree: we know that the world is not like this, but it suits us for the moment to pretend that it is.

Because for us the chaos of political events in the 1850s is structured into coherence by the Civil War that followed, we tend to forget that people witnessing the occurrence of those same events had to turn elsewhere for structuring devices. Melodrama helped to perform that function; it also could organize emotions and provide some of the satisfactions of action without the dangers. Yet in the act of imposing structure on the seeming randomness of events, melodrama distorted the passing scene in crucial ways. In seeing the world as a contest between virtue and vice, it grossly simplified complex problems and lent support to the idea that all adverse change was ultimately caused by the malevolence of a few individuals rather than anything grander, less personal, or beyond the control of the will and efforts of good men. In seeing virtue as unfailingly triumphant, it encouraged an optimistic view of events that permitted people to take a passive stance toward them, and to doubt that the crisis must be taken altogether seriously.

Lincoln in the House Divided passage and elsewhere took these risks with the plainly calculated hope that the crisis of the Union would be redefined—and ended. He repeatedly suggested that the locus of the problem facing the Republic was "the public mind" and that the solution he sought was to put that mind at "rest."[51] If he could move public opinion to a certain kind of expectation, events would then take care of themselves. Thus in Lincoln's view two issues dominated the crisis of the Union as he challenged Douglas for the Senate in

[51] This is most conspicuously the case in the House Divided speech. Basler, *Works of Lincoln*, 2:461.

1858. Whether slavery would in fact expand—its *actual* future—was one of them, but more immediately pressing was the question of public opinion on whether slavery should or should not expand. To settle the second would (he believed) settle the first. Thus to Lincoln the crisis ultimately involved a question of sensibility.

In an undated fragment found among his papers he wrote that American prosperity (by which he evidently meant well-being in a very broad sense) rested on the Constitution and the Union, but these in turn rested on the love of liberty "entwining itself more closely about the human heart." It was this sentiment, and not simply the desire for independence, that drove "our fathers" to fight.[52] It was this sentiment that Douglas was seeking to destroy. Lincoln did not disagree with the sentimentalists' central idea that feeling was the great conservative social force, and he sought, as they did, a solution that was fundamentally emotional. "To the salvation of this Union, there needs but one single thing," he told an audience in Indiana in 1861: "the hearts of a people like yours."[53] The people must be emotionally involved. What better way to achieve this than to evoke and dramatize the powerful fantasy of the besieged house?

To Lincoln, as to others, the house metaphor was a conventional way of (as he put it) "figuratively expressing the Union." In his rhetoric after 1854 he often spoke of political matters in the language of domesticity. Government was "national house-keeping," the nation, "our national homestead." Cast into domestic terms the problem of class conflict proved to be no problem at all: "Let not him who is houseless pull down the house of another; but let him labor diligently and build one for himself, thus by example assuring that his own shall be safe from violence when built." Slavery he called "an

52 Ibid., 4:168–69. See also 2:271.
53 Ibid., 4:193.

element of division in the house." "By the Nebraska bill, a door has been opened for the spread of slavery in the Territories."[54] Like Harriet Beecher Stowe, Lincoln used domestic imagery to bring complex political issues to people in their own ancient and daily language, thereby enabling and finally compelling them to feel the slavery problem as their problem.

Although he agreed with the Union-saving sentimentalists that "the Union is a house divided against itself," Lincoln reworked their image for his own purposes.[55] In his hands it ceased to be a warning of disunion to be inevitably followed by civil war. It became instead a warning that Douglas and his allies were conspiring to destroy liberty—a very different danger. The sentimentalists warned of separating brothers who would end up fighting each other. As if sensing that this prospect was almost as attractive as it was horrible (and thus truly dangerous in a political situation where the brake of compromise no longer worked), Lincoln reimagined the danger so as to divest it of all possible appeal. He invoked the deeper, primordial fear of the monster trying to get into the house.

To convey an adequate sense of the danger he saw, Lincoln on more than one occasion associated Douglas, the Kansas-Nebraska Act, and slavery generally with the imagery of monsters. Douglas's position on slavery in the territories was "monstrous" and a "serpent." When Douglas asserted that despite the *Dred Scott* decision the people of a territory could keep slavery out by passing unfriendly legislation, Lincoln responded that "there has never been so monstrous a doctrine uttered from the mouth of a respectable man." "When it came upon us," Lincoln said of the predatory Kansas-Nebraska legislation, "all was peace and quiet." The idea of extending slavery was "the great Behemoth of danger." Slavery itself was a "monstrous

54 Ibid., 3:309; 4:13; 5:529; 7:259–60; 3:18; 2:362–63. See also 2:237, 238, 241, 258; 3:211, 213.

55 Ibid., 3:18.

injustice." Lincoln once compared the institution to a "venomous snake" which if found "in bed with my children,"—his image for the existing situation in the South—he would treat with surpassing caution. But if the snake were found out on the prairie, no one would *"put it in bed with other children, I think we'd kill it!"*[56]

Lincoln thus set up a confrontation between good and evil, but good did not correspond to North, nor evil to South. Because the metaphor of the house divided has almost always been used in this historical context to refer to the conflict between the sections, it was and is natural, although incorrect, to assume that like everyone else Lincoln was talking about disunion. Nothing about the reaction to the House Divided speech so perplexed him as the prevalent interpretation that he was talking about coming civil war. "I said no such thing and . . . I thought of no such thing," he insisted. The famous passage is clear on the point: "I do not expect the Union to be *dissolved*—I do not expect the house to *fall*."[57] People who thought the way Lincoln did, and evoked an image of the Republic as a besieged house, quite naturally did not tend to be preoccupied with the possibility of secession. The man who believes that his brother is trying to take all of the inheritance they were meant to share is not likely to spend time supposing that his brother is going to disappear altogether. Moreover, from the standpoint of arousing Northern emotions, the melodramatic formulation made strategic sense. It was easier to arouse people to the prospect of the house being taken over than to the less horrific, and progressively less plausible, prospect that the South would move out of it.

From the start of the political conflict over slavery, it was obvious that the stakes of the sections in its outcome were very

[56] Ibid., 2:237; 2:500; 3:317; 2:270; 2:255; 4:10–11. See also 3:306; 4:5.
[57] Lincoln to Oliver P. Hall, Jacob N. Fullinwider, and William F. Correll, February 14, 1860, in ibid., 3:520; 2:461.

different. It was a commonplace for Southerners to say, as one did to a Northerner at its climax, that "with us the question at issue involves our property, our lives, and those of our families, while with you it is but a political abstraction." Southerners claimed that they were defending homes and firesides "as if . . . hordes of insatiable desperadoes threatened domestic security."[58] Henry Clay reminded Northerners in 1850 that they were "safely housed, enjoying all the blessings of domestic comfort, peace, and quiet in the bosom of their own families." Southerners, on the other hand, lived with a sense of siege, a fear that as a result of antislavery agitation, their dwellings would be attacked and burned.[59] Lincoln appreciated the way that the fire-eaters were able to "maintain apprehension among the Southern people that their homes, and firesides, and lives, are . . . endangered" by the abolitionist- and Black Republican-inspired monster of slave insurrection.[60]

It was precisely because there was no plausible way any longer to argue that Northern homes were in any sense similarly endangered by prosecessionists that Lincoln attempted to restructure the conflict along party rather than sectional lines.[61] Except for Taney, who came from Maryland, the men Lincoln named as conspirators were all Northerners. They were also all Democrats. Partisan conflict adhered to a ritual of its own that promised to move toward a resolution that was both decisive (which sectional conflict had never been) and peaceful

[58] Henry T. Tuckerman, *The Rebellion: Its Latent Causes and True Significance* (New York: James G. Gregory, 1861), pp. 35, 22.

[59] *Congressional Globe,* 31 Cong., 1 Sess. (January 29, 1850), p. 246. See also A. G. Brown, ibid., 31 Cong., 1 Sess. (January 30, 1850), p. 257; Abraham W. Venable, ibid., 31 Cong., 1 Sess. (February 19, 1850), appendix, p. 161; Clement C. Clay, Jr., ibid., 36 Cong., 1 Sess. (December 13, 1859), p. 121; James D. Richardson, ed., *A Compilation of the Messages and Papers of the Presidents,* 10 vols. (Washington: Government Printing Office, 1897), 5:627.

[60] Basler, *Works of Lincoln,* 4:142.

[61] Ibid., 2:385.

(which sectional conflict was no longer so likely to be). Thus to place the struggle on a party basis was to take advantage of the built-in and well-practiced ways that parties handled aggressive tensions, channeling them toward the climax of an election which produced a result that normally dissipated those tensions rather than escalated them to violence.

Lincoln set up a conflict that implicitly defined its own resolution—the defeat of the villain or, in more prosaic electoral terms, the defeat of Douglas, the Democrats, and popular sovereignty, and the triumph of the principle of the federal prohibition of slavery extension. The purpose of the formulation of the besieged but rescuable house was not to solve intractable problems of race relations. It was not intended to solve the problem of slavery for the slave or for the slaveholder, but to solve it for Northern whites in psychological terms by permitting their minds to rest in the belief that slavery was back where it had been in the beginning days of the Republic. This was what Lincoln meant by the restoration of the house. Thus in meeting the danger of the possible extension of slavery by popular sovereignty and, even more, the triumph of despotism, the good (but up to now passively preserving) sons were given a chance to act at last by rescuing and restoring the fathers' work.

Countless times after 1854 Lincoln made statements to the effect that Republican policy "is exactly the policy of the men who made the Union. Nothing more and nothing less."[62] He sought only to "reinaugurate the good old 'central ideas' of the Republic," and to "restore the government to the policy of the fathers."[63] In broad terms, the Republicans, once in office, would "treat you . . . like Washington, Jefferson, and Madison treated you."[64] As for the slavery question in particular,

[62] Ibid., 3:502.
[63] Ibid., 2:385; 3:93. See also 3:118, 538.
[64] Ibid., 3:453.

"All I have asked or desired anywhere is that it should be placed back again upon the basis that the fathers of our government originally placed it upon."[65] Placing slavery "where our fathers originally placed it" meant treating it in such a way that the public mind would conclude that the institution was on the road to eventual extinction.[66] In New York City in 1860 he insisted that

> this is all Republicans ask—all Republicans desire—in relation to slavery. As those fathers marked it, so let it be again marked, as an evil not to be extended, but to be tolerated and protected only because of and only so far as its actual presence among us makes that toleration and protection a necessity.[67]

Restoration involved change at the level of policy, but more importantly it also involved emotional regeneration. "Let me entreat you to come back," Lincoln once pleaded in words that received wide distribution. "Return to the fountain whose waters spring close by the blood of the Revolution."[68]

Resolving the crisis in this ritualistic way promised also to solve the problem of the post-heroic generation—at least for some of its members. Action in the service of restoring slavery to the place it had held in the paternal vision would be a deed of heroic quality. "If we do this," Lincoln believed, "we shall not only have saved the Union; but we shall have so saved it . . . that the succeeding millions of free happy people, the world over, shall rise up, and call us blessed, to the latest generations."[69] He, of course, received the immortality he desired, although hardly in the way he intended or expected. The melodramatic ritual he created led not to a psychological solution

[65] Ibid., p. 117.

[66] Ibid., 2:515, 492, 501, 513, 514.

[67] Ibid., 3:535. The entire statement is italicized in the original.

[68] Ibid., 2:547.

[69] Ibid., p. 276.

to the crisis of the Union, but to secession and civil war. Thus it failed, and the failure was anything but innocuous.

The results of the rivalry between Lincoln and Douglas are perhaps as well known as any other sequence of events in American political history. Lincoln narrowly lost to Douglas in the contest for the latter's Senate seat in 1858. The formal result may have served briefly to hide, but it did not retard, the increasing erosion of Douglas's centrist political base, a process that Lincoln assisted with effect. Douglas won re-election to the Senate at the cost of exacerbating his tense relationship with the Southern, proslavery wing of the Democratic party, which had been growing increasingly wary of him ever since he decided to oppose the proslavery Lecompton constitution in Kansas on the grounds that it did not represent the will of the people there.[70] Strained as it was, however, this relationship in 1858 was not necessarily any further beyond repair than was Douglas's relationship with the Northerners who burned him in effigy in 1854 only to talk four years later of supporting him for president after he took his anti-Lecompton stand. There was nothing preordained about the Southern rejection of his candidacy in 1860. Indeed, as Harry Jaffa has plausibly supposed, if Douglas in 1860 had seemed headed for victory, Southern Democrats probably would not have deserted the party.[71] Repudiating him would not bring them Kansas, but tolerating him might well bring them Cuba. By leading Douglas repeatedly to emphasize his belief that popular sovereignty was a means to free soil, Lincoln prevented Douglas from taking the steps to repair his standing with the

[70] Robert W. Johannsen, *Stephen A. Douglas* (New York: Oxford University Press, 1973), pp. 576–613, 685–705.

[71] Harry V. Jaffa and Robert W. Johannsen, eds., *In the Name of the People: Speeches and Writings of Lincoln and Douglas in the Ohio Campaign of 1859* (Columbus: Ohio State University Press, 1959), pp. 45–46.

South that this endlessly resourceful man might otherwise have been able to initiate.

The second isolating effect of Lincoln's pursuit was to prevent the offsetting of Douglas's Southern losses by Northern gains. As he approached his showdown with Lincoln, Douglas was attempting to win the backing both of Northerners who were willing to accept free soil in the territories as long as it did not threaten the Union, and of Northerners who very much wanted free soil but were not overly fastidious about the means of getting it. He was making gains in this direction, and by 1858 Douglas represented to many Northerners the prospect of free soil neither tainted by abolitionism nor accompanied by the danger of disunion. He was not without potentially expanding attraction, after all, to the vast middle of the electorate—many of them still wandering homelessly in search of political calm and security after the decay of the Whigs and the Know-Nothings—the very people, in other words, who were responding to appeals of the sort made by Edward Everett. Douglas's article in *Harper's Magazine* was intended, among other purposes, to enhance his own restorationist credentials. But by evoking in vivid language the fear that Douglas offered neither calm nor free soil but continuing agitation, expanding slavery, and ultimately despotism, Lincoln reduced his opponent's acceptability to the political center, probably by a decisive degree. It is hardly fanciful to suppose that if Lincoln had not opposed him in 1858, Douglas might have been able not only to retain but also expand his centrist base and win the presidency in 1860. At the very least, this result would certainly have had the effect of postponing disunion and civil war, for with slavery restrictionists held at bay, Southern Democrats would have been (nominally at any rate) on the winning side of the electoral contest.

In his struggle with Douglas, Lincoln sought to restructure and help resolve the crisis of the Union and also to win election to the United States Senate. He achieved neither object. Instead, within little more than two years, he became president and led the Union into a civil war with the eleven Southern states that seceded from it. One of the three other candidates Lincoln defeated in the election of 1860 was Stephen A. Douglas, the candidate of the Northern wing of the Democratic party, whose Southern leaders left it rather than march behind him. He had long since lost any control over the current of political events; now he lost even the ability to ride it. In 1861, after watching helplessly as the country fell into the war he had both tried to prevent and helped to bring, Douglas became one of its first casualties. A combination of maladies not then or since clearly diagnosed carried him off in the first spring of the war. He was forty-eight years old.

There are two ways then, opposite sides of the same coin so to say, in which the events of 1858 contributed to the coming of civil war. Everyone knows the first: the prominence Lincoln achieved in 1858 put him on the course (a winding one, to be sure) that led to his election to the presidency, which in turn led to secession, which in turn led to civil war. The second way is the other side of the first: the victory that Douglas won in 1858 ironically narrowed his base and weakened his power, which led to the split of the Democratic party in 1860, which led to Lincoln's election and to the subsequent disasters. There is a subtle difference in the nature of Lincoln's role in these two formulations, and his moral stature is perhaps affected by whether one emphasizes the first or the second. In the first, he appears to be almost a passive figure who happened to be in a crucial position when he was struck by the historical lightning from a long-darkening sky. In the second, he appears in a much more active role, as the man who set in motion a sequence of events that might not otherwise have occurred.

In 1860, the year of Lincoln's election, a writer calling himself "Procrustes, Jr." analyzed the long-term effects on a nation's history of a heroic age and great men. One of the results of their sway was that their successors attempted to imitate them whether or not the times required imitation. "Such men create war for the purpose of showing their heroism. It is like setting a house on fire for the purpose of showing our skill in putting it out."[72] People who live in dull ages cast up imaginary challenges, so that they can meet them and demonstrate to themselves and others that they are not, after all, degenerate sons of heroic sires. Procrustes was writing about the national situation generally, and gave no sign that he had Lincoln in mind. Even if he had, one might respond that the challenge that preoccupied Lincoln was hardly imaginary, and that the house was already on fire when he came upon it. But to concede this is still to leave room for the possibility—which is what the writer evidently had in mind—that when an ambitious man perceives that because the house exists he cannot satisfy his ambition by building it, and that the only way he can rise is defensively, by saving it—that these circumstances increase the likelihood that he will tend, consciously or not, to create or contribute to a situation that will put the house in danger, thereby permitting him to act not only defensively but also heroically to save and restore it.

If Lincoln had not played the role that he did, would the Republican party in Illinois in its first years have been more moderate than it was, thereby permitting the practical Douglas to avoid either breaking with the Buchanan administration or alienating the South? Would the Republicans in 1860 have nominated someone perceived to be more radical than Lincoln—say, William H. Seward of New York, who might have lost the election, thereby electing Douglas and blunting the secessionist drive? Would the Republicans have nominated someone perceived to be more moderate—say, Edward Bates of Missouri, whose election might not have inspired a secession

[72] "Great Men, a Misfortune," *Southern Literary Messenger* 30 (1860): 312.

movement that could not be peaceably contained? Would some other president have abandoned Fort Sumter? Would peaceable reunion have eventually taken place if Fort Sumter had been abandoned? Of course we cannot know the answers to these questions, but that fact suggests the point: Abraham Lincoln, who had every reason to ask them and others, could not have known the answers to these questions either. What the questions reveal is that, step by barely perceptible step, symbolic fratricide edged over into the real thing, that there is a straight line from the melodrama of the house divided to the tragedy of the house divided.

THE NEW BIRTH OF FREEDOM

The nation in its childhood needed a paternal Washington; but now it has arrived at manhood.

JOHN T. TROWBRIDGE, 1864

The story of Oedipus, as Freud made the world know, is endlessly instructive to observers of conflicts between fathers and
sons.[1] While in horrified flight to avoid fulfilling the prophecy
he heard from Apollo that he would slay his father (who he
mistakenly thought was Polybus, the king of Corinth), Oedipus fulfilled the prophecy when he killed Laius, the king of
Thebes, who turned out to be his father. Abraham Lincoln
did not hear, but rather made, a prophecy that an ambitious
genius would emerge in American politics to commit an act
of patricide in the sense of destroying the temple of liberty

---

[1] For Freud's use of Oedipus see *The Standard Edition of the Complete
Psychological Works of Sigmund Freud,* ed. and trans. James Strachey, 24 vols.
(London: Hogarth Press and the Institute of Psycho-Analysis, 1953–73), 1:265;
7:226n; 11:171.

(later the house) that the fathers had built. Like Oedipus he consciously sought to prevent the deed, although by a flight that was psychological rather than physical. He stayed where he was, in Springfield, and coped with his own unrecognized (because forbidden) hostile feelings toward the fathers by projecting them onto an imagined being who finally appeared in the representative figure of Stephen A. Douglas.

Thus Lincoln's own powerful patricidal desires, generated (I have argued) by the obstacles that the immortality of the revolutionary fathers placed in the way of his towering ambition, but blocked from consciousness by the successfully repressive force of an equally powerful filiopiety, found an outlet in a symbolic act of fratricide. The good son banished the bad son, who was made to play the scapegoat role, and rose first to power and then to an immortality that matched that of the fathers. But in this process events slipped beyond the reach of the man who had sought to confine political tensions within the structure of melodramatic ritual. The way that Lincoln cast himself into the center of the political conflict between the sections over slavery transformed that conflict into a civil war that created a modern nation while it destroyed forever the old Republic of the fathers. To formulate the descent into fratricidal violence in this way is not to assert that the Civil War was Lincoln's war. He probably would have gotten nowhere—with his love of the fathers or his hatred for them—if his generation had not shared the conflicted emotions he contained within himself and acted out for them.

Lincoln's behavior after 1860 invites the analogy to Oedipus to proceed. Following his election to the presidency he passed into virtual seclusion for three months, reappearing to stage a scene that as much as announced that the good son had become a man: he now wore a beard for the first time in his life, he was leaving home perhaps (and so it turned out) forever, "with a task before me greater than that which rested upon Washington."[2] Which meant that the guidance of Washington and the other fathers, who had never been confronted with the challenging reality of a broken Union, was less useful than before. So saying, he left on his journey east to take up the office Washington had held. (Never mind that there is no obvious Jocasta in this analogy. Since the invention of psychoanalysis it has been easy to forget that Oedipus got more than his father's wife; he also got his father's job. Moreover, the wife came with the job rather than the other way around.)

Neither side in the Civil War ceased at any time to appeal to the revolutionary fathers.[3] Throughout the conflict Lincoln continued to make filiopietistic pronouncements and to explain the Union cause in traditional sentimental terms. He said in 1864, as he might have said in 1854 or 1834, that "we are striving to maintain the government and institutions of our fathers, to enjoy them ourselves, and transmit them to our children and our children's children forever."[4] But the statements concerning preservation and restoration were balanced and then overbalanced by arguments for fundamental change not directed by precedent. In 1848, when he was a member of Congress, Lin-

[2] Roy P. Basler, ed., *The Collected Works of Abraham Lincoln*, 8 vols. (New Brunswick, N.J.: Rutgers University Press, 1953), 4:190.

[3] For examples of such appeals, see "Editor's Table," *Southern Literary Messenger* 31 (1860): 468; ibid. 36 (1864): 184; statements by Joel Parker, John Pendleton Kennedy, Wendell Phillips, and Robert Dale Owen in Frank Freidel, ed., *Union Pamphlets of the Civil War, 1861–1865*, 2 vols. (Cambridge, Mass.: Harvard University Press, 1967), 1:85, 91, 99, 315–16; 2:618; statements by John A. Dix, Caleb Lyon, and Robert Barnwell Rhett in Frank Moore, ed., *The Rebellion Record: A Diary of American Events, with Documents, Narratives, Illustrative Incidents, Poetry, etc.*, 11 vols. (New York: G. P. Putnam, 1861–63; D. Van Nostrand, 1864–68), documents, 1:84, 94, 399; Edward Everett, *Orations and Speeches on Various Occasions*, 4 vols. (Boston: Little, Brown and Co., 1850–68), 4:337, 405–6, 530; [Woodbury Davis], "Political Problems, and Conditions of Peace," *Atlantic Monthly* 12 (1863): 252; Robert C. Winthrop, *Addresses and Speeches on Various Occasions*, 4 vols. (Boston: Little, Brown and Co., 1852–86), 2:556.

[4] Basler, *Works of Lincoln*, 7:528. See also ibid., 4:439; 7:512.

coln had spoken against even thinking about changing the
Constitution. "Better, rather, habituate ourselves to think of it,
as unalterable. It can scarcely be made better than it is. . . .
The men who made it, have done their work, and have passed
away. Who shall improve on what *they* did?" In the second
year of the war, when he proposed to Congress several constitutional amendments that would have provided for the
gradual, compensated emancipation of the slaves, Lincoln concluded his argument as if he were speaking to an earlier version of himself: "The dogmas of the quiet past, are inadequate
to the stormy present. . . . As our case is new, so we must
think anew, and act anew. We must disenthrall our selves,
and then we shall save our country."[5] Our case is *new;* then
at Gettysburg a *new* birth of freedom: the man who throughout his career had opposed the attitudes and projects of Young
America adopted the language of Young America at last. The
more open and direct patricidal assaults of the transcendentalists in culture, and the displaced assaults of the Young America
adherents in politics, had succeeded in arousing psychological
and social defenses in support of tradition, thereby contributing
to their own defeat. The community had easily protected the
fathers against the openly hostile or the casually indifferent
sons. It is always the good and obedient son who ends up
slaying the father.

The tragedy in Sophocles' drama, which is the greatest telling of the Oedipus myth, does not center on the killing of the
father, which occurs long before the play itself begins, but on
the murderer's developing realization of what he has done.
This realization is not inevitable, but is the result of Oedipus's
own willed, persistent pursuit of truth—an investigation set off
by the plague sent to devastate Thebes as a result of the un-

punished murder of Laius. Oedipus's pursuit of the killer does not flag—indeed it grows more intense—when it begins to seem that the person he seeks is himself. The movement in the drama, for Oedipus and the community, is from ignorance to knowledge and the true manhood that comes with taking responsibility for one's acts. Nothing that Lincoln—and little that anyone else of his generation—ever said matched Oedipus's explicit acceptance of responsibility for the ruin he helped to bring. On the contrary, Lincoln's course lay quite the other way. Where Oedipus came to understand the plague of Thebes as divine punishment for his unatoned patricidal deed, Lincoln came to see the American Civil War as divine punishment upon his generation for sins committed predominantly by the preceding generations that Americans collectively called "our fathers." In this formulation, the fratricide of Civil War becomes a continuation of the displaced patricidal quest that the contest with Douglas may be said to have begun.

Before the American Civil War began Lincoln did not consider civil war inevitable. "There is no need of bloodshed and war . . . no necessity for it," he said in February 1861, two months before the showdown at Fort Sumter.[6] He plainly considered that events were within the control of men. But when war came, and persisted, and grew in its effects, he started making statements asserting that he was controlled by events rather than the other way around.[7] By 1864 he looked upon the struggle as a "mighty convulsion, which no mortal could make, and no mortal could stay."[8] The Civil War had been made by God.

[6] Ibid., 4:240.

[7] See, for example, ibid., 7:282, 301.

[8] Lincoln to Eliza P. Gurney, September 4, 1864, in ibid., p. 535. On the question of Lincoln's perception of responsibility for the war, see Don E. Fehrenbacher, "Lincoln and the Weight of Responsibility," *Journal of the Illinois State Historical Society* 68 (1975): 45–56. Lincoln's "not me" habit of projection served to ease him in a number of situations. Everyone knows that,

Lincoln's departure from home may have signaled the end of his apprenticeship to the fathers, but it was no more a departure in the service of autonomy than was his departure from Thomas Lincoln's house thirty years earlier. "Our fathers" could assist him no longer, and he transferred his filial affections again, this last time to "our Father in Heaven."[9] During the Civil War Lincoln came to see himself—he said so in public—as the agent of God, chosen by Him to perform a "great work."[10] He seemed to many people to model his behavior on that attributed to God's most famous Son. The gentleness, compassion, forgiveness, and extraordinary kindness, combined with the ineffable sadness he displayed, seemed to be the qualities of a man who had taken the suffering of a whole people for his own. Not lightly or for nothing did his secretary call Lincoln "the greatest character since Christ." The course this last transference would ultimately have taken we cannot know, of course: the relationship was cut off on Good Friday, 1865 by the same event that seemed to many Americans to validate its existence.[11] But in the years between 1861 and 1865, the dependence grew quite strong, and the idea that God was using

a few nights before he was assassinated, Lincoln had a dream in which he came upon the corpse of a murdered president lying in state in the East Room of the White House. It is less well known that he was able to find comfort in what others considered ominous. "Don't you see how it will turn out?" he said. "In this dream it was not me, but some other fellow, that was killed." Ward Hill Lamon, *Recollections of Abraham Lincoln, 1847–1865,* ed. and pub. Dorothy Lamon Teillard (Washington, D.C.: 1911), pp. 115–18.

[9] See, for instance, Lincoln to Gurney, in Basler, *Works of Lincoln,* 7:535.

[10] Ibid., 5:279. See also ibid., 4:236.

[11] [Ralph Waldo Emerson], "The President's Proclamation," *Atlantic Monthly* 10 (1862): 638–42; John Hay to John G. Nicolay, August 7, 1863, in Tyler Dennett, ed., *Lincoln and the Civil War in the Diaries and Letters of John Hay* (New York: Dodd, Mead & Co., 1939), p. 76; John Hay to William H. Herndon, September 5, 1866, in Emanuel Hertz, ed., *The Hidden Lincoln: From the Letters and Papers of William H. Herndon* (New York: Viking Press, 1938), p. 308; Paul Roazen, *Freud: Political and Social Thought* (New York: Alfred A. Knopf, 1968), p. 134.

him to effect His purposes moved to the very center of his thought.

Lincoln liked to think that God supported the Union cause. But the duration of the war (indeed, even the existence of it) led him to consider that God's purpose was not simply congruent either with his own wishes for a quick victory by the North over the South, or with the opposite result. "God wills this contest, and wills that it shall not end yet," he wrote in a memorandum to himself in 1862.

> By his mere quiet power, on the minds of the now contestants, He could have either *saved* or *destroyed* the Union without a human contest. Yet the contest began. And having begun He could give the final victory to either side any day. Yet the contest proceeds.

It occurred to Lincoln that "God's purpose is something different from the purpose of either party."[12]

The emancipation of slaves, a goal different from that of "either party" before late 1862, might have been that purpose. But when the war had not ended several months after Lincoln issued the Emancipation Proclamation, he came to the idea that the catastrophe was God's punishment—not on the South for attempting to destroy the Union (for the North, which sought to preserve it, was suffering greatly too), but on the entire nation for its sinful life. Apparently only gradually did Lincoln identify slavery as the great national sin. Proclaiming a National Fast Day in the spring of 1863, he reminded the country of an idea that had come to America with the Puritans. God can punish individual souls by consigning them to hell, but cannot punish erring nations anywhere but in this world. "May we not justly fear," he asked, "that the awful calamity of civil war, which now desolates the land, may be but

[12] Basler, *Works of Lincoln,* 5:404.

a punishment, inflicted upon us, for our presumptuous sins, to the needful end of our national reformation as a whole People?" Americans had for most of their history enjoyed "the choicest bounties of Heaven": peace, wealth, and power. So accustomed had they become to these blessings that they had forgotten God's role in providing them.

> We have vainly imagined . . . that all these blessings were produced by some superior wisdom and virtue of our own. Intoxicated with unbroken success, we have become too self-sufficient to feel the necessity of redeeming and preserving grace, too proud to pray to the God that made us!

Now the pattern of success was broken; God was punishing national ingratitude.[13]

A year later, in the spring of 1864, Lincoln was prepared to say that slavery was the sin that brought God's wrath. He wrote to a Southern editor that "God now wills the removal of a great wrong, and wills also that we of the North as well as you of the South, shall pay fairly for our complicity in that wrong."[14] At his Second Inaugural, which came six weeks before he was murdered, Lincoln devoted nearly half of his address to the development of the theme. Once again he quoted Luke: " 'Woe unto the world because of offences! for it must needs be that offences come; but woe to that man by whom the offence cometh!' " Slavery was the offence that God "now wills to remove," and "if God wills that [the war] continue, until all the wealth piled by the bond-man's two hundred and fifty years of unrequited toil shall be sunk, and until every drop of blood drawn with the lash, shall be paid by another drawn with the sword . . . it must be said 'the judg-

13 Ibid., 6:156.
14 Lincoln to Albert G. Hodges, April 4, 1864, in ibid., 7:282.

ments of the Lord, are true and righteous altogether.' "[15] Paying for two hundred and fifty years: once he began to comprehend the war in this way Lincoln could see that in some respects the fathers were more guilty than the sons, for the fathers had founded the institution of slavery as well as the institutions he was trying to preserve. They were the men "by whom the offence cometh." The sons were the inheritors of the institution of slavery as well as the institutions that protected liberty. Always before this, the spokesmen for the post-heroic generation had agreed among themselves that the well-being they enjoyed was attributable to the fathers, and the reason for their unending debt of gratitude. Now that they could also believe that the calamity of war that they were suffering was also attributable to the fathers, and that they were paying off in blood their ancient accounts, the sense of their own debt to the founders virtually disappeared.

If the sons were no longer so beholden to the fathers, neither were they so in awe of them. The post-heroic generation had preserved the Union, as it had always told itself it must, and had moreover put the very question beyond raising again. The sons had secured the immortality of the Republic, which once was the only kind of immortality that seemed within reach, but now many of them had also attained personal immortality. Those, like Lincoln, who tested "whether that nation, or any nation so conceived, and so dedicated, can long endure," and who died "that that nation might live," made certain that the great wish of the most conspicuous members

[15] Ibid., 8:333. For anticipations of this theme, see "Shall we vote to Perpetuate Slavery?" *New-Englander* 2 (1844): 597; John P. Hale, *Congressional Globe,* 36 Cong., 2 Sess. (December 10, 1860), p. 34; Freidel, *Union Pamphlets,* 1:102–3, 504; George Bancroft to Abraham Lincoln, November 15, 1861, in Basler, *Works of Lincoln,* 5:26n. Harriet Beecher Stowe considered the war to be "the purifying chastening of a Father, rather than the avenging anger of a Destroyer." Quoted in Alice C. Crozier, *The Novels of Harriet Beecher Stowe* (New York: Oxford University Press, 1969), p. 152.

of the post-heroic generation would also be fulfilled: they would never be forgotten. In matching the fathers' deeds in this respect, the sons had a diminished need for them.[16]

Lincoln's gesture to "our fathers" at the beginning of the Gettysburg Address was one of the last significant public characterizations of the revolutionary heroes in the close, possessive terms that were characteristic of the post-heroic period.[17] After 1865 they were known more distantly and less personally as "the founders," "our forefathers," or "the founding fathers." The change is not explained simply by the passage of time, which had never before demonstrated any power to affect this usage, but rather by the events of the American Civil War. Whatever else it did or failed to do, the war brought the post-heroic age to a close by ending the psychological thralldom to the past that had defined it. Thus the ironic result of the sentimental attempt to recover the American beginning was its important contribution to the precipitation of a crisis that sharply and forever separated Americans from their heroic origins, and in the process made irrelevant the role of sentiment in preserving the Union. "The nation in its childhood," wrote John T. Trowbridge when the Civil War was far advanced, "needed a paternal Washington; but now it has arrived at manhood," and the need was gone.[18] Another writer attri-

[16] The quotations are from the speech at Gettysburg, the various versions of which appear in Basler, *Works of Lincoln*, 7:17–23. Three important works on the meaning of the Civil War for people who were involved in it are Edmund Wilson, *Patriotic Gore: Studies in the Literature of the American Civil War* (New York: Oxford University Press, 1962); George M. Fredrickson, *The Inner Civil War: Northern Intellectuals and the Crisis of the Union* (New York: Harper & Row, 1965); Daniel Aaron, *The Unwritten War: American Writers and the Civil War* (New York: Alfred A. Knopf, 1973).

[17] But see James Russell Lowell, "Ode Read at the One Hundredth Anniversary of the Fight at Concord Bridge," *The Poetical Works of James Russell Lowell* (Boston: Houghton Mifflin Co., 1882), p. 408.

[18] [John T. Trowbridge], "We are a Nation," *Atlantic Monthly* 14 (1864): 773. When a Connecticut senator voted in 1864 against repeal of the Fugitive

buted the achievement of national maturity to Abraham Lincoln. "Washington taught the world to know us, Lincoln taught us to know ourselves," Donn Piatt said. "The first won for us our independence, the last wrought out our manhood and self-respect."[19] Their experience in the Civil War, and the "new birth of freedom" they needed to believe they had achieved in fighting it, permitted the sons to recognize that they were free of the fathers, and that at last their fathers' house had truly become their own.

Slave Law on the grounds that "our fathers" would disapprove, E. L. Godkin wrote that he doubted "if the worship of ancestors has ever been carried much further than this even in China." "The Constitution, and its Defects," *North American Review* 99 (1864): 126.

[19] Allen Thorndike Rice, ed., *Reminiscences of Abraham Lincoln by Distinguished Men of His Time* (New York: North America Publishing Co., 1886), p. 500.

INDEX